Anita Flegg

D1367427

The RRSP Secret

The RRSP Secret

Defend and Build Your Wealth with This Powerful Investment Strategy

Greg Habstritt

Compliments of
Flegg Investments
Anita Flegg
613-769-3034

John Wiley & Sons Canada, Ltd.

Library and Archives Canada Cataloguing in Publication

Habstritt, Greg
   The RRSP secret : defend and build your wealth with this powerful investment strategy / Greg Habstritt.

Includes index.
ISBN 978-0-470-73652-4

   1. Registered Retirement Savings Plans.   2. Real estate investment—Canada.
3. Finance, Personal—Canada.   I. Title.

HD7129.H33 2010   332.024'0145   C2009-905916-9

The material in this publication is provided for information purposes only. Laws, regulations, and procedures are constantly changing, and the examples given are intended to be general guidelines only. This book is sold with the understanding that neither the author nor the publisher is engaged in rendering professional advice. It is strongly recommended that legal, accounting, tax, financial, insurance, and other advice or assistance be obtained before acting on any information contained in this book. If such advice or other assistance is required, the personal services of a competent professional should be sought.

Production Credits
Cover Design: Adrian So
Interior Design: Pat Loi
Typesetter: Thomson
Printer: Friesens Printing Ltd.

Editorial Credits
Editor: Don Loney
Project Coordinator: Pamela Vokey

John Wiley & Sons Canada, Ltd.
6045 Freemont Blvd.
Mississauga, Ontario
L5R 4J3

Printed in Canada

1 2 3 4 5 FP 14 13 12 11 10

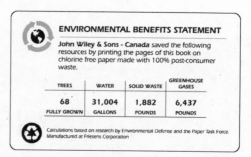

ENVIRONMENTAL BENEFITS STATEMENT

John Wiley & Sons - Canada saved the following resources by printing the pages of this book on chlorine free paper made with 100% post-consumer waste.

TREES	WATER	SOLID WASTE	GREENHOUSE GASES
68	31,004	1,882	6,437
FULLY GROWN	GALLONS	POUNDS	POUNDS

Calculations based on research by Environmental Defense and the Paper Task Force. Manufactured at Friesens Corporation

Table of Contents

Foreword

Are you tired of low returns, high mutual fund fees and no one taking responsibility for your financial plan's performance? Afraid to open the RRSP statement that comes in the mail each month, worried about how much worse things are getting for your financial future?

Then this is the book for you.

If there's one thing that the 2008–2009 economic downturn taught Canadians, it was this: *financial success and early retirement are not guaranteed.* It also taught us that we must take back control of our personal financial situation by becoming much more aware of what we invest in and what our desired outcome is. And that is exactly what this book is going to enable you to do: take control and create a financial future based on reality, while reducing the underlying risk.

The financial industry in Canada has long held the advantage over the average investor, because most people never get the inside view of how things really work. As a result, most Canadians are playing the financial game without even understanding the rules. This book is going to change that for you.

Ever since RRSPs were created, Canadians have been obsessed about them; obsessed, but often not well informed. Most information we receive has been filtered through the eyes of the financial community, and then watered down to the point where most investors have false assumptions about RRSPs and don't understand how to truly capitalize on them and maximize their benefit.

One simple example of this is that the financial industry has convinced many Canadians that there is a "season" for RRSP contributions every year in February. Even though this isn't true, it serves the purposes of the financial industry, and keeps Canadians doing things that do not necessarily serve their own interests.

Your RRSP is a part of your overall financial plan, a plan that should take advantage of the RRSP tax advantages *but not rely upon them*. It's a plan that should be designed not to help you "stop working," but a plan that shows you how to "start doing the work you love to do" in your community, business or charity. It's time that Canadians start to live their financial life with a whole life picture in mind, instead of just a retirement plan.

The book you have in your hands will play a major role in opening your eyes to how the financial industry *really* works and to the significant potential role that your RRSPs can play in your overall plan. You'll discover many of the secrets that the financial industry has held for so long, designed to maximize their profits while ignoring the financial health of the average Canadian.

This book is controversial, because it reveals many of the things that some in the financial industry would prefer you didn't know. In addition, for the first time ever, it shines a light on innovative options you can use to take advantage of the tax savings an RRSP provides you while increasing your returns and limiting your downside risk.

You'll finally learn how to turn the tables so that *you*, rather than the financial industry, are in a position of advantage. You'll learn how to create your own investments that generate double-digit returns without a laundry list of commissions, fees and expenses.

The concepts you'll read about have been used by wealthy Canadians for decades and now, for the first time, they're being shared in a very straightforward, step-by-step guide.

I have known the author of this book, Greg Habstritt, for several years, and have always appreciated his integrity, honest approach, and willingness to "tell it like it is." I believe there is a lack of solid, practical, high-integrity educational material in the marketplace, and I believe that *The RRSP Secret* will begin to fill this void.

In this book, Greg has revealed the secrets and myths that hold back most Canadians financially, and provided the blueprint for you to follow to create success for yourself. Using this powerful information, anyone can start tapping into these strategies and never again have that anxious feeling in their stomach every time their RRSP statements show up in the mail.

Pay close attention to what you read in this book. Enjoy it, and above all else, *use it* and start to see how the real financial world is nothing like what the RRSP commercials tell you. It is a much larger world out there, and this book will give you the tools to enjoy it.

Sincerely,
Don R. Campbell
President of the Real Estate Investing Network and bestselling author of *Real Estate Investing in Canada 2.0*

Introduction

It was July 5, 2002, and it was what I refer to as a "moment of truth" in my life. I believe that we all have a few of these crucial, life-changing moments. And usually, they're tremendously painful realizations that cause us to make an immediate decision on the spot, a decision that forever changes our life. For me, this was the day I had gotten out of bed early to impress Raylene, my girlfriend, with breakfast in bed.

I woke up in my custom-built 5,000-square-foot mansion on the outskirts of Calgary, which I had built shortly after selling my communications company. I thought I was pretty clever. After all, I had become a millionaire the day before I turned 30 years old, and I was on top of the world.

As it turned out, selling my company was more luck than anything else, because it sold at the absolute peak of the dot-com bubble. In fact, I had consummated the deal in March 2000, the very top of the tech bubble that was just about to burst. At the time, of course, I didn't realize it, and figured that my success had come because I was such a genius.

I was about to learn the truth. I got up to make breakfast, quietly going into the kitchen and preparing all the ingredients for the perfect meal. When I went to turn the stove on, however, it wouldn't fire up and there didn't seem to be any gas. Since it was brand new, that seemed odd, so I went downstairs to investigate.

The gas water heater was off as well, so it seemed like there was a problem with the gas. As I went outside, I assumed that it was probably an interruption from workers in the area, since our community was relatively new and still undergoing construction.

As I rounded the outside of the house to look down the street, something caught my eye—a big, red tag hanging from the gas meter on my property. As I approached it, the reality began to set in, even though I didn't want to process it.

The gas company had turned off my gas for lack of payment.

Here I was, this supposed brilliant young entrepreneur, living the life that most people only dream of, and my gas had been shut off. Soon I would discover that this wasn't the only financial problem I had.

I went back into the house, and as my primary focus was Raylene, I tried to figure out how to hide this embarrassing fact from her so that she didn't find out I wasn't as put together as she probably thought I was.

Fortunately for me, when she woke up she was in a rush because she had to get back into town to her photography business. That day happened to be the first day of the Calgary Stampede, a busy time for her, and she had a million things to get done.

I drove her into town and dropped her off for work. Crisis averted—for now.

Of course, I then had to immediately go to the gas company and plead to get my gas turned back on. Since I had no money in the bank, I had to get an advance on my credit card in order to pay cash and clear the delinquency on my account. I will never forget the way that I felt that day. It was like I was living in a dream, and then suddenly, someone came along as I slept and whacked me across the back of the head with a baseball bat. It was painful, humiliating and life-altering. It was then that I decided I would never be in that position again.

THE JOURNEY BEGINS

If you're like most Canadians, you've never received much in the way of formal education or training when it comes to money, investing and wealth. It really is astonishing to think that no one gets proper training on how to create, protect and manage their money, even though money is an important resource in every person's life.

I'm a typical Canadian, born to middle-class parents that worked hard to give their children every opportunity and chance for success. My brother, Jim, and I grew up in a very loving family. Like most children, we learned from our parents most of what we knew.

While we were fortunate that my father was an accountant and understood how numbers and accounting worked, he also spent most of his career with one employer and never started his own business. There was a time when this worked for most people. Go to school, get good grades, find a good job, stay there for 30 years, and then eventually you'll retire and they'll take care of you. That plan worked for my dad quite well, but the world has changed and this is now a recipe for disaster.

I started my own businesses when I was very young, and both my brother and I seemed to have the entrepreneurial bug in us. My first memories of running a business are of being eight years old and selling drinks to thirsty golfers through the fence just down the alley from my childhood home, which happened to back onto a golf course.

Over the years, I've started and run more than twenty different businesses, and decided early that I wasn't going to rely on someone else to employ me and take care of me. My vision was to run my own business, be my own boss and determine my own destiny. And for the past twenty-odd years, that's exactly what I've been doing.

The start of my journey towards financial fluency started that day, July 5, 2002, when I realized I didn't understand money. It was painful to admit that I was doing a terrible job managing my finances, and that I was actually in very poor financial condition. To the outside world, I looked like a success story—winning awards for my companies and entrepreneurship, living in a million-dollar mansion with all the toys—but inside I was a financial wreck. And getting my gas cut off was the wake-up call I needed.

It was at that moment that I decided I was going to learn how money really works, and was going to do whatever I had to in order to ensure I would never feel that way again. For the past several years, I have dedicated myself to the study of money, investing and financial success. I've spent hundreds of thousands of dollars to be educated by some of the best and brightest mentors, teachers and speakers in the world when it comes to success and prosperity.

Early on, I recognized that I had to choose an investment strategy that I would focus on, because it's difficult to be successful in something if you don't focus on it. I chose real estate, primarily because I had always been interested in it, and also because the research I'd done told me that our local real estate market in Calgary was poised to perform well over the next several years. I had started dabbling in real estate in 1997 when I bought my first investment property (I lived upstairs and rented out the basement suite), but I decided to get serious about it the same year I had my moment of truth.

I began educating myself on investment principles, how money really worked, and the habits and traits of successful and wealthy investors. I quickly gained insight into all the mistakes I had made in the past, and began to discipline myself not to repeat them.

At the same time I was increasing my financial fluency, I started to investigate real estate and to develop a system that would allow me to create wealth by buying properties. I focused on properties I could acquire with little cash down, and quickly began using my selling skills to get other investors to partner with me and provide the necessary cash to buy the properties. Before long, I had built up an impressive portfolio of about forty properties, and people began asking me if I could show them how I was doing it. In fact, I had decided to get a real estate licence early on, because I realized that I couldn't find a real estate agent that understood what I was trying to accomplish.

Using my real estate licence, I started helping others buy real estate for investment purposes, and created more income from the commissions. Eventually, I realized I had enough people wanting my help that I could probably hold a seminar and teach them all at the same time, instead of trying to help people one by one. Soon enough, my one-day training seminars blossomed into multi-day, international training programs, which now have attracted thousands of students from more than twenty different countries. But it all began because I made a decision to focus on real estate and learn everything I needed to know to be successful.

All along, I continued to buy real estate and increase the size of the properties I was acquiring. The result was a sizable real estate portfolio, most of which I continue to hold today, along with a growing training company called SimpleWealth, which provides people inspiration, knowledge and tools to create financial success for themselves.

Another blessing I have is that not only do I have an incredible business partner, Kourosh, who allows me to do what I do best, but also I get to work with my best friend every single day because that happens to be Kourosh as well. His influence and impact on me has been incredible, and I have been fortunate to attract such world-class people into my life because of the realizations and decisions I've made on the road to becoming a professional investor.

I'm truly grateful for the life I have now—in fact, my girlfriend Raylene stuck with me through the learning journey I went on, and did me the huge favor of becoming my wife in 2005. She's also the mother of the most incredible gift I've ever received, our baby boy Cooper. The two of them are really why I do what I do, and why I love my life so much.

I tell you all this about myself for one reason only: to help you recognize that no matter how uneducated you feel you are about money, or how little you know about the financial industry, you do have the power to change your financial future. You simply need to *decide* that you are going to learn what you need to know, so that you'll always be able to take care of yourself.

That's what I did back in 2002, and it changed my entire life. Only one thing is for sure: I did not know anything more about investing, finance or money back when I started than you do today. Even if you know nothing, that puts you on the same level I was at when I started down this path.

I hope to help you avoid taking several years to get to the point where you are confident enough to make your own financial decisions and begin creating wealth for yourself and your family. No one will ever take better care of your money than you will, and this book is intended not just to show you why you shouldn't trust the financial industry with your money, but to share with you some practical and simple ways to create double-digit returns for yourself, without taking massive risks or paying outrageous fees.

If you've picked up this book, I'm going to assume that it's because you're looking for better financial answers than what you've been getting from the financial industry and the media at large.

It's truly amazing to me that in a time when we have more access to information and resources than ever before, more people are making disasters of their financial lives than ever before. If it were as simple as getting "the right information," we'd see the average person getting into better financial shape. But we know this isn't the case.

My plan with this book is pretty simple. First, I want to wake you up and help you realize that the financial industry is a massive machine that will eat your financial lunch if you let it. It's not there to help you, it's there to make massive profits for its shareholders. It's really that simple. If you're going to take control of your own finances, you must realize that the financial system will take from you as much as it possibly can, and it won't feel bad about doing it. So our first job together is to make sure you understand the game you're playing.

Next, I'm going to show you why so much of the traditional thinking when it comes to investing and money is completely wrong, and in fact doesn't work. This won't come as a surprise, as you'll see that many of the traditional investment strategies and ideas come from the financial industry itself. We'll break through some of these myths and, as we do, I think you'll start to see a new light shine through. You'll begin to feel more engaged and optimistic that you *can* take control of your own finances, and be successful.

Then, we'll look specifically at registered accounts in Canada, such as RRSPs, RESPs and TFSAs, and see why so many Canadians are taken advantage of when it comes to these types of accounts. If the mention of these terms scares you, don't worry. I'll explain them in a very simple way. As a key part of this book, I'll show you specifically what you can do to create impressive returns without having to take huge risks.

I'll walk you step by step through what I believe is one of the most powerful investment strategies that you can begin to implement immediately, so that you're in a position to finally feel confident, empowered and able to create your own financial future. This is a little-known method of creating double-digit returns that most people aren't aware of, and I'll explain why it is that the financial industry doesn't want you to know about it.

I am humbled that you are reading this book, and I want to sincerely thank you for spending your valuable time with me on this journey. Also, I want to point out that this book will not be the end of your learning process. Through my website, which you can find at www.rrspSecret. com, you will be able to access a wealth of articles, tools, resources and bonuses that will help you gain even more confidence and control over your financial future. You can go to the website and register for free to receive all of the bonuses and articles. This is my way of thanking you for investing your trust and time in me.

I hope that this book introduces you to new ways of thinking and to innovative ideas and strategies that will allow you to beat the financial industry at their own game and create prosperity and security for you and your family.

To your success,
Greg

How to Use This Book

Welcome to *The RRSP Secret*! You're about to embark on an exciting journey, designed to help look "behind the curtain" and see what's really going on in the financial industry. My goal in this book is to help you see things for what they really are, and then to provide you with some powerful tools you can use to maximize your own financial success.

But here's the really important point that I want to emphasize: this book is only where you should start—not where you should finish!

One of the challenges in teaching an investment strategy is that the environment, rules and documents are always changing. As a sophisticated investor, it's important that you're always aware of any changing rules, and getting access to the most up-to-date versions of the documents and information you need. That's why I created the powerful www.rrspSecret.com website, which will support your education and learning process. On the website, you'll find current versions of all the documents, forms, agreements and applications that I refer to in the book.

Your first step should be to register at www.rrspSecret.com. Your second step should be to download the resources so you can refer to them as you read the book.

Once you are a registered member, you'll have access to the **Bonus Resources** section of the website, which is full of bonuses and added benefits that I've created to maximize your value from reading this book.

How to Claim Your Free Bonuses

As a thank you for purchasing this book, I've arranged for you to get access to a number of powerful bonuses and resources that will fast track your financial success and progress.

I've created a very powerful website that you can access by virtue of purchasing this book. Once you register, you'll have complete access to this online resource, which will provide you all of the most recent documents, forms, rules and updates that you need in order to make full use of this book.

You'll also benefit from additional Special Reports, audio and video training sessions—in total, there is more than $850.00 worth of bonuses that will provide you additional education, training and support as you begin to make better financial and investment decisions.

To access these exclusive bonuses, go to my website at www. rrspSecret.com, and register as the owner of this book.

When you visit the site, simply look in the top right corner of the home page for the "Register Your Book" link, and follow the simple instructions!

SOME OF THE BONUSES THAT ARE WAITING FOR YOU

You'll find a variety of important resources at www.rrspSecret.com, including

Sample Documents, Forms and Agreements (that you can edit and use)

Throughout the book, I refer to sample documents and forms that you'll need to understand as you execute this strategy. Rather than embedding these documents into the book (and killing thousands of trees in the process), I have placed them on the website so you can always access the most up-to-date, current versions of every document and form. Wherever possible, the documents are also provided in Word format so that you can actually download and utilize them in your own investment journey.

Additional Training Resources

On the website, you'll find that I have provided a number of very powerful video training clips, audio recordings, and special reports and articles that will help you learn even more about the strategy I teach in this book. You can access these resources for free, as my way of thanking you for purchasing this book.

For example, you'll find a very powerful conference call recording that I held with one of the top financial planners, where he reveals some of the most shocking and concerning realities about the financial industry. You don't want to make any major financial or investment decisions until you've heard this call! The financial industry does not like this information to be shared publicly, but you'll have free access to the recording when you register for the site.

Greg's Q&A

Once you've read the book, I expect you're going to have questions that you need answered—and I'm going to be there to help you get the answers you need! I will be hosting a regular Q&A session for all registered members of the website, allowing you to ask me whatever questions you have about the strategy or anything contained in the book.

Updates and Alerts

When you register on the website, you'll also then be on my insider list so that you receive updates of new changes to legislation, as well as alerts when we've added or changed any of the resources on the website.

Discussion Forum

On the website, you'll also find a discussion forum where you can connect with other investors from across Canada, and talk about how you're implementing the strategy. You'll also find this is a powerful place to network with other investors, and ask questions about specific situations or issues that you come across.

Mutual Fund Calculator & Other Tools

One of the most significant things for Canadians to understand is the devastating effect of fees and commissions on their investments. I've created a calculator that provides you a simple way of revealing the *true* cost that you're paying when you invest in mutual funds. I refer to this in detail in Part I, as you'll see. This will be an eye-opening tool for you to use and share with your friends, I assure you!

I've also provided you free access to my "Market Matrix" Calculator, which allows you to do market research that will assist you in implementing what I teach you in this book.

I Want To Hear From You!

Once you've read the book and registered on the website, please submit your comments and feedback on this book! My goal is to inspire Canadians to ask better financial questions, and take control of their financial futures. If anything I share in this book helps you think differently, please let me know. On the website, you'll find a link to submit your comments.

WHAT THE FINANCIAL INDUSTRY DOESN'T WANT YOU TO KNOW

1

I've Met the Enemy, and the Enemy Is Me!

When I'm left on my own, I'm my own worst enemy.
—Ron Wood

I'm going to start with the single most important thing for you to understand if you're going to change your financial circumstances and create prosperity for yourself and your family. You're probably not going to like what I'm about to tell you, but here's something I can guarantee: your financial future depends on your ability to believe and accept what I'm about to reveal to you. In fact, I'm starting with this because without question it is absolutely the main reason that most people never achieve financial success.

The reality is that the biggest reason you've been held back financially is *you*. You are literally your own worst enemy when it comes to money and investing. Most people don't like to hear this, but let me remind you that this applies to everyone, including me.

It's important for you to understand some of the thinking and behaviours you have right now that are hurting your financial future, because once you're aware of them, you can change them. Sadly, most Canadians never take the time to try and learn anything about how investing, finance or money works. They simply listen to the "experts," hand their money over to others who claim to be professionals and hope for the best. To many people, investing and money management are some kind of voodoo magic, and they don't really understand it. It's too painful to try and learn it, so they avoid the topic—and their financial statements reflect this sad reality.

So why is it that so many investors are fearful of making decisions? Why do so many people avoid learning about simple concepts when it comes to investing and managing their own money?

This can be easily explained by what I call the "Financial Overwhelm Loop."

THE FINANCIAL OVERWHELM LOOP

As you grow up and get through high school and then possibly university or college or go directly into the workforce, you become acutely aware of all the financial things out in the world you know nothing about. You begin to hear about the stock market, RRSPs, mutual funds, real estate, taxes, corporations, stockbrokers, cash flow, contribution matching, market timing, diversification, dollar-cost averaging—the list is endless.

Predictably, since you've never formally been taught any of these things, they cause you anxiety and concern, because you have no idea what they are or what you should be doing about them. As you accumulate some money, you have a sense that you should be doing *something* with that money, but you just don't know *what* that should be. You begin to feel a sense of being overwhelmed by trying to figure out what to do. Fear and trepidation set in, too.

There doesn't appear to be any other logical solution. Your parents don't seem to be able to offer any intelligent advice and your friends don't seem to understand things any more than you do, so you do what most people do in this situation and turn to a financial advisor to ask for some help. And then it begins.

You feel a sense of relief as you hand your responsibilities over to an "expert" who will take care of your money. When you meet with him (or her, as the case may be), he sounds very smart and he gains your confidence that you've selected the right person.

Of course, since you don't know to ask, he doesn't discuss his compensation or how he is going to profit from working with you. Rarely is the nature of your relationship with him discussed in detail. All you know is that he is going to manage your money and grow it so that you can enjoy a wonderful retirement.

You then essentially ignore your financial situation, trusting it to someone else. You don't educate yourself, or learn about new products and services coming out in the marketplace. You don't pay a lot of attention to the fundamentals of the markets. In fact, you can't, because you wouldn't know where to start.

But you carry on with your career or your business, your family and all the other priorities you have. Besides, you've got enough going on in your life, and the last thing you need to do is try to become a financial expert. You've never been good with numbers, and it's just not your skill set. You do what you need to do, your advisor manages your money, and everyone lives happily ever after. Right?

Unfortunately, most investors find out at some point that while this fairy tale is easy to believe, it rarely comes true. Eventually, out of nowhere, some kind of financial problem arises. There's a meltdown in the stock market, or interest rates are increased without warning, or your portfolio takes a hit for some reason that you're not clear on.

And here you are, looking to your advisor for help and reassurance. And what does he tell you? "Don't worry," he says. "Now is not the time to panic. We're in for the long haul, and now is a terrible time to pull out." He tells you that he thinks the market's about to come back, and tries to calm you down.

You're feeling trapped, because you don't have any idea how to interpret what's going on and you're blindly relying on someone you hope knows what they're doing. You're again feeling overwhelmed, because you don't know whether you should fire your advisor, or if you should stick with it "for the long run."

And this vicious circle continues over and over, blindly trusting others with your money and then failing to become educated so that you can make better decisions in the future. For many investors, this cycle repeats itself for their entire lifetime. Some investors switch advisors during a downturn, while others stick with theirs, hoping that at some point things will turn around.

Now, don't get me wrong—as I'll outline in the next chapter, I don't think that the entire financial industry is out to get you, or that you can't trust any financial advisor. While there are definitely some serious problems in the way that the system is structured (and works against the interest of the individual investor), I do believe that most of the people in the financial sector are honest and want to help you. Unfortunately, as you'll see, many of them don't even know the damage they're causing to their clients.

In any case, the point you need to get right now is that no one will take better care of your money than you will.

PATH OF LEAST RESISTANCE

One of my key beliefs is that in life, when something negative happens to you, there are three primary ways in which you can respond.

1. **Blame.** One response might be to place blame on why the negative outcome occurred. For example, let's assume that an investor places $10,000 in a stock that his stockbroker recommends. The stock goes to zero, and he loses his entire $10,000 investment. He immediately jumps up and down, and points his finger at the broker, blaming him for putting him into a bad investment. Placing blame is the primary method in which most investors respond to losses.

2. **Justify.** Another response to a negative situation is to work to find good reasons for why it happened—investors attempt to justify the outcome. For example, a real estate investor who loses money suggests that the reason for the loss is that the market is soft, and there's not much he can do about something like that. The cause of the problem is out of his control, and he just shrugs his shoulders.

3. **Take Responsibility.** The third response to something negative is to take responsibility for the outcome. The investor accepts that the reason for the negative outcome was either in whole or part due to the actions (or inactions) that he personally took. If you look at the first example above, where the investor lost $10,000, instead of blaming his broker he could instead look at what he did personally to contribute to the negative outcome (the loss).

Out of curiosity, how did you respond to the last loss that you took on an investment? When you checked your portfolio and saw that it has gone down several percentage points, did you blame anybody and anything but yourself?

If you look carefully at these three ways of responding to something negative, you'll notice that the first two—placing blame and justifying—put the power into the hands of someone or something else, and you cannot control the outcome. That's another way of saying that you are a victim.

You're really saying that it's not your fault, and therefore it must be the fault of someone or something else.

In the third response, taking responsibility, you are forced to step up and recognize what role you played in the negative outcome. Of course, most investors don't like to do this, as it's much easier to point the finger at someone else, or come up with a good reason (excuse) as to why things didn't turn out as hoped.

Accepting This Important Truth

Until you are willing to identify and take responsibility for negative investment outcomes, you'll be powerless to stop them because you are putting yourself in the role of victim. Let me go back to the examples above to illustrate my point.

In the situation where the investor lost $10,000 because he trusted his broker, it's easy for the investor to point at the broker and blame him. After all, the broker suggested that stock. But what role did the investor play? Or, more importantly, what role *could* the investor have played?

If the investor had been willing to be responsible and accountable, one of the things he likely would have done is tried to learn more about the investment that the broker was recommending. He would have played an active role in the investment, as opposed to just sitting back and hoping that his broker had made a good suggestion.

Blindly throwing money at an investment without understanding it is no different than placing a bet in Las Vegas. Any time you invest in something you don't understand, you're gambling, not investing.

In this case, the investor needs to accept responsibility for investing in something that he really didn't understand. By the way, this isn't the exception, this is the rule! Most investors are putting their money into investments in which they have no knowledge or understanding, so it's not surprising that most investors do not do very well.

In 2005, Ellen Roseman reported in the *Toronto Star* on a survey of Canadian investors in mutual funds that underlines this point. Of those surveyed, 60% didn't know what an "MER" was (it stands for "management expense ratio"), and 40% couldn't name the fund that they were invested in.

Think about that for a moment: 40% of the investors didn't even know what it was that their money was invested in! That's like having money invested in real estate, but not knowing in what city or province.

THE H.A.P. INVESTING STRATEGY

I'm about to reveal to you the most popular investment strategy in the world today. It's particularly popular because it takes virtually no time to learn or to apply, and you can use it in any kind of investment vehicle. You don't even need a financial planner or stockbroker to utilize this strategy and, in fact, most investors do it themselves because it's so easy. It also happens to be the most popular strategy used by Canadians, and has been since the dawn of time. My guess is that at some point, you've applied this strategy yourself and perhaps still are.

What I'm talking about is the Hope and Pray (H.A.P.) Investing Strategy—what most investors are relying on to create their financial future and retire in comfort. It involves simply hoping and praying that things are going to turn out okay, but my guess is that if you're reading this book you already know that this is a fairy tale. The H.A.P. strategy hasn't worked for you.

Hoping and praying is what you have to do if you decide to hand over your money to someone and let them take care of it. You have to hope they know what they're doing, and pray that they make decisions in your best interest and don't lose it all. It's truly a loser's strategy, and it's one that I hope you'll never apply after reading this book.

VICTIM NO MORE

At this point, I hope it's clear why being a victim is so damaging to your net worth and your financial future, and I hope I've inspired you to decide that you're not going to choose to be a victim anymore. I'm also hoping you're recognizing why this discussion of psychology is as important, if not more important, than talking about investment principles, facts and figures!

If you're prepared to STOP being a victim with your money and investing, I have a very effective tool that I personally created when trying to overcome the desire to be a victim.

Asking "What Role Did I Play in This?"

"What role did I play in this?" This is a question I created for myself many years ago, I find that it immediately takes me out of the victim mentality and plants me squarely in reality. It forces me to think about what role I've played in an outcome, and helps me avoid the trap of blaming and justifying.

Asking yourself this question forces you to be accountable for at least some portion of the outcome. The more you ask the question, and the more honestly you answer it, the more you begin to realize that you—not someone or something else—were primarily responsible for the outcome.

Let me again look at the $10,000 investment loss to demonstrate the use of this powerful tool. In that case, when the investor lost his $10,000 in the stock recommended by the broker, he was quick to condemn and blame the broker for making the bad decision.

However, if that investor stopped and asked himself what role he played, he would soon have to face the reality that *he* invested his money without understanding the stock. He would have to admit that he was blindly hoping and praying that the broker was going to do a good job. Thinking about it further, he'd likely come to the realization that if he had done some research on the stock and was able to ask intelligent questions, he may have been able to see a reason why that stock wasn't the best choice.

I certainly feel that the broker played some role here, since providing good advice is supposed to be part of the job. But when we're talking about an investor who doesn't even pretend like he wants to learn anything or be involved, it's rare that this situation works out well for everyone.

Let me emphasize this point by looking beyond the investment world and sharing with you what I believe is one of the most profound and important statements that I'll make in this entire book.

> I believe that a direct indicator of how successful you will be in life (not just financially) is based on your willingness to be accountable for your results.

This applies not only to investing and money but equally to relationships and other areas of your life. For example, if you continually blame your spouse for the problems you have in your marriage, and you're not willing to step up and assume responsibility for some of your faults, then that relationship is doomed.

Taking Full Responsibility, No Matter What

If you want to be successful, you must immediately begin assuming responsibility and being accountable for all the negative things that happen in your life. The more that you can eliminate blame and justification from your vocabulary, the more successful you will be.

I often get challenged on this, because someone will say to me, "Well, my car got broken into last night, and they took my briefcase with my laptop. I lost all of my documents for the past three years. And you're telling me this is my fault?"

Actually, yes I am. Before you decide to return this book, I'm not saying that you caused the break-in, but you did make several decisions that brought about the negative outcome. First, you decided where to park your car. That likely contributed to the outcome. Next, you left a valuable asset in the car, when I think most of us realize that's usually not a good idea. You chose not to take the briefcase with you, wherever you were going. Maybe you felt you had a good reason for this—perhaps you were going for dinner with your spouse, or going to the gym. In any case, whether you had a good reason or not, recognize that you made the decision that led to the outcome. All of the documents for the past three years are gone. That would imply you didn't have a backup of your documents. And whose responsibility was that?

Hopefully you're getting the point here, and not resisting what I'm saying. Believe me, it has taken practice and time to get accustomed to taking responsibility in as many areas of my life as I can. But I also share with you that the moment I became accountable, my life changed. And you have the very same opportunity. You simply need to make the decision.

DON'T WORRY, THAT'S NOT YOUR ONLY PROBLEM

If all of this weren't enough to contend with, the reality is that as human beings we are wired with instincts, habits and responses that have evolved over thousands of years, all with one purpose: to help us survive this dangerous world.

I'm not going to delve into a deep discussion about psychology, but I think it's important to help you recognize that the way our brains are wired is in direct conflict with good, fundamental investment habits. Put another way, the things that we do by instinct actually hurt us as investors. It doesn't seem very fair, but it's true, and becoming aware of such things gives us a fighting chance to work around these weaknesses instead of being blind to them as most investors are.

In fact, this realm is a fascinating field that continues to develop. Behavioural finance and behavioural economics are fast-growing areas of knowledge that apply scientific research to the study of economics and the investment world, and attempt to identify the reasons why investors do seemingly irrational things. Personally, I've always been intrigued by what causes people to do the foolish things they do. Why do people hold onto a stock well after it's dropped, and has little hope of ever coming back? Why do investors buy real estate at the very top, thinking they're getting in at the bottom, when the market indicators clearly are saying otherwise?

Recognizing Investor Biases

I refer to each of these problematic instincts as "investor biases," because you have a natural bias to respond in a certain way when presented with a specific scenario. A bias is simply a false assumption or judgment you've made that isn't based on fact or truth. Investor biases are automatic reactions that you likely have to specific investing situations that are based on an emotional response, not an intellectual one.

It's worth noting here that a powerful psychological influence is at work twenty-four hours a day on all of us, which helps explain some of the strange things we do, not just with our money but in other areas of our life as well.

Psychologists have proven that the human mind only does something for one of two primary reasons: a desire to either (1) obtain pleasure or (2) avoid pain. And they've proven that our instinct to avoid pain is stronger than our desire for pleasure. In other words, your brain will go out of its way to avoid pain, regardless of whether there's an opportunity to obtain pleasure. The avoidance of pain overrides your desire to obtain pleasure, and this is something that's hard-wired into us as human beings.

What does. this have to do with investing? Everything. Your psychology will dictate your investment success more than anything else you can learn or understand. That's why I feel it is appropriate to spend just a few moments on this.

Investor Bias #1: Aversion to Loss (The Need to Be Right)

One of the most powerful human instincts ingrained in us is that each of us has some deep desire to be right about the decisions we make. We gain a sense of pleasure when we are correct. Conversely, when we are wrong, we experience some degree of psychological pain, and therefore we try to avoid being wrong. Again, remember the two things our brain is constantly seeking out: experiencing pleasure and avoiding pain.

To demonstrate this bias, consider an investor who buys a stock at $1.00. After a couple of weeks, she checks her account and finds that her stock is down to $0.85. What does she do? If she's like most investors, she holds onto her position and uses a number of reasons (excuses) to rationalize that decision:

1. "I've already taken the 15% loss, so selling now locks that in and that would be foolish."

2. "The decline is temporary and the stock's going to come back."

3. "It's a good company and the market isn't seeing the potential." (And she tells herself this, even though she has never reviewed the company's financial statements or prospectus.)

What's really going on here is quite simple. Subconsciously, the investor is trying to avoid a painful experience. As a result, she's avoiding the decision to sell at a loss, because she would have to admit that she was wrong and that creates pain, which she is desperate to avoid.

Most investors aren't even aware of this inner dialogue going on, but the net result is that they decide to keep holding the stock, which usually means that what could have been a short, quick pain turns into a long, dull, slow pain that lasts for weeks, months or even years.

If you're not sure whether you are vulnerable to this bias, consider the following scenarios based on the excellent work of Van K. Tharp in *Trade Your Way to Financial Freedom*.

Given the following two options, which would you choose?

1. A sure loss of $15,000

2. A 20% chance of no loss at all, and an 80% chance of a loss of $20,000

If you're like 80% of the population, you would select the second option. The problem is, the second option works out to a larger loss because, on average, the second option produces a loss of $16,000 (i.e., 20% × $0 loss + 80% × $20,000 loss = $16,000 average loss). Therefore, the first option is the one that a professional investor would choose.

The reason that most people choose the second option is because it provides some potential of avoiding loss. Most investors would prefer to take the risk that the market is going to come back and help save them from the loss. Unfortunately, this leads to a larger loss, which then makes it even more difficult to get out.

Let's try another example. Which of the following options would you choose?

1. A sure gain of $15,000

2. An 80% chance of $20,000, and a 20% chance of no gain at all

Again, about 80% of the population chooses the first option in this case—the sure gain. However, the second option is actually the best, because the gain in that case would be $16,000, which is higher than the sure gain. Taking the sure gain violates the investing rule of letting your profits run.

Most investors are afraid of losing, and end up taking a profit whenever they can. This satisfies their need to be right, and helps avoid the loss. Unfortunately, being blind to the bias at play means that they are likely making poor investment decisions, even though their decisions may seem logical.

I've felt this very bias many times, and none more than when I bought Nortel in 2000, the year of the dot-com collapse. I bought Nortel at $80 per share, after it had come down from $120 per share, on the advice of a broker that I had at the time. Because I thought I was such a brilliant investor I decided to use leverage (using a margin account), and borrowed money from the brokerage so that I could buy even more stock. I bought three times the amount of stock that I had the money for, because that would mean I'd make triple the killing!

Soon after I had bought it, it dipped to $60 per share, and I spoke to the broker. He told me that he thought it was headed back to $120, and that this was just a temporary decline. I quickly agreed (recognizing now that it was because I was looking for a reason to avoid selling) and held on. The stock started to climb back up, making me feel great pleasure that I had made such a genius decision. It slowly moved back up towards $80, but never made it. The rise in price was temporary and soon it was headed back where it came from.

When the stock dropped again like a rock, I was forced to sell my major position at $12 (on margin). The pain of being wrong was intense. I blamed the broker at the time, since it was he who convinced me to hold on. I had a gut feeling I should sell, but I overrode that thought and stayed in . . . only to lose all of my money on that investment.

In hindsight, this was one of my greatest learning experiences as an investor, because it taught me the lesson of accountability, and made me realize first-hand how dangerous the need to be right can be to an investor.

As a side note, it is usually when we take a loss or make a mistake that we truly grow and evolve as investors, because it is through those experiences that we learn how the investment world really works.

Investor Bias #2: Overconfidence

Another dangerous bias that many investors experience is that of overconfidence. It comes in many forms, but the result is that an investor makes decisions out of courage or false belief that they know more about the situation or strategy than they really do.

You've probably heard of the studies that show that when surveyed about their driving abilities, 80% of all drivers rank themselves as "better than average." Of course, this is impossible. Clearly, many of those surveyed are incorrect and would actually fall in the category of "poorer than average." But most drivers are not willing to accept this, and assume that they are better drivers than they really are—they are overconfident in their abilities on the road.

Yet another cause of overconfidence is the *illusion of control*. Many investors falsely believe that they have more control over a given situation than they really do, leading them to make decisions based on poor assumptions.

As a look into how profits are made by taking advantage of human biases such as the illusion of control, let's consider the lottery industry. As you probably know, when you are buying a ticket for Lotto 6/49, you have the choice of allowing the computer to select your numbers or choosing your own "lucky numbers" for the draw. What do you expect most people prefer to do?

As you'd expect, most people would prefer to choose their own numbers because they feel they're better in control of their odds of winning, yet logically we know that the odds are identical whether you choose your own numbers or they're randomly generated by a computer.

It's actually quite humorous to think that we have better control of the outcome of the lottery if we are able to choose our own numbers, but this is something that most people never even stop to think about.

And you can bet the lottery industry reaps billions of dollars of profit as a result.

The truth is, as human beings, we want to believe that we're in control of what is going to happen and that we can influence outcomes such as winning the lottery or investing in a stock that goes up in value. However, the cold, hard fact remains that when it comes to money, the only way to create success and prosperity for yourself is to understand what you're investing in and to reduce (to the best extent you can) the biases and instincts that are constantly working against you.

And as a last comment regarding overconfidence, another challenge also can develop that many investors don't see coming: the challenge of being successful out of the gate. Early success, sometimes referred to as beginner's luck, is often the worst thing that can happen to an investor. It causes newbie investors to quickly think they're more capable and talented at investing than they really are. Early successes often lead investors to take bigger and bigger risks, putting them in a position where they end up taking a loss they can't afford. This is why it is so important to be aware of these biases, and recognize them when they begin to show up in your investing efforts.

Aversion to loss and *overconfidence* are two of the most powerful biases that you will likely need to wrestle with on your path to investment success, so be on the lookout for them.

* * *

In this chapter, my goal was to help you understand why it is that from the outside looking in, so many investors seem to do things that do not make a lot of sense and appear to be irrational. The reality is that as human beings, we are vulnerable to emotional and biased decision-making, and this can be disastrous when those decisions are about our money and finances.

Successful investors recognize that investment decisions need to be based on practical, proven investment principles, and spend time not only learning solid strategies but also paying attention to their own emotions and biases.

In an ideal world, we could eliminate our emotions from any decisions we made that involve money. But the reality is that this is impossible. Your goal shouldn't be to eliminate emotion from your decision-making, but rather on managing your emotion and identifying when you're letting it seep into your investment decisions.

Managing your emotions and biases is the internal challenge that we all face. However, in the next chapter, I'll introduce you to the external challenge that's also waiting for you, and I'll warn you now: what we're about to go into is a much more challenging adversary than your own emotions and internal dialogue.

2

Why the Financial Industry Isn't Your Friend

The greatest trick the Devil ever pulled was convincing the world he didn't exist.
—from the movie, *The Usual Suspects*

Several years ago, I received a call in response to an ad I was running in the local classifieds. The headline of the ad was "We Buy Houses," and the goal was to find people interested in selling their homes easily and without hassle.

On the other end of the line was Edith, a lady I estimated was about 70 years old. As it turned out, she was living in a duplex on the west side of Calgary and had been there for more than twenty years. Her husband had passed away a decade before, and their home was paid off by the proceeds of his life insurance.

She lived alone in this property with no mortgage and had a small basement suite rented out to a quiet tenant, which helped cover her living expenses. She lived a simple life, and mostly because of her age, had decided that it was time to sell her property and move into a seniors' care centre.

When I went to meet her and look at the property, it was clear that the property had not been maintained for quite some time and would need a number of repairs. I approached the door and rang the doorbell, and a sweet, elderly lady came to the door. In one hand she had a cane that she used to get around, and in her other hand a lit cigarette. As I went inside, it was obvious that smoking was her primary pastime. You could barely see out the windows in the kitchen because of the grime that had accumulated on them.

As I proceeded to learn more about her situation and her property, my goal was to try and understand what she intended to use the proceeds of the property sale for. As an investor, I feel that if I can help someone get what they need, and at the same time structure the deal so it makes sense for me, then that's a win-win scenario where everyone gets what they need.

In her situation, she didn't really need all the money from the sale, as she had no immediate use for it. I asked her what she was going to use it for, and she didn't have any idea. She was going to move into a seniors' care facility that her friend had helped her find; it would cost her about $1,200 a month. If she sold her property for cash, it would likely just sit in a bank account somewhere, earning almost nothing.

A WIN-WIN OUTCOME

After leaving her property and doing some research, I determined what the property was likely worth and created a couple of options for her to consider. Because she didn't owe any money on a mortgage, she would need to figure out where to place that money, and it was from this perspective that I presented her a couple of creative ideas.

Since she had lived in the property for more than twenty years, she knew it and the area well and knew that her property was solid. As an investor, I was looking for ways that I could buy real estate without having to put down a big down payment and go through the pain of getting a mortgage from the bank. What I suggested to her was that if I put down a reasonable amount, such as 10% to 15%, she could "carry" the balance as a first mortgage on the property, and I would pay her 7% on her money.

If you're not a real estate investor, I don't want you to get confused by what I'm explaining. The idea here was simply that instead of paying her the whole amount up front, I would pay her some of it, and then she would wait for the rest of it, effectively "lending" me the unpaid balance and receiving interest on it until I paid her off.

If she would have listed the property for sale with a real estate agent, she likely would have listed at approximately $150,000. After negotiations and real estate fees, she would have ended up netting out somewhere around $135,000. On top of that, she would have to put up with people wandering through her house for viewings, sometimes with little warning, and this would be highly inconvenient because of her age and lack of mobility.

To save her the hassle of listing the property, I proposed to her that I would pay her $133,000 for the property, which was only $2,000 less than what she would have received if she listed it, but it allowed her to sell it immediately and avoid the hassles of listing.

Why would I do this? The other part of my proposal to her was that if I paid $133,000 for the property, I would put down 15% (which would be $19,950 in this case) and she would give me a mortgage for the 85% balance (which would be approximately $113,000).

All this really meant was that when I purchased the property for $133,000, I would put down the $19,950 and she would wait to receive the rest of the amount according to the terms of the mortgage. I offered to pay her 7% on her money, which was approximately 2% more than the going rate for mortgages at the time. I also suggested a three-year period for the loan, which would mean that I would need to come up with the balance and repay her in full in three years or less.

To make sure you're following my numbers, here's a summary showing what I was proposing to her:

Purchase Price:	$ 133,000
Less Down Payment:	$ 19,950
Balance Owing:	$ 113,050

Since she wouldn't be receiving the $113,050 up front, to secure that balance owing she would hold a mortgage on the property after the sale, giving her first charge on the property.

I could have arranged to get a loan from a bank, but the qualifying process and running around involved in doing that was worth avoiding. In addition, at the time, I was a full-time real estate investor with no reportable income, and the banks do not like lending money to people who cannot demonstrate an income stream (whether you have one through a business or not).

The difference in this case was that instead of going to a bank and having them lend me the $113,050 against the property to pay off Edith, I was asking her to carry the mortgage herself. She would hold the mortgage and receive monthly payments based on the mortgage terms, and then I would pay her off in three years.

Why would Edith want to do this? The first reason is that it would allow her to put her money into an income-producing investment that is low risk. Since her property would be the security on the investment, she would know that it was backed by a solid asset. Second, it would enable her to earn 7% on her money, as opposed to putting the money into a GIC (Guaranteed Investment Certificate) or government bond that might pay her 1%–2%.

In addition, doing this deal would have made it very easy and simple for her to sell her property, and end up making almost exactly what she would had she gone through the process of listing her property with a real estate agent.

At the time, the Calgary real estate market was rising slowly, and all of the indicators in the market suggested that the market would remain healthy into the future. All around, this was a deal that made a lot of sense for Edith because it put her money to work for her, and offered solid security to ensure her risk was very low.

I remember feeling a sense of pride in how I was going to help this elderly woman take care of her money, and make sure that she was treated fairly in the process. I had worked hard to create a deal that would benefit both of us and get us both what we wanted. I remember looking at her with a big smile and having a sense of satisfaction.

And then it happened.

After presenting this win-win scenario to her, she looked at me and smiled, and said, "This sounds good. I just have to talk to my bank manager to make sure he thinks it's a good idea."

Huh? Why on earth would she need to speak to her bank manager about this?

She went on to explain that she never made a financial decision without consulting her bank manager. I found this curious, so as I asked her more questions, I found out more about her financial situation—and I didn't like what I heard.

As it turned out, this bank manager had been "with her" ever since her husband had died. He happened to be the bank manager at the time of the death, and began giving her financial advice and helping her sort through all the financial decisions that fell upon her shoulders after the passing of her husband.

So, what kind of insightful financial advice had this "expert" been giving her? I found out that she originally had about $200,000 after paying off her mortgage. Her bank manager then placed her into a series of mutual funds and government savings bonds.

After close to ten years, her $200,000 had blossomed into about $43,000. And it was clear to me that she didn't understand any of what had happened, other than what she started with and what she had now. I asked her what funds she had been invested in, whether she knew what the fees and commissions were, and details around her investments. She couldn't answer any of my questions.

It saddened me to think about all the fees, commissions and charges that had been extracted from this poor lady, all without her even understanding what was going on. The worst part was that this woman felt sorry for the bank manager. Why? Because he was not able to manage her account directly any more—she didn't have enough money in her account! She still called him occasionally for "advice," and apparently listened to everything he said.

I don't know the specifics of what he invested her money in, but it was clear to me that he hadn't explained anything to her or based the investments on her situation. For someone in their late sixties or seventies, being invested in something that can drop 75% is not appropriate.

These kinds of situations make me extremely upset. There was no doubt in my mind that the bank manager was taking advantage of this lady. In any case, I left her home, saddened with having seen this unfortunate situation up close. However, I also was enthusiastic that I was going to help her take better care of her money.

A few days later, my phone rang and Edith was on the other end of the line. She thanked me for the time I had spent with her to explain everything, but she had decided that she wasn't able to accept my offer. I asked her why and, not to my surprise, she said, "Well, my bank manager thinks that it is very risky for me, and doesn't think it is a good idea at my age."

I was speechless, but I knew I wasn't going to change her mind. She then told me she was planning to refinance the house instead of selling it so that she could get some more capital to invest and make up for the money that had been lost.

That's right, the bank manager offered to put a new mortgage on her house for only 5%. The really good news was that if she did this, she would have enough money for her bank manager to have oversight of her account again, and they could work together once more!

I thanked her kindly for her time and wished her well. Sadly, I knew she needed all the good fortune and wishes she could get, because her financial future was bleak.

The 10/80/10 Rule

At this point I want to make it clear that I don't think most people in the financial industry are this predatory or devious in the way that they profit at their clients' ignorance and expense. My belief (and hope) is that examples like this bank manager are few and far between.

There are some great people in the financial industry, but as in all sectors, there are a lot of mediocre ones and then some dishonest thieves as well. Whether you're looking at financial planners, real estate agents, lawyers, doctors or any other group, you'll typically find that the 10/80/10 Rule holds true.

The 10/80/10 Rule suggests that the top 10% of that industry are high achievers, high-integrity players that everyone else wants to emulate. There's the 80% in the middle, who are the average, typical performers in that industry. And then we have the bottom 10%, the people that you have to watch out for because they're either incompetent, dishonest, criminal or all three.

I believe that Edith was dealing with someone in that bottom 10%, which was fatal to her financial future. The problem we all have is that we can't easily identify which category someone fits into until we've had a chance to work with them (and likely lost money)!

Some of the more public cases of fraud and criminal activity, such as Bernie Madoff, make it clear that you cannot easily distinguish the top performers from the thieves. Many of Madoff's clients were with him for decades, never thinking twice about his integrity or competence.

The only way you can protect yourself as an investor is to take an interest in your money and make sure you understand what it is you're investing in. I'll be reiterating this bit of advice throughout the book. If you don't heed it, then you are at risk of being taken advantage of by someone like Bernie Madoff, or Edith's bank manager.

As I said before, my intention isn't to have you believe that everyone in the financial industry is out to get you, or that they'll take advantage of you any chance they get. In fact, I believe that most people in the financial services business don't even realize what the game is really all about.

The Truth About the Financial Industry

It probably doesn't come as a shock to you that the financial industry is in business to make money for its shareholders and stakeholders. Just like any business, the goal of people in the industry is to maximize profits and do the best job they can at increasing profitability. There's nothing wrong with this, provided that you understand that they're playing a completely different game, with different rules, than most Canadians realize.

To that end, they have developed the entire industry in a way that increases their profits as their primary objective—and taking care of the individual investors is absolutely a secondary consideration.

It's important to remember that the financial services sector is a massive industry, creating approximately 6% of Canada's entire GDP (gross domestic product). Employing about 750,000 Canadians, the industry is a significant component of our economy, and very sophisticated. Its sheer size also gives it major influence when it comes to lobbying the government for laws and policies that benefit the companies involved in financial services.

While the industry's growth has been incredibly successful and profitable, this success has been detrimental to the average Canadian investor looking to grow his money with certainty.

If you ask Canadians what the financial services industry is all about, in particular from the investment perspective, most Canadians will say something along the lines of "helping Canadians invest their money" or "providing planning and advice to investors."

However, most Canadians don't realize that financial companies are really in two specific businesses: (1) asset accumulation, and (2) the marketing and selling of products. These are the two ways that the financial companies are able to grow their record profits into the billions of dollars every year. They are not interested in trying to help you make money as an investor. Their goal is to attract under their management as many assets as they possibly can, because they get rich from charging fees for "managing" those assets. They then manufacture and sell financial products that primarily benefit themselves and not necessarily the investor.

When you step back and look at the financial industry, it's actually genius how they've set it up and have Canadians playing right into their hands! Just consider some of the things that we've become accustomed to, based on how the financial services industry works.

Lending Your Money to Others at a Higher Rate

It's common knowledge that when you deposit money into your bank account, the bank then turns around and lends out that money to someone else, through the form of a mortgage, credit card limit, personal loan or some other form of debt. They're likely paying you nothing on your money (unless you maintain significant minimum balances), yet they're charging anywhere from 5%–6%, to as much as 29%, when they lend out your money to another customer!

Now that's a great business model—borrow something from one person at a very low rate and then turn around and lend that same asset out at a much higher rate, and make billions. In fact, this is the essence of what banks do. They borrow money at a low rate from customers (or they just create the money out of thin air, as you'll soon learn) and lend it out at a higher rate to other customers, charging a laundry list of fees, commissions and expenses.

Charging You to Hold Your Money

Does it make any sense that most Canadians pay some kind of monthly service fee to a bank, for the privilege of holding onto their money? This might make sense if the funds were held carefully and kept safe, but as you know the reality is that when you put money into your bank account, the bank takes that money and lends it out.

You may not have thought about this in the past, but I want you to think about this just for a second. In no other industry would this ever be possible, but because the financial services industry is so powerful and has spent a hundred years "teaching" Canadians how to be good customers, rarely does anyone even recognize what's really going on.

Imagine if you rented a stall at a parking lot, and each day you parked there the owner of the lot took your car and rented it to someone else. That's what the banking industry does with our money, and yet no one complains because it's "just the way it is"!

Lending Money They Don't Even Have!

What you may not realize is that banks are legally allowed to lend money that they don't actually have. Canada has the dubious distinction of being one of the few countries in the world that essentially allows its banks to lend out as much money as they wish, without requiring them to have some amount of money backing their lending activity.

Long ago, as the banks would take deposits from their clients, they realized at some point that they had all this money in the bank and clients rarely came back to take it out, especially all at the same time. As the money piled up in their vaults, they realized that if they were to lend some of that money out to other customers, instead of just letting it sit in their bank, they could actually make a lot of money. In fact, they could make more money than they were from charging their customers to store their money.

Using complex statistical models, they figured out that they really only needed to keep a small amount of cash on hand for those times when a customer came in and asked for cash. In other words, they only needed to keep a "fraction" of the deposits on hand as a "reserve" in order to meet the demands of any customer that might want some cash from their account. And thus, the fractional reserve system was created and standards were developed.

As an example, if you deposit $10 into a bank account and that bank is operating with a 10:1 fractional reserve, the bank is immediately able to lend up to $90 to other customers, even though it only has $10 from you in the bank. Because most banking is done electronically, the bank can simply "create" more money with a few keystrokes. For the sake of keeping this discussion simple, the point here is that banks are lending trillions of dollars that do not actually exist.

Until 1991, Canada employed this fractional reserve concept, where it would require a bank to have some amount of cash on deposit in order to back any loans or debts it was creating. However, in December 1991, the financial industry's lobbying power showed its strength and Bill C-19 was passed, which effectively eliminated the need for any reserves at all.

This opened the door to banks charging fees and interest on money that didn't even exist. If this is the first time you've heard about fractional reserves, this might sound a little crazy, but it's true. Please review the Additional Resources section at www.rrspSecret.com if you're interested in reading more about this fascinating process (or do some Google searches on "Bill C-19" and "fractional reserves in Canada").

As a side note, you've likely heard the phrase "a run on the bank." That's exactly what can happen in a fractional reserve system. If enough bank customers come in at the same time and demand their cash, the system falls apart because the bank doesn't hold enough cash on hand to pay back everyone. We saw this occur in some of the recent bank failures in the U.S. because enough customers became concerned their money was at risk.

Okay, enough praise of the innovation and creativity of the financial industry. While I do think it's pretty incredible how they've built such a profitable machine that benefits their shareholders, the fact remains that the financial industry is a very dangerous animal if you don't understand it.

THE DIFFERENCE BETWEEN FINANCIAL PLANNERS, FINANCIAL ADVISORS AND STOCK BROKERS

These terms are often used interchangeably, but I wanted to give you a simple view of the differences between each title that you'll see in the financial industry.

All three are intended to be individuals who contribute to some component of your overall financial plan. Most people think of financial planning as investing, but there are actually several other important areas—taxation, insurance, savings, retirement and estate planning are some of them. However, since your investments are just one part of your bigger financial picture, the role of a financial planner is to provide a complete view of your finances, so that you can make the best possible use of your money in trying to reach your financial goals.

A good Financial Planner can be an important key to financial success, but here's the problem—most financial planners don't actually DO any financial planning. They're too busy selling investments to worry about tedious financial plans.

Now remember, I'm not talking about all individuals, but any honest insider from the financial industry will tell you that most financial planners are focused on the investments and not on the planning. Who can blame them—they make their money from selling investments, so it shouldn't come as a surprise that's where their attention goes.

The Financial Advisor, on the other hand, is someone who holds a securities license and focuses on providing guidance for selecting investments. In other words, their role is not to provide overall financial planning, but to assist you in making investment decisions.

And finally, there is the Stock Broker, whose job it is to sell you investments, such as stocks, and they typically do not even pretend to offer you financial planning advice.

And in the end, even though they go by different titles, the truth is, they're all really in the same business, doing a lot of the same thing—and that's going to be the first secret that I share with you now.

SEVEN UGLY SECRETS OF THE FINANCIAL INDUSTRY

1. Advisors, Planners and Stockbrokers Are Salespeople.

While they certainly work hard to place themselves into a position of expertise and build up their professional reputation, individuals you are buying investment products and services from are salespeople. Their goal is to create a great income for themselves by selling a lot of financial products and services to their clients. The vast majority of them are compensated by commissions paid for products they sell to you. If they don't sell investment products and services to you on a regular basis, they don't eat.

This in itself isn't evil or bad, it's simply a fact of life. A lot of these salespeople truly are interested in trying to help their clients create wealth, and hope that their advice and guidance brings positive results for not just their own bank account but their clients' accounts as well.

The entire financial industry has been structured so that it motivates and compensates its salespeople to work at selling as much product as possible. Again, this makes great business sense, but what you have to recognize is that this means that the advice being dispensed isn't always coming from the right place.

If you look at the training programs and continuing education that are offered by the big financial firms to their salespeople, you see that the emphasis is on how to generate more sales, how to become more effective in closing transactions and how to be a better marketer.

The financial companies regularly send their salespeople on conferences and incentive trips to exotic locations, rewarding them for how much product they've sold or the amount of net margin they've created for the firm. I have yet to see a financial services company give awards to their salespeople based on how much money they've made for their clients—and I'm not holding my breath to see this anytime soon.

The bottom line is that while most salespeople hope to be able to generate positive returns for their clients, that isn't the underlying motivation for many of them.

2. There's a Built-In "Conflict of Interest" Between Clients and Commissioned Salespeople.

One of the biggest problems in the financial system is that the salespeople who are selling the investment products often are placed into a situation where what's good for them isn't good for their client, and this creates a conflict of interest that the industry really doesn't like to talk about.

A good friend of mine was one of the top financial planners at a major financial firm for more than a decade, and he recently gave up his licence and got out of the business because of this very fact. As someone with integrity and a commitment to his clients, he regularly was placed into a situation where he had to choose between doing what he felt was the right thing for his client, and making his living.

During the major market downturn in 2008, he came to the conclusion that because of the massive volatility in the marketplace, and because fundamentals simply were not holding true, the best thing to do for his clients was to put them into a cash position. This meant his clients wouldn't hold any assets other than cash in their accounts for some period of time.

He felt this would be the right thing to do. The problem was that if he were to call all of his clients and tell them he was putting them into cash, two things would happen. First, he would make no commission or fees, because a financial salesperson doesn't make any money when a client holds cash in their account. Second, his clients likely would take their money and go somewhere else or just hold onto their money themselves. They would recognize that it didn't take any skill or expertise to hold their accounts in cash and that they could do it themselves. By doing what he believed would be the right thing, he essentially was shooting himself in the foot, because it meant he would take a hit on his personal income. What did he do?

He took the least obvious option and actually left the business altogether, because he wasn't willing to be placed into this conflict of interest anymore. Unfortunately, most people in the business don't have the option of simply leaving because they don't like the politics or the ethics. He was fortunate that he was in a financial position to make such a move.

As it turned out, he did put most of his clients into cash before he left the business, and being in cash was the single most profitable strategy for that time period because everything else was so volatile and lost significant value. As a result, his clients did very well, but he would have made no money from doing so had he kept his licence.

Because of the way the industry is structured, always choosing based on the best interest of the client is not a sustainable business model for most salespeople. It's not that most advisors and planners aren't interested in helping serve their clients, but the reality is that everyone has to make a living. The way that the financial industry has set things up makes it difficult for advisors to serve both the clients and themselves at the same time.

3. Most Advisors or Planners Don't Even Realize the Damage They're Doing to You.

If it sounds like I think the problem in the financial industry is the advisor, planner or broker, that's not the case. In fact, I believe that they are often unaware of the damage they're causing their clients when they sell them investment products. While there are those bottom 10% that knowingly mislead and defraud their clients, I think the biggest problem in the industry is that most salespeople just don't realize the harm they're causing their clients. They are simply cogs in a very powerful marketing machine. And they have been drinking the proverbial Kool-Aid for a very long time.

Just in the way that the financial industry has convinced the average Canadian that it is working for them, the industry also has done a great job of convincing those it brings in as salespeople that they are doing their clients a service by selling them these products.

Most financial advisors and planners are not sophisticated money managers or highly experienced investment professionals. Let's face the facts—most financial planners enter the business right out of college or university, with absolutely no financial experience whatsoever. They are salespeople first, and financial experts a much distant second. The financial institutions that hire them are the ones who ultimately train them and skew their perspective.

Most Canadians assume that financial planners are experts, when in fact they've been taught mostly how to sell the products, not analyze or understand them. While this may seem astonishing to you, a significant number of advisors and planners are not able to accurately calculate out the real cost of hidden fees and expenses that are charged when you invest in certain kinds of investment products.

If you look at the top 10% of the financial planners and advisors, I think you'll find an incredibly bright and talented group of individuals who can provide good advice. Unfortunately, for the remaining 90%, most of them are not able to critically evaluate investments. They are simply told what to say to clients and how best to sell the products they offer. I liken this to calling a customer service line for help on a specific problem but all you get are automated, scripted responses instead of true service based on real expertise that can really help you.

Again, this isn't much different than a lot of other industries. As long as you remember what business the financial industry is really in, that of accumulating assets and selling financial products, then all of this should not come as a big surprise to you.

4. You May Already Be More Financially Successful than Your Advisor/Planner.

If you ask Canadians how much money a financial planner or advisor makes, most would tell you that they make a lot of money and many of them are wealthy. This is logical, because you'd assume that the people who are providing financial advice would be successful themselves. It only makes sense that you need to be financially successful to advise other people how to achieve that same success.

This may come as a shock, but the average financial advisor/planner in Canada makes approximately $49,000 a year. According to a 2009 Government of Alberta study, the average financial planner's annual salary was $49,266, and according to PayScale Inc., based on a survey of 586 respondents, the average annual salary of a personal financial advisor is $48,776. Those with the designation of "CFP" (Certified Financial Planner) earned an average of $51,190 per year.

Depending on your own circumstances, that income may seem like either a lot of money or not very much at all, compared to what you would have thought the average financial planner or advisor would make. A proven principle in creating wealth is that you want to be learning from those that are achieving higher levels of success than you are. It doesn't make sense to take financial advice from someone who's earning less money than you are; if they knew how to make more, then they would!

The financial services industry has really done a fantastic job convincing the average investor that financial planners and advisors have the expertise and knowledge to give good advice, even though their own earnings do not support this idea.

Warren Buffett, undoubtedly the best investor of modern times, said the following:

> "Wall Street is the only place that people ride to work in a Rolls-Royce to get advice from those who take the subway."

And I agree with Warren on this matter. For years, I have been teaching investment principles and strategies to students from around the world, and one of my key prosperity principles is what I call "The Do and Get Principle," which is this:

> Only take advice from those who are doing and getting what it is you want to do and get.

It seems almost too obvious, but think about how often people are not following this practical rule. And as an investor, you should be following this rule as well.

It doesn't make sense to take financial advice from someone who is earning the same, or less, than you are. You need to take advice from those who are well beyond your earning level (because they obviously know something that you don't). Unfortunately, the financial industry has convinced the average Canadian that they need to take advice from anyone who calls themselves a "planner" or "advisor."

5. Keeping Investment Products Complicated Is Good for Business.

As I've already laid out for you in this chapter, making money for clients is not the highest priority for the financial industry. The main objective is to create profits for its own shareholders first, which means manufacturing a never-ending supply of financial products that can be sold to clients.

By making these products increasingly more complex and adding hidden fees, commissions and charges, financial companies have built a very profitable model that continues to work. The only thing that will change this is having clients ask more questions, which is what I'm hoping this book will give you the confidence and courage to do.

"Hold on," the industry will say, "we don't 'hide' our fees and commissions! They're right there, in the 96-page prospectus that every investor is offered the chance to read!" And this is usually true. The problem is that the individual investor generally isn't able to read and interpret a typical investment prospectus, because it's written in such complicated and legal language.

As just one simple and somewhat humorous example, here is an excerpt from a prospectus that is supposed to explain the structure of the fund you would be investing in.

The Company works as an umbrella structure which means that it is comprised of Sub-Funds, each of which represents a specific class of assets and liabilities and has a distinct investment policy or any other specific feature, as further described in the Sub-Funds' Particulars.

The Company constitutes a single legal entity, but the assets of each Sub-Fund shall be invested for the exclusive benefit of the shareholders of the corresponding Sub-Fund and the assets of a specific Sub-Fund are solely accountable for the liabilities, commitments and obligations of that Sub-Fund.

To the average investor, this simply doesn't provide any insight or clarity into the investment.

If the industry really wanted people to understand the facts behind an investment, they'd create a single page that outlines all of the important things in plain English. Don't hold out for this to happen anytime soon though because that would have a dramatic (negative) impact on profits, so there's very little motivation for the financial industry to do something like this.

6. Independent Advice Is Almost Impossible to Obtain.

Another inherent problem in the financial industry is that the major financial companies are involved in both the manufacturing of financial products and the marketing and sale of those products. This is no different than any business that manufactures a product that it then turns around and sells.

For example, all of the big Canadian banks have their own mutual funds and various investments that they manufacture and sell. They also have salespeople responsible for selling those products, who are usually compensated more for selling the "house" products (i.e., the ones that it manufactures and owns itself) than the investments manufactured by others.

As you might guess, it's far more profitable for the bank to sell you its own financial products than to sell you a product created by another, competing firm.

Again, from a business perspective, this makes a lot of sense and it's no different than most other industries. For example, if you go into an Apple Store, you don't expect them to show you the latest version of Microsoft Windows, and you're unlikely to see a Dell computer as one of your purchasing options.

On the surface there's nothing wrong with this, but it helps illustrate the point that independent advice is very difficult to obtain in the financial industry. The conflict I see is that the financial industry doesn't clearly disclose a lot of the important details that the consumer really needs to understand, and the lack of transparency means that the consumer isn't on fair ground when trying to make investment decisions.

The main reason for this is that over the years, the financial companies have figured out that it's far more profitable to manufacture the investments than it is to distribute and sell them. As a result, the entire industry has seen massive consolidation and merging, where companies that typically have been the sales force marketing the products have become involved in the manufacturing of them as well.

Historically in Canada, there were the companies that manufactured the financial products, and then there were independent advisory firms that marketed the various financial products. One by one, those independent firms have been bought up by the major financial institutions so that they could control the distribution and ensure that only their products were being sold by the salespeople.

Unfortunately for the individual investor, this means that it's become more difficult to get independent advice, because the vast majority of financial planners and advisors are working for firms that have their own investment products to distribute and sell. It's the classic fox-guarding-the-henhouse scenario.

7. Advisors Are Often Given Sales Quotas, and Told What Needs to Be Sold.

We've already discussed the fact that professionals in the financial industry are salespeople, first and foremost. Their job, and how they are compensated, is based primarily on the financial products and services that they sell to their clients.

However, it doesn't stop there. Many financial companies impose sales targets and quotas on their salespeople, which means that financial products must be sold to someone, and it has little to do with what's in the client's best interest. In order to meet a certain sales target, the salesperson needs to find someone they can convince to buy more product. Now again, stepping back from this, having a sales quota is not unusual in many businesses, since it helps drive revenues and profits for the company. But when it comes to your own money, I think it's pretty important that you understand that this is going on behind the scenes.

Even more concerning is that financial companies routinely manufacture an investment product, and then direct their sales force (the advisors, planners or brokers) to go out and sell that product—without really knowing much about it. My friend, who formerly was a financial planner and worked for one of the biggest financial services companies in Canada, told me a story about this problem. His company would come to the sales team, and tell them a new product had been created, and they needed to go and sell it. They provided no training or insight as to what the product was about and the salespeople had no way of determining whether it was something that was good for their client, or what the risk profile of the investment was. And this wasn't a 'boiler room' type of company—it was one of the most respected names in the financial industry! These clients were not receiving unbiased advice that was in their best interest—they were being pitched products that needed to be sold because of quotas, or because the company selling them was going to make a lot of money through their distribution.

> As a special bonus, I've arranged for you to hear a powerful interview that I did with the former financial industry insider—it is one of the most revealing and shocking interviews you'll ever hear! Simply go to my website at www.rrspSecret.com and look for the "Mr. X Interview" after you register your copy of this book!

WHERE DO YOU FIND UNBIASED FINANCIAL ADVICE?

My goal here isn't to convince you that all financial planners and advisors give poor advice, and that you shouldn't try to find good outside help. As I've said before, there are a lot of good people in the financial industry and all sophisticated investors are wise to have good advisors in their corner.

Ultimately, the best way to get unbiased advice is to find a "fee only" financial planner or advisor. They're referred to as "fee only" because they will charge you a fee for the advice they give you, but not earn any commissions or fees from any of the investments they suggest for you.

This is a powerful thing because in this situation, you know that they're giving you the best advice they can based on your situation, not the advice that's going to lead to them making the most commissions and fees from you.

Sadly, according to the 2008 Financial Planners Standards Council report "Profile of the Profession," only 6% of all financial planners and advisors are "fee only." This is largely due to the fact that many investors are too short-sighted to pay for their advice up front.

When a fee-only advisor suggests to the average investor that they will have to pay several hundred dollars or a couple of thousand dollars for a financial plan, that investor thinks it's cheaper to go to a traditional planner or advisor that doesn't charge a fee but gets paid through the commissions and fees they earn from the products sold.

I believe this is tripping over the dollars to get to the dimes. Chances are, the advice you'd receive from a fee-only planner is going to help you make (and save) far more money than the up-front fee would have cost you, because you're likely to get better advice for your situation. However, most investors don't recognize this, and think that they're saving money by going to a planner or advisor who doesn't charge a fee.

If you're really looking for unbiased advice, the best thing you can do is seek out a fee-only planner that will provide a review of your financial situation and help you develop a financial plan that will work for you, all without the potential conflict of recommending investments based on the commissions that are generated. The reality is that unless you have a signifi-cant amount of assets to invest (in the range of $1 million or more), most of the top advisors are not available to you because they have minimum account thresholds. Therefore, it's in your best interest to first get some unbiased advice, and then to begin educating yourself so that you're able to make more intelligent financial decisions for yourself.

And here's a final piece of advice if you're looking for a financial advisor or planner. I would suggest that you stick with individuals who hold the "CFP" designation. This stands for Certified Financial Planner. While this won't ensure the quality of your advisor, those who carry a CFP designa-tion have gone through more education than non-CFPs and adhere to an industry code of ethics and standards.

• • •

The financial industry has been built specifically to make massive profits for its shareholders, and it has been a huge success from this perspective.

Unfortunately, the interests of the individual investor have not been served very well.

The problem isn't that financial planners and advisors are unethical, dishonest or don't care about their clients. With some exceptions, most advisors and planners are good people that are trying to make a living and help their clients as well. However, because of the compensation structures in place, selling products and services often comes before serving the best interests of clients.

It's absolutely essential that as an individual investor, you recognize the rules of the game before you try to play it. The financial sector has created the rules, so don't be surprised that it ends up winning most of the time. Your job is to become aware of the traps and myths that doom most investors. We've started that process in this chapter.

As you'll learn in the next chapter, I've only touched the surface of the problems inherent in the financial industry, and I'm about to show you two of the biggest reasons that most Canadians will not retire in comfort and style.

Now hold on, because we're about to dig into a couple of areas that the financial industry *really* doesn't want you to know about.

3

The Trillion-Dollar Heist

If you think education is expensive, try ignorance.
—Derek Bok

Now that we've looked at the financial industry from a 30,000-foot view, you're aware of many of the dangers you face as an individual investor. The truth is, you've got a target on your back and it's up to you to protect yourself and make smart investment decisions.

In this chapter, I want to focus on one of the most popular investment vehicles there is, and that the financial industry aggressively sells. I believe this is one of the greatest problems in the financial industry, and it robs more individuals of wealth and freedom than anything else. It's important to remember that this monster was created by the financial industry in order to serve their interests first and the investor's interests a distant second.

If you're a typical Canadian investor, it's likely you're falling victim to this strategy without even knowing it. But don't worry, awareness is the first step to fixing the problem! Stick with me and I'll give you not only the evidence of the problem, but we'll explore the solutions as well.

Yes, I'm talking about mutual funds, the most common investment that Canadians make—without really understanding what's going on behind the scenes.

THE CLASSIC MUTUAL FUND SALES PITCH

Just as it happens every year, it's "RRSP season" and time for you to make some decisions with your money. You've got some capital saved up, and your goal is to get it invested in a solid vehicle that will help bring you closer to financial freedom. You're feeling that pressure that you should be invested in something, but the truth is you're really not sure what that should be.

You receive a flyer from your local bank branch or a financial planning company around the corner, promoting its financial advisory services, and since you don't already have a financial planner you make an appointment to go see the financial advisor at the local branch.

When you show up, the advisor listens to what you are interested in doing and that you have some money to invest. After listening intently to you, she pulls out three different brochures, each for a different investment product.

"This first investment fund," she tells you, "is a growth fund that is a little more aggressive than average, which means that there is a little more risk. But that means that you can usually make higher returns in this fund."

She goes on to the second brochure. "This is a value fund, which means that it is more conservative. Generally speaking there is less risk, but it also means that your returns may not be as high as the growth fund."

And then she points at the third flyer and says, "This fund is a blend of the two. It is a little more conservative than the growth fund, but also has the potential of generating a higher return as well."

Then she looks you in the eye and says, "So, which of these makes the most sense to you?"

And at this point, most clients think carefully and then choose one of those funds to invest their money in, based on the elementary discussion of risk versus reward. Do you want high returns and are you willing to take a risk, or would you rather be conservative and accept lower returns?

The paperwork is drawn up, and the investment is made.

What the salesperson (and that's what they are, remember) didn't mention to you is that all three funds are owned by the bank, that there are other funds out there, and that there are other possible investments that might (better) suit your needs! You're never offered a choice of the best investment alternatives on the market, but rather you are shown only investments that the bank itself owns.

Make no mistake, there are very good reasons that the financial industry desperately wants to sell you as many mutual funds as they possibly can, and I believe that's because *mutual funds are one of the greatest threats to your financial freedom.*

THE WOLF IN SHEEP'S CLOTHING: MUTUAL FUNDS

As you're likely aware, mutual funds are one of the most popular investment vehicles in the world, and this is no different in Canada. According to the Investment Funds Institute of Canada, at September 2009, approximately $583 billion was invested in various forms of funds.

Quite simply, a mutual fund is a managed pool of capital where the management team selects specific equities or stocks to invest in. It allows an individual investor to become invested in a range of stocks and investments with one purchase. The fund is managed by professional money managers, who presumably have more insight and experience in making wise investment decisions than the average investor does on their own.

Over the past several years, I've spoken to thousands of investors around the world and virtually every one of them is familiar with mutual funds. But it's shocking how few actually understand how they work (since many of them admit to owning mutual funds already).

Normally, when I am doing a presentation, I start with asking the entire audience to close their eyes to help me with an experiment. Once their eyes are closed, I ask them to raise their hand if they do not know what an "MER" is. Without exception, regardless of the group I'm speaking to or training, approximately 75% to 80% of the room raises their hand.

I then tell them to open their eyes and look around. People are always astonished to find out that they're not the only one who doesn't understand the most basic principles of mutual funds. If you're not familiar with what an MER is, don't worry. I'm going to explain that to you now, and then you'll realize how crazy it is that most investors own mutual funds yet don't even understand this fundamental thing.

When you invest in a mutual fund, that management expertise doesn't come for free. The mutual fund manager charges a management fee, referred to as the Management Expense Ratio (MER), for managing the funds. This is simply a percentage of the holdings that is deducted and paid to the management team.

For example, if a particular mutual fund carries a 2.5% MER, that simply means that 2.5% of the assets under management are paid to the manager each year (the MER is an annual fee). Using real figures, if your investment in a mutual fund was worth $10,000 at the end of the year, $250 would be deducted from your account for a 2.5% management expense.

Now, if you've never heard of the MER, it's not by coincidence—they go out of their way to hide it. In fact, if you have mutual funds as an investment right now, go and pull out the last statement you received and find where the MER is detailed.

Good luck—because they don't disclose it on your statements! They only show you the returns "after fees," so you really have no way of seeing the fees that you're being charged. This means if you didn't read the prospectus, there's really no way for you to know what the MER is that you're paying.

It's also important to understand that the management expenses are not kept entirely by the management team of the mutual fund. Included in the MER are "trailer fees," which are how the financial advisor or planner that originally put you into the mutual fund is compensated over time.

In other words, your financial planner/advisor generally continues to get paid as long as you stay in that particular mutual fund. This varies according to the investment and fund set-up, but trailer fees are the bread and butter of the Canadian financial industry. And most Canadians have never heard of them.

If you don't believe me, here's what Morningstar had to say about trailer fees and commissions in their *Fund Research Report* (published May 2009): "Assets tend to flow into average- or higher-fee funds because Canadian investors use financial advisors to help them make decisions. Advisors direct client assets to funds that pay better trailers. And since the trailer is included in the MER, the result is that assets flow into higher-fee funds."

In other words, it's a standard practice for investors to end up with their money in investments that have higher management fees because their financial advisors are "helping" them to make better decisions, and coincidentally those decisions include funds with higher commissions.

> In this example and throughout the book, I try to keep things simple so that it's easy to follow what I'm saying. In many mutual funds, other expenses and fees are involved that actually make your returns even worse. However, at the risk of those who may say my examples are not perfectly accurate, I'd rather keep this simple to understand than get dragged into unnecessary detail. Remember, the financial industry loves complexity because then it's easier to confuse and distract you.

For most investors, paying a 2.5% fee to a professional money manager seems reasonable, since they're doing all the heavy lifting. Real estate agents get 5% or 6% of a transaction when you buy or sell a house, so 2.5% for a professional service seems more than fair, doesn't it?

As you'll soon see, this seemingly "fair" fee actually prevents financial freedom for many Canadians.

Why have mutual funds become the most common investment for Canadians to hold? There are a number of reasons for this, which the industry eagerly tells you about in building the case for why mutual funds should be owned by everyone. Here are the key reasons consumers should hold mutual funds, as advertised by the banks:

- **Mutual Funds Are Convenient.** This is the major reason why Canadians invest in mutual funds. They're sold as a very simple and easy way to hold a diverse range of quality assets with one transaction. Rather than having to manage several transactions or buy multiple stocks or investments, you simply make one decision and end up owning a basket of well-selected equities and assets.

- **They Save You Time.** According to one of the big Canadian banks' websites marketing mutual funds, saving time is a key benefit: "The most important benefit of investing in mutual funds is that it saves you time! By having the mutual fund manager manage your investments you no longer have to spend your time analyzing and worrying about individual stocks."

- **You Get Professional Money Management.** Mutual funds are managed by professional money managers who have access to detailed company research and economic data and an understanding about how world events will affect your investments. This feature has particular value for investing in foreign markets where information is not always readily available to a retail investor and local laws and accounting practices are different than those in Canada and therefore difficult to interpret.

- **Mutual Funds Offer Diversification to Offset Risk.** "Don't put all of your eggs in one basket." By investing in one security only you take on a great deal of risk of that investment underperforming. By spreading your portfolio over several different investments this risk is lessened, thus reducing the overall risk of your portfolio. Since many investors cannot afford to split their portfolios into several different securities because they'd be paying a fortune in commissions, mutual funds are the ideal solution. By pooling the resources of several retail investors, mutual funds can get better pricing and much lower commissions than a retail investor can get. This provides the benefits of diversification at a much lower cost.

- **Mutual Funds Are Transferable.** Since most mutual fund families offer more than one type of mutual fund, mutual fund investors have the ability to move their investments from one sector to another and from one country to another, easily and (usually) without cost. An investor who purchases their own stocks would have to sell their old stocks and buy their new stocks, paying commissions on both trades.

Gee, it all sounds so wonderful. Why wouldn't you want to invest all your money in mutual funds?

Let me go back through all of these points from my perspective, and provide you a different way to look at many of these supposed "benefits."

- **"Convenience."** While it's true that it's convenient to invest in mutual funds, that's like saying it's convenient to stop for fast food three times a day, rather than trying to eat a healthy, balanced meal. The reality is that any time you choose an investment option for convenience, you likely are not making the best financial decision you can. The financial industry makes it as easy as possible for you to buy packaged investments like mutual funds because they make so much money from them. They rely on the Financial Overwhelm Loop that I discussed in chapter 1, hoping that you'll just throw up your hands and buy a mutual fund. Don't be fooled—in the investment world, convenience has a cost to you!

- **"Save You Time."** It seems like too much for the individual investor to do their own research and understand what they're investing in, in part because the financial industry has built it this way. It's true, it takes more time to be an active, intelligent investor. But the choice you're making isn't one of time management. You're literally trading away your financial potential when you take the lazy approach, and investing in something simply because you don't want to invest the time to really understand what you're doing.

- **"Professional Money Management."** On the surface, this seems like a logical argument. Why try to manage your own money when you can let a professional do it for you? If it were that simple, this would make sense; however, there are a number of reasons why this logic doesn't hold true, which I will explain shortly. In the meantime, consider this: if mutual fund managers are so much smarter than the average person, why is it that approximately 80% of all mutual funds underperform the market after fees? That's right—on average, if you invest in a mutual fund, you can expect to underperform the market eight out of ten times. Gee, I don't remember that being a part of their advertising! Another thing to ask yourself: if professional money managers are so great at investing, then why aren't they all super rich and retired?

- **"Diversification."** Here's a great example of how the financial industry takes a seemingly intelligent principle and completely manipulates it for its own benefit. This classic thinking is also known as "don't put all your eggs in one basket." That seems like good advice your mom would have given you; however, in the investment world, this is dangerous advice and usually leads to mediocre returns. Warren Buffett says this about the subject: "Wide diversification is only required when investors do not understand what they are doing." Why is this? Because in the investment world, you need to understand what you're investing in, and focus your efforts. Spreading your money around into fifteen different asset classes and not understanding any of them is a recipe for disaster. But that's what the financial industry wants you to do, because they make more money as a result.

- **"Transferability."** This "benefit" suggests that because you can move your money around into different funds that a particular company has, you get flexibility. Don't like the fund you're invested in now? No problem, switch it over to one of the other funds we own. But here's the challenge: what if all of their funds are not good investments? When you restrict your choices down to only those that are offered by one company, you significantly reduce your chances of success.

Aside from the problems I've outlined above, there are other serious problems associated with investing in mutual funds. If you're invested in mutual funds right now, get ready to feel a sudden knot in your stomach, because you're about to learn why mutual funds are the most popular investment vehicle . . . and it's not because they're good investments.

Going back to the MER, the financial industry has ingeniously created this seemingly small and insignificant cost so that it doesn't raise the alarm of most investors. After all, paying a fee of 2.5% or so doesn't seem unreasonable.

The problem is that the true cost to you is nowhere near 2.5% in the big picture. Let me show you why and how it is that a measly fee of 2.5% can actually crush your financial future.

Losing 50% of Your Returns on a 2.5% Fee

Let me use an example I've been presenting to investors for several years that illustrates the point very well.

Let's assume that you have $100,000 to invest and you decide that you're going to invest in a mutual fund with strong historical returns and a great management team. This particular fund has generated gross returns averaging 8% per year (before fees) for the past several years and charges a fairly typical MER of 2.5%. (Ignore for the moment that there are very few, if any, mutual funds that can claim this kind of long-term return, but I want to be as fair to the industry as I can so you can see that even when we use optimistic numbers the results are still tragic.)

Doing just what the financial industry wants, you take their advice, and "buy and hold"—you invest your $100,000 for a twenty-year period, with the hope that you're going to build that nest egg into a nice little retirement fund for you and your family.

As it turns out, your mutual fund returns 8% gross per year, just as you had hoped. Congratulations, you should be rich now! An 8% return every year for twenty years is excellent, and should have grown that nest egg substantially.

First, let's look at what would have happened if you had invested that $100,000 at an 8% return but didn't pay any fees on it. If you refer to the chart on page 45, you can see that before fees, your $100,000 would have turned into $466,095.71 (your original $100,000 plus the return of $366,095.71) after twenty years—pretty impressive!

But let's look at what happens when we include that little 2.5% management fee in the mix. Believe it or not, after the 2.5% fee is applied, your $100,000 turns into $280,910.14 (your $100,000 investment plus the reduced return of $180,910.14). That's right, your 2.5% MER has reduced your overall return by more than $185,000!

Put another way, *you've lost about 50% of your potential return*, simply because of a little 2.5% fee that you thought was reasonable.

Understanding How This Is Possible

Here's a chart that shows you what happened to your money:

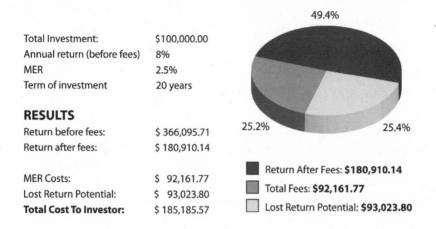

Total Investment:	$100,000.00
Annual return (before fees)	8%
MER	2.5%
Term of investment	20 years

RESULTS

Return before fees:	$ 366,095.71
Return after fees:	$ 180,910.14
MER Costs:	$ 92,161.77
Lost Return Potential:	$ 93,023.80
Total Cost To Investor:	$ 185,185.57

■ Return After Fees: **$180,910.14**

▨ Total Fees: **$92,161.77**

☐ Lost Return Potential: **$93,023.80**

As you can see, there are two places that your returns are diluted substantially.

First, the 2.5% fee actually ends up costing you 25.2% of your investment returns. This is because every year, the 2.5% fee is charged against your *entire* investment account, even though you're only earning 8%.

The reality is that you're not incurring a 2.5% fee each year; you're actually paying out 2.5% of the 8% total return that you made that year. This means the MER is actually costing you more than 31% of your total investment returns (i.e., 2.5% fee on an 8% return is actually a fee of 31.25%).

Second, every time the MER is removed from your account, you've lost the potential earnings you could have made from compounding had that money remained invested. The 2.5% that you paid out in fees last year isn't in your account to work for you this year, and over time, this creates a significant loss of 25.4% because of those expenses being deducted and reducing the benefit of compound returns for you.

I want to emphasize again that this example assumes a consistent 8% gross return by the mutual fund. It goes without saying, you'll spend a long time searching for this kind of return in the real world. Imagine what your returns look like if you don't achieve an 8% return, or worse, if your fund actually loses money!

> Interested in seeing how different MER and return rates impact your returns? You'll find a free Mutual Fund Calculator on my website at www.rrspSecret.com, which allows you to enter your own data to see the real damage that fees cause to your wealth.

SEVEN DIRTY SECRETS OF MUTUAL FUNDS

1. They're Not In Business to Make You Money.

While you'd think that the primary goal of every mutual fund manager is to help you make money, the truth is that whether you make money or not doesn't matter much to them. This is, as mentioned, because making you money is not what they're in business for—the primary objective of every mutual fund manager is *to accumulate as many assets under management as possible*.

Because the manager takes a percentage of all of the assets they manage, their primary objective is to attract as much investment capital into the fund as they can. Once it's there, as long as they can keep those investors from leaving, they continue to make their management fees on the entire pool of funds.

Whether you make any money in that fund or not doesn't materially affect them, because they get paid their fees regardless of whether you gain or lose. This is another great example of how the financial industry places itself in direct conflict with the interests of the individual investor.

If you make a little bit of money, they make a little bit of money.

If you make a lot of money, they make a little bit of money.

If you lose a lot of money, they make a little bit of money.

Do you see the problem? They take very little risk and get the predictable return, whereas you invest YOUR money and take all the risk of loss!

2. Canadians Pay the Highest Fees in the Developed World.

According to the Morningstar's *Fund Research Report* (May 2009), based on research of sixteen developed countries, Canada has the highest fees in the world for mutual funds. The report states, "The typical investor in a Canadian equity fund pays [an] MER of between 2.00% and 2.50%. Canadian investors do not pay much attention to fees. Canadian investors are comfortable with the fees because they don't know how low these fees should actually be."

The sad reality is that the Canadian financial industry has done a fantastic job with their marketing and "education" of the individual investor. This leads not only to record profits for the industry, but to devastating financial futures for Canadians.

Why is it that Canadians put up with the highest expenses in the world? I can't tell you for sure, but one contributing factor is that our education system does a poor job teaching people the basics about money. The financial industry then picks up where the education system leaves off, keeping investors in the dark about some of the most important and critical elements of understanding an investment.

Interestingly enough, Canadian cellphone expenses also are among the highest in the developed world. It would seem that Canadians are just too polite or timid to demand better value for the services and products they purchase. Additionally, it appears that perhaps Canadians are willing to trust the big financial institutions much more than they should.

3. The MER Isn't the Only Fee You're Paying.

If it's not bad enough that you're already paying the highest management expenses in the world as a Canadian, then you're about to get even more depressed.

The MER is only one of the fees that you incur by investing in a mutual fund. In addition to the MER, which covers the management costs and marketing expenses of the fund, there are what the industry refers to as "trading costs." These additional expenses cover things that are not included in the MER, such as

- **Brokerage Commissions.** Every time the manager executes a trade and buys or sells stocks or investments inside the fund, a commission is paid. No different than if you buy or sell a stock online, the mutual fund managers have to pay trading commissions as well. Since the average fund turns over their portfolio about 80% per year, these costs can add up significantly and have a material impact on the net results of the fund.

- **Market Impact Costs.** This is a cost that results, in part, from a mutual fund having a huge holding of a particular asset, and trying to sell off that large holding quickly. Depending on the liquidity of the asset, the bid/ask spread may be high and that means the cost to make the trade is increased. In other words, sometimes a mutual fund manager wants to buy or sell a large block of shares in an asset. If buying they may have to pay more than the going price in order to acquire that large block, and if they are selling off a large block they may have to accept a lower price because there are fewer buyers willing to take on that amount of stock at the going rate.

- **Sales Charges.** According to *Investor Economics*, approximately 75% of funds in Canada have sales charges, either front-end or deferred. Front-end charges or loads are charged to the investor when the investment is first made, while deferred charges end up being incurred when the investment is sold (or, if the investor holds long enough, eventually the deferred charge reduces to zero). Typical deferred charges start at 6% and then decline each year for seven years, finally falling to zero. The problem is that most investors never hold a fund for seven years, so they end up paying some amount of deferred charge when they sell.

Here's the bottom line: the industry has built in a series of expenses and fees over and above the MER and the vast majority of investors have no idea.

What these added expenses cost investors is difficult to estimate, but a 2007 analysis by Virginia Tech, the University of Virginia, and Boston College revealed that the average additional cost to an investor, over and above the MER, is 1.44% per year. That means if a mutual fund has an MER of 2.5%, the real cost to the investor is close to 4% once these additional (sometimes hidden) costs are factored in.

By the way, this analysis doesn't even take into account the negative impact that taxes can have on a mutual fund's returns. I don't want to completely depress you (though it may be too late), but I'm trying to make the point that there is a significant cost to the decision to invest in mutual funds.

4. They Don't Follow Their Own Advice.

One of the most glaring problems in the financial industry is that the mutual funds don't take the same advice that the industry gives to individual investors.

A classic mantra of the financial industry is that you should buy an investment and hold onto it for the long term, referred to as "buy and hold" investing. In fact, one of the major Canadian investment institutions proclaims as their tagline "Buy. Hold. Prosper."

Another piece of advice the industry likes to give clients is "don't try to time the market." Essentially, this means trying to buy a stock that you think is going to go up in the short term, and selling off investments that you think may decline for whatever reason. The overall guidance is to buy good companies, hold them for the long term and ignore the short-term movements that might occur.

Yet, when you look at the mutual fund industry, you rarely find anyone practicing this investment wisdom. A variety of studies have shown that the average mutual fund turns over approximately 80% of their portfolio per year. This means that each year, they're selling 80% of what they own, far from the "buy and hold" advice that investors are given. Many of these trades are done with a short-term view, going against the market-timing advice that most financial advisors dispense.

The result of this turnover is higher trading expenses to the fund, since commissions are paid every time a transaction takes place inside the fund. Remember that these trading expenses are not included in the MER of the fund, so that works to reduce the net returns to the investors even more.

It would seem that the old saying of "do as I say, not as I do" is precisely how the financial industry is run.

5. There Are More Mutual Funds than There Are Individual Stocks.

It surprises many investors to find out that there are approximately three times as many Canadian mutual funds to choose from than there are individual stocks that trade in Canada. With approximately three thousand individual stocks trading on the two major Canadian exchanges, there are more than nine thousand mutual funds to choose from, including ETFs, hedge funds and traditional funds.

The problem with this is that many of the mutual funds are very similar and own a lot of the same investments. There are only so many investments that a multibillion dollar investment fund can make, and their choices are generally restricted to the biggest Canadian stocks. As a result, what appears to be a lot of choice ends up being a great deal of duplication and confusion for the individual investor.

6. Mutual Funds Have to Invest, Even When There's Nothing Good to Buy.

A further challenge to optimizing returns in a fund is the fact that many mutual funds are mandated to remain "fully invested" at all times. What this really means is that they're not allowed to sit on a large percentage of cash in their portfolio, because when they set out the objectives of the fund they didn't list cash as a major component of the portfolio.

On the surface this makes logical sense, because it allows an investor to see what that particular fund intends to invest in and whether the manager intends to hold any cash inside the fund.

However, what seems like a good intention ends up working against the mutual fund investor, because it restricts the manager's ability to respond to the marketplace. For example, if you were a fund manager in 2008 and could see the upcoming crashing markets, you would have done very well if you had put your fund into an all-cash position early in the decline.

Unfortunately, and as I illustrated earlier, even if a mutual fund manager wanted to do this, he or she likely was unable to do so because their fund guidelines required them to leave the vast majority of the fund invested in the market.

They're literally forced to go out and try to find "the best of the worst," because their money has to remain invested. They can only try to pick investments that are "less bad" than many of the alternatives. This explains in part why, according to the Investment Funds Institute of Canada, *in 2008 Canadian mutual funds lost an average of more than 20%.*

7. Their Historical Performance Is Worse than What They Tell You.

Mutual fund managers recognize that most of their investors are not particularly sophisticated and are attracted primarily by large returns. As a result, managers devise creative ways to try and improve their "historical returns" in an effort to attract investors.

You'll often see ads in magazines and newspapers from mutual funds trumpeting their amazing one-year or three-year returns, but the reality is that those numbers rarely reflect the big picture.

It's common for mutual fund companies to have a range of different investment funds, and over time, some of those funds underperform more than others. When it becomes obvious that a fund is a loser, the manager will close that fund down and stop reporting those historical returns.

The industry refers to this as "survivorship bias," which simply means that the returns you see quoted don't really reflect all of the firms' investments funds—only the ones that they haven't shot because they underperformed!

When a fund is closed down, the returns from that fund no longer need to be disclosed to investors. As a result, when historical returns are quoted by a company, they are only quoting the returns of the funds that are doing okay, which skews the overall track record of that company to be higher than it really was. If not shut down altogether, these underperformers get merged into more successful funds in order to hide their poor performance.

Chasing high historical returns in the mutual fund industry is always a bad idea, because studies show that when a fund is a leader in its class one year, it almost always falls out of the lead position in the next year. In other words, investing in a fund because it produced high returns last year is a terrible investment strategy. Yet this is how most mutual investors (and many financial advisors) decide which funds to invest in going forward.

• • •

Hopefully by now, you're seeing why it is that so many Canadians never achieve their financial goals, and how important it is to be educated and to understand what it is you're investing in. The mutual fund industry has done a terrific job of convincing the average Canadian that mutual funds are a very profitable place to invest for the future. And as it turns out this is true—only it's very profitable for the industry, not for the investor.

Since mutual funds are the largest investment for most Canadians, I wanted to pull back the curtain and show you what's really going on with this investment vehicle. This isn't to say that mutual funds are the only danger you face in the investment world, but given the size of the market, this information affects a lot of Canadians. I hope this revealing look into mutual funds helps you make better decisions for yourself and your family.

Let's move on to another topic that I believe is robbing millions of Canadians from a comfortable, enjoyable financial future, and not coincidentally, it happens to be another area where the financial industry makes billions of dollars from investor ignorance.

CHAPTER 4

Understanding Registered Accounts

It would be so nice if something made sense for a change.
—*Alice in Wonderland*

Ask the average Canadian investor what they're invested in and one of the most popular answers you'll get is "RRSPs." Without knowing it, these investors actually have revealed that they don't know a lot about investing, because you cannot invest in RRSPs.

An RRSP (or any other kind of registered account) isn't an investment in and of itself, it is simply a vehicle from which you can make investments. Therefore, saying that you are investing in an RRSP is incorrect. Think of a registered account as a special type of bank account that's registered with the Government of Canada, because that's exactly what it is.

Registered accounts such as RRSPs (Registered Retirement Savings Plans) and RESPs (Registered Education Savings Plans) are among the very few tax breaks that Canadians are able to enjoy. When used properly, they provide you a unique opportunity to build wealth outside the eroding impact of taxes. However, when misunderstood or used incorrectly, they can make a bad investment much worse.

Once you open a registered account like an RRSP and you've placed funds into it, you still need to invest those funds into some kind of investment, such as stocks, bonds, mutual funds, etc. There is a long list of investments you're allowed to invest in, which we'll look at later in the book.

In Canada, there are several types of registered accounts. What follows is a brief overview of the major registered accounts we have in Canada. If you're interested in learning more detail about the account types, restrictions and uses, I would encourage you to visit www.rrspSecret.com, where you'll find more resources.

The **RRSP** is the most common retirement account in Canada. Virtually every Canadian that earns income in Canada is eligible to have an RRSP, and Canadians currently hold about $700 billion collectively in RRSPs. The amount you're allowed to contribute each year to your RRSP is limited according to your income, and any contributions you make can be deducted against your personal income. For this reason, the higher your income bracket, the more beneficial RRSPs become. You can withdraw from your RRSP at any time, but if you do, whatever amount you remove becomes taxable the moment it is removed. In most cases, the trustee or brokerage that holds your account is required by law to withhold the estimated taxes you will owe.

The **RESP** is specifically designed for parents to save money for a child's post-secondary education. Similar to an RRSP, any gains incurred on investments inside the RESP are tax free; however, you don't get a tax deduction when you contribute the funds into the RESP. There's no annual contribution maximum, but generally speaking, your total contribution is limited to $50,000 per child. There are different types of RESPs, but the overall intent of an RESP is to provide funding for a child's education.

The **TFSA (Tax-Free Savings Account)** is a relatively new type of registered account that the Canadian government introduced in 2009. Any Canadian over the age of eighteen is allowed to open a TFSA and contribute up to $5,000 per calendar year. Contributions made to the TFSA are not deductible against your personal income, but the upside of a TFSA is that when you take money out of the account, any gains you've made inside the TFSA are not taxable.

The **LIRA (Locked-In Retirement Account)** and **LRSP (Locked-In Retirement Savings Plan)** are similar in nature, both designed to hold "locked-in" pension funds for former plan members, former spouses or common law partners, or spouses or partners that are surviving (widows and widowers). The term "locked-in" refers to the fact these accounts cannot be cashed out at any time like an RRSP can. The investment held can't be removed until certain conditions are met, and is based on the province in which the original pension was registered.

Whether or not somebody refers to their account as a LIRA or an LRSP really is dependent on where the account was set up. In Alberta, Saskatchewan, Manitoba, Ontario, Quebec, New Brunswick, and Newfoundland and Labrador, they're called LIRAs. In B.C., Nova Scotia and PEI, as well as those accounts which are registered under Federal legislation (including the Northwest Territories, Nunavut and the Yukon) they're generally referred to as LRSPs.

And finally, the **RRIF (Registered Retirement Income Fund)** is a tax-deferred retirement plan under Canadian tax law similar to the RRSP. The main difference is that the RRIF is not designed to be a savings account like the other accounts I've outlined here. Rather, the RRIF is intended for Canadians who turn seventy-one, and are required to begin making regular withdrawals from their registered plans. The purpose of the RRIF is to generate income, as opposed to saving money.

Before the end of the year in which you turn seventy-one, it's mandatory to either withdraw all the funds from your RRSP account, or to convert the RRSP over to a RRIF or a life annuity. If you take the money out of the RRSP, it will be taxed as ordinary income. You can avoid this taxation, however, if you transfer from an RRSP and convert into a RRIF.

Once you've got the money in a RRIF, it then continues to grow tax deferred just like an RRSP. But there are two key differences between an RRSP and a RRIF. Number one, you're not allowed to contribute any more to the RRIF. The government won't let you continue to contribute once you've converted to a RRIF. Another way of looking at it is once you turn seventy-one, you cannot contribute to a registered retirement plan.

The second difference is a minimum withdrawal requirement. The government essentially tells you that you've got to withdraw a certain amount every year, which you cash out of the RRIF. Of course, you're taxed on any amount that you withdraw. Remember I mentioned the government eventually gets its tax revenue? This is where it starts to happen because now you're forced to withdraw certain amounts every year, whether you want to or not. That withdrawal minimum amount is determined by a percentage depending on your age, the total value of the plan, and so on.

As the holder of a RRIF, you can choose to take out a higher amount than you have to, but again you'll be taxed on it. It helps to think of a RRIF account as an income account designed for you when you retire. Unfortunately, the idea sounds better than it works out in reality. For many Canadians who were counting on the income from their RRIF to support them in their later years, the market meltdown in 2008 wiped out much of that retirement income.

A lot of people wonder why the government forces people to begin withdrawing their savings when they turn seventy-one. Because your assets have been compounding without the impact of tax, the government's hope (as well as yours) is that you've been able to grow a large nest egg. And now the government gets to take its share of it. They're happy to let you do the hard work of growing your assets tax free, because they end up taking a piece of a much larger asset base.

In addition, the government recognizes that it needs to have tax revenue in order to pay its bills in the future. Hence, the government has carefully figured out that as long as it starts recovering tax revenues from you in the future, it's going to be okay. There will be plenty of citizens turning seventy-one in any given year to help generate those tax payments. So the entire registered account concept is essentially a future savings account for the Canadian government itself.

Other countries have similar types of registered accounts. For example, in the United States they typically refer to their version of the RRSP as an Individual Retirement Account or IRA. American corporations offer so-called 401Ks to their employees, which you hear about routinely in the media. In Australia, an account similar to the RRSP is called a "super" (short for the official term, which is "superannuation") and in the United Kingdom it's called an "ISA" (Individual Savings Account).

The reason we call these accounts "registered" in Canada is because they are literally registered as a trust account with the Canada Revenue Agency (CRA). All the investment accounts I discuss in this book are of the registered type because it's these types of accounts that provide a unique tax benefit that you can't get with a non-registered account, such as a simple bank account or trading account with a brokerage firm.

THE BUBBLE CONCEPT

The easiest way to think of a registered account is this: imagine that you have a protective bubble that's in front of you and you're able to put your arm through its skin and place assets inside. For instance, you can take a $10 bill, reach through the bubble and drop it safely inside. Anything inside the bubble is not affected by taxes like it is the outside world, but only as long as the money remains inside the bubble.

Let me give you a more concrete example. Let's say you buy a share of a public company and place it inside your bubble. If that stock goes up in value while the stock is inside the bubble, you're not going to have to pay taxes on the proceeds of that increase because it's inside the bubble. In other words, your gains are protected from being taxed by virtue of being inside the bubble.

Not all bubbles operate exactly the same way, hence the different types of registered accounts, but in most cases there are several advantages to putting assets into this bubble.

The government restricts what you're able to put into the bubble as an eligible investment, which we will go into later. For now, let's say you've got $10,000 and you place it inside your protective bubble (whether it's an RRSP, RESP or TFSA). The reason you would do that is because you want to invest that $10,000 without being affected by taxes, and as long as you leave that money invested inside the bubble, you won't incur them.

Let's pretend that you invest your $10,000 well, and you create a gain of $2,000 (i.e., 20% on your money). If you made that money outside the protective bubble, then that 20% gain you made would be subject to taxes. Assuming you were in a 40% personal tax bracket, that would mean you'd have to write a cheque for $800 to the CRA and you'd be left with $1,200.

However, if that $2,000 profit was made inside the protective bubble, you wouldn't pay any taxes on it at the time. This would mean that you'd still have the full $2,000 to reinvest, instead of only the $1,200. Keeping your investments (and profits) inside the bubble mean you can grow your capital much faster, protected from the damaging effects of tax.

Where the TFSA is unique is that if you were to remove that $2,000, you would not incur any tax on it, whereas all the other registered account types would create a tax consequence. Of course, you wouldn't have received a deduction for contributing to your TFSA either. This is a good example of how each account has its own pros and cons, and you need to get good financial advice from an expert that can advise you on which type of account is the most appropriate for your situation.

SPECIAL CONSIDERATIONS FOR RRSP ACCOUNTS

When it comes to RRSPs, there are a number of specific considerations and issues that are important to understand.

First, you get an additional tax benefit; you're able to deduct from your personal income whatever you contribute to your RRSP in that tax year. For example, if your personal income this year is $100,000 and you contribute $10,000 to your RRSP, you're able to deduct the $10,000 from your $100,000 income, and only pay taxes on $90,000 of personal income. This deduction isn't available with the RESP or the TFSA.

When you contribute to an RRSP, you may end up getting a tax refund at the end of the year. As an aside, remember that when the government pays you a refund after you've paid your taxes at the end of the year and you file your tax return, getting any money back just means that you've been lending money to the government tax free. In other words, you've been overpaying your taxes; it's *your* money that they're giving back to you. They essentially borrowed it from you and didn't have to pay you any interest.

In Canada we have what's called a progressive tax system, which means that the more money you make, the higher the tax rate becomes at those higher levels. So how much you make on an annual basis factors into how much tax you have to pay. Someone who doesn't earn a lot of income, and therefore doesn't pay a lot of taxes compared to higher-income earners, won't benefit as much from allocating assets to an RRSP. But if you're a high-tax payer or a high-income earner, you're going to get substantial benefits from the tax deduction that comes with putting money into an RRSP.

Paying Taxes Eventually

Just because the government lets you deduct that RRSP contribution today from your income doesn't mean you're totally off the hook. As you might guess, the government isn't that kind-hearted. The taxman will catch up with you later. When you eventually remove your assets from your RRSP account, he's going to collect tax on the entire amount of gains that you've amassed inside the RRSP.

Overcontributing

The amount you're allowed to contribute to your RRSP is limited each year, and that limit is based on the income that you report. Your RRSP contribution limit is generally limited to 18% of your total income, or to a maximum dollar amount, whichever is less. For 2010, the RRSP contribution limit is $22,000, and for 2011, the limit is $22,450. This means that even if you earn a million dollars in 2010, the most you can contribute to your RRSP is $22,000.

What happens if you contribute more than the limit? You're allowed to overcontribute by up to $2,000, but if you exceed this buffer, you are penalized on the overcontributions and the penalties add up quickly, so as a general rule there's no benefit to overcontributing beyond what you're allowed by the CRA.

SPECIAL RRSP PROGRAMS

The RRSP also has a couple of unique programs that, under specific conditions, allow you to take money out without triggering taxes.

The **Home Buyers' Plan** is designed to help first-time home buyers. Although the original purpose of RRSPs was obviously to help Canadians save for retirement, the government introduced this unique part of the plan to allow for people who were trying to save for the down payment to buy their first home. Under the Home Buyers' Plan, you're allowed to borrow up to $25,000 tax free from your RRSP in order to buy a house, and if you're married your spouse can take $25,000 out of his or her RRSP or a spousal RRSP, thus allowing you to potentially take out up to $50,000 to use as a down payment.

The loan has to be paid back in fifteen years, and contrary to what most people think you can actually use this plan more than once, but only if you have not owned a house in the previous five years. So if you don't currently own your home right now and you're thinking about buying one, and you've got some funds in your RRSP account, this might be something that you want to consider.

Another special program related to the RRSP is what's called the **Lifelong Learning Program**. This is similar to the Home Buyers' Plan except the difference is the Lifelong Learning Plan allows you to temporarily use your tax-free RRSP money to pay for the cost of post-secondary school for you or your spouse (you can't use this program to pay for your child's education; you have to use an RESP for that). You're allowed to withdraw up to $10,000 a year to a maximum of $20,000, and obviously you've got to pay the funds back in the future. This can be a good place to get funds if you're looking to return to school.

BENEFITS OF RRSP ACCOUNTS

Let's talk more about RRSPs as being similar to a protective bubble because this analogy makes it easy to explain the basics of these accounts, including the advantages and disadvantages of each.

Time. It's important to remember the consequences of taking assets out of the bubble once they're inside. If you remove anything from the bubble it's back in the real world and suddenly you trigger taxes to be paid to the government. The longer you can leave the assets inside that bubble, the longer they're going to grow without the corrosive effect of taxes on them.

Time is on your side here. Keep in mind, too, that once you reach the age of seventy-one, even though the government requires you to start removing funds from your RRSP, chances are good that you'll be in a lower tax bracket because you will have surpassed your major income-earning years. That is to say, your income may not be as high as it was when you were forty, forty-five or fifty, but as a result your tax burden won't be so bad.

That said, I'll warn you now that when you do take your money out of an RRSP, every penny of it is taxed at the same rate regardless of the type of income. What this really means is that inside your RRSP if you own stocks, for example, which would normally qualify for a capital gain, you lose the benefit of the 50% exemption on the capital gain because you can't claim it as a capital gain in your RRSP when you take it out. It's the same with dividends; you lose your dividend tax credit. So the bottom line is that interest income is much more attractive as an RRSP investment than outside an RRSP because interest income is typically taxed at a higher rate, but inside an RRSP all income is taxed at the same rate. So if you're going to accumulate interest income, there's an advantage to having it inside your RRSP. Remember this—it'll be important later in the book when we discuss specific strategies.

Flexibility. Most people don't understand that once your assets are inside the bubble, you can move the assets around inside the bubble without triggering a tax consequence. Let me give you an example. Let's say you've got an investment account at a specific financial institution, but you decide that you want to move those assets to another financial institution. That transaction can happen between those two financial institutions without ever removing the assets from the bubble, so you continue to protect them from taxes even as they are moved. This is like passing a beach ball (a bubble) between two people. You simply instruct the new institution to go and retrieve the assets inside your RRSP from the old institution. Allowing the institutions to manage the transfer means you don't take the assets into your own hands, and you don't trigger a tax consequence.

Some people make the mistake of saying, "I've got $20,000 in this RRSP account at institution X. I'm going to ask for my money back, get it out of that account, and then open a new account at institution Y, open an RRSP account there, and put my money back in."

Transferring funds this way is problematic, because what you've done is "deregistered" your account. The simple way to think of this is that the moment that you can touch the money or assets inside your registered account, you've deregistered it. The whole purpose of a registered account is to keep you away from your own money. When the account is registered, the government puts a third party in charge of your money so you can't access it directly.

> When you deregister an RRSP, you essentially put a hole in your bubble, making your assets inside vulnerable to penalties and taxation.

HOW TO CREATE A REGISTERED ACCOUNT

Because registered accounts have very specific guidelines and rules to follow, it won't come as a surprise that there is a very specific process that must be followed to create a registered account.

From a legal perspective, a registered account is actually a "trust" account, with the person who owns the account as the **beneficiary**, and a third party (typically a financial institution) that acts as the **trustee** (often referred to as the **administrator**).

Even though you own the registered account and the assets ultimately belong to you, your registered account is considered a separate legal entity from you. This means that the financial company where you hold your registered account acts on your behalf as a third party to hold the account. This has the effect of creating a metaphorical gap between you and your assets, ensuring that you don't have direct access to your own investment or money. When you want to make an investment within this account, you instruct your administrator or trustee to act on your behalf.

Having that distance between you and your assets through a trustee can benefit you in ways you might not think about. Trustees are well versed in the rules and regulation of these accounts; that alone can help protect you from doing something wrong and jeopardizing your accounts. This can be incredibly helpful if you're dealing with multiple registered accounts of various types, each of which comes with a different set of rules.

If you do try to take money out of the bubble, then whichever company is acting as your trustee is required by law to withhold a certain amount of the money. The government has this law in place to make sure it gets its cut, before you take your money and spend it. Remember, the moment you take any money out of an RRSP account, you trigger tax consequences.

For example, if you went to the institution that manages your RRSP account and asked for $20,000 cash from your account, your trustee will likely keep a percentage of that money and give you what's left after that (the withholding amount depends on how much you are taking out). In this case, you'd likely get a cheque for $14,000 and the remaining $6,000 would be retained by the trustee, who would then submit it to the government.

At the end of the year, you'd reflect this withholding amount on your tax return, and if they withheld more than you owed, you would get a refund for that amount. Of course, that means you've lent money to the government tax free for all that time—but they've built this system to win, as you can appreciate.

Most of the financial institutions, brokerages and advisory firms in Canada are registered to act as administrator for registered accounts. Generally speaking, anywhere you can invest in stocks, bonds, GICs, mutual funds and other financial investments can act as a registered account administrator.

Suffering the Downside of Registered Accounts

Although it sounds great so far, there are a few pitfalls when it comes to registered accounts.

Perhaps the most important pitfall is that you cannot write off losses incurred in a registered account. An investor may have had an account of $200,000 or $300,000 a couple of years ago, and they were investing in stocks. Through the market crash of 2008, their portfolio lost 50% of its value, so an account worth $300,000 went down to $150,000. And here's the painful lesson: that $150,000 loss cannot be written off against their income to help offset the loss. Sadly, this is how a lot of Canadians are finding out the hard way that they didn't really understand their RRSP accounts.

Had they invested in stocks outside their RRSP using regular cash, at least they would have been able to write that $150,000 loss against other investment income they had generated. This is a critical distinction that most investors don't understand, and leads to a very important principle that you need to follow.

The secret is to invest registered account funds in types of investments that have minimal risk of losing value, which I'm going to teach you about in this book. It's great to be in a position whereby you don't have any losses in your RRSP, and that's what your goal should be. Since applying the strategies that I'm going to teach you later, I've never lost a dime and none of my investors have either.

In the previous chapter, you got an earful of wisdom about the financial industry and how it hopes to keep people like you and me in the dark about some of the most powerful investment strategies. They'd rather keep you invested in mediocre investments that pay high commissions, instead of introducing you to high-return investments that don't pay commissions or fees.

"THAT'S IMPOSSIBLE!"

There are a number of different types of investments that you're allowed to hold in a registered account, but here's the problem: the financial industry only tells you about the ones that pay commissions and make them a lot of money. For this reason alone you're already way ahead of the curve by reading this book. You're going to learn all the secrets that most people don't understand, even many of the people in the financial industry itself!

If you don't believe me, then after you read this book, take some of the strategies I teach you and ask your local bank manager if he or she can help you do what I'm going to show you. They're going to look at you like you're from another planet, and tell you point blank that "this can't be done" or "that's illegal" or "I've never heard of that." Remember this powerful thought: **a confused mind always says no.**

When somebody says it can't be done, often what they really mean is that it can't be done *by them*. Remember that my goal in this book is to give you all the understanding you're going to need to make this work for you, including how to find the right person to help you proceed. It's easier than you think, and it can literally help you unlock financial freedom for yourself and your family.

HOW TO TAKE CONTROL OF YOUR RRSP ACCOUNT

There are actually two primary types of RRSP accounts that you can create, and it is critical to understand the difference.

A **managed account** is the type of RRSP account that typically has some kind of broker, advisor, planner or other kind of asset manager who is managing the account (and its contents) for you. You'll be charged directly every time something is bought or sold in your account, and you also may pay a percentage of any profits you make. There are different versions of the managed account, including nominee accounts, intermediary accounts and others. The details on this are not important to our discussion, because what I'm going to suggest for you is that you do not focus on having a managed account.

A **self-directed RRSP account**, on the other hand, is exactly what it sounds like. It's an account that you manage or direct yourself. No one else is involved, so there's no one else to pay. Aside from very minor administration fees for maintaining the account, you don't pay commissions to anyone for making decisions. As you might expect, that's the kind of account we're going to be talking about a lot in this book.

I don't know about you, but I'd rather manage my own money than pay somebody else to do it for me, especially since I (like many others, and soon you) understand what's really going on in the financial industry!

Don't let the words "self-directed" lead you to believe it entails a lot of work and a long learning curve to do this yourself. That's the whole point of this book: to show you how, with some information and a little bit of effort, you can take control of your finances and do a much better job than someone else will do.

I'll remind you again that I am giving you a simple view of the types of accounts, without getting into all the unnecessary details. Ultimately, the point I want you to understand is that in order to begin truly taking control, you need to establish a self-directed RRSP account for yourself.

NOT ALL SELF-DIRECTED ACCOUNTS ARE CREATED EQUAL

As you can probably guess, the investment strategies I'm going to talk about do not involve investing in the typical things that a bank or financial advisor would suggest you buy. In fact, for the strategies I'm going to reveal to you, most of the banks, brokerages and advisory firms won't even let you hold them in their accounts.

A lot of people say, "Well, I've already got a self-directed RRSP account at my bank, so why can't I just go in there and invest through that account?"

The answer is because the investments that we're going to be talking about don't pay commissions and fees. Remember, the entire financial system is built on the business model of getting paid commission every time you do something, and even when you don't do anything.

The small handful of companies that allow these advanced kinds of investments are designed to serve a small niche of investors like you and me. Rather than basing their business model on commissions, they rely on volume.

As I said before, if you try calling your local bank or financial planner and telling them you want to execute the strategies I'm going to teach you in this book, they'll probably tell you that you're not allowed or that it's illegal.

In chapter 7, I'll outline the various administrators that I suggest you consider for setting up a self-directed RRSP account, because they'll allow you to execute the investment strategies you're going to learn.

• • •

Believe it or not, at this point you probably know more about RRSP accounts than 95% of Canadians. I've only scratched the surface of these accounts, but my goal isn't to teach you every detail. Frankly, what matters is that you understand that the financial industry will not provide you the range of investment options that are in your best interest.

This chapter was intended to give you a brief overview of registered accounts and give you the foundation that you'll need in order to apply the strategies I'm going to teach you in Part II of this book, as well as to optimize the benefits of these accounts.

I hope to get you into the top 1% of Canadians so that you can be one of those "one percenters" who tap into the real power of these accounts, and take control of your financial future.

Now that we've looked at the things that hold most investors back from success, let's move on to Part II of the book, where I will share with you what I believe is the single most powerful investment strategy for Canadians.

THE BEST-KEPT INVESTING SECRET FOR CANADIANS

5

The Best-Kept Secret Strategy for Creating Double-Digit Returns with Low Risk

Stop trying to do what's popular, and start doing what actually works!
—Anonymous

What if I told you that there was a strategy available to you that delivers the following incredible combination of benefits:

- It's among the most stable and predictable investments you can make.

- It can consistently produce double-digit returns without taking significant risk, and you're in control of how much risk you take.

- It doesn't require you to pay commissions or high fees to advisors or "experts."

- It's virtually immune to what the markets are doing, whether they're up or down.

- It's 100% eligible for RRSP, RESP, RRIF, TFSA and LIRA investing.

- It's what the financial industry *really* doesn't want you to know about.

In this chapter I'm going to tell you what I believe is the single most powerful investment strategy that can be used with RRSPs. In fact, you can use this strategy without having an RRSP if you want, but I believe doing it within the RRSP provides you the ultimate in power and control.

I'll remind you that when I'm talking and I use the phrase "RRSPs," I'm not just talking about RRSP accounts. This also applies to RESPs, Tax-Free Savings Accounts, RRIFs and Locked-In Retirement Accounts. But I'm going to refer to using RRSPs because that's the biggest category and that's the one that most people think of. Whether you're looking for a better way to invest your registered funds, or you're a real estate investor interested in attracting other people's money to your deals, this chapter is definitely one that you're going to get a lot of information from.

The strategy that I'm going to discuss here is a very similar strategy that the banks follow in order to generate significant returns with very little risk. When I first introduced this concept to clients and workshop attendees, I was taken aback by how many people thought that the strategy was risky and not very smart. However, I'll tell you this: anything is risky if you are ill-informed. For example, most people think of investing in mutual funds as a very safe way to invest your money. Well, at this point you already know how false that assumption really is.

The fact remains that if you follow the strategy as presented to you, you will set yourself up for success with one of the most secure forms of investing that there is.

THE STRATEGY UNVEILED

This strategy utilizes a simple financial product that you're probably already very familiar with: the mortgage. Most Canadians have a mortgage (perhaps even a couple) on their personal residences, and also may have a mortgage on a recreational property.

Let's think about wealth creation from the perspective of a Big Bank. Why do you think the biggest financial institutions rely on mortgage lending as their bread-and-butter business? It's because it is so profitable! Mortgage lending is one of the oldest wealth creation tools in the financial world, but until now, it's largely been protected and kept under wraps by those who understand how powerful and profitable it is. They have no interest in sharing the money or the power.

If you're like most Canadians, you've probably never thought about how mortgages can become a wealth-building tool for you, but in this chapter, my goal is to help you think differently and see the opportunities. I'm about to reveal a very specific method of investing in mortgages that you can do within your registered accounts that provides attractive returns (often in the double digits), with very limited risk (provided you know how to do it properly).

First, let's briefly review the concept of investing in mortgages to make sure you understand the fundamentals. Then I'll show you why it's even more powerful when you start to utilize registered accounts for this.

Understanding Mortgage Mechanics

A mortgage is simply a loan, secured against real estate, that is provided by a lender to a borrower. For example, if you currently own a home, chances are very good that you have a mortgage you pay down monthly or bi-weekly, and the title of your house is the security against which the bank has loaned you the money. This means that you've borrowed money from the lender, you have allowed the bank to register a mortgage and that mortgage was registered on your title, and the funds the lender provided were used to pay for some or all of the property when you bought it.

Having the mortgage registered against the property title is critically important, because that is exactly how the lender protects its interest. As I'm sure you're aware, if you stop making your mortgage payments, it's not going to be long before the lender begins the process of taking your house back so that it can recoup its money by foreclosing on the property and selling it.

Canadian banks lend billions of dollars on mortgages every year simply because they know that *mortgage lending is a very safe and secure way of investing as long as they mitigate their risk.* Even that risk is decidedly minimal, as fewer than 2% of all mortgages go into default. The banks take savings and deposits on account from their customers (and pay next to nothing in interest), and they lend the money back out to property owners at higher interest rates than they're paying to borrow those funds.

If you think about it for a minute, what's the lowest interest rate loan that you can get from a bank? Credit cards are really just loans under a different name and credit card companies charge anywhere from 10% to 30% interest. A car loan from the bank will typically be in the range of prime plus several percentage points. These days, a typical car loan might be 7% or 8%. If you have a personal line of credit—in other words, it's on your signature and you're not pledging specific assets—then typically, a personal line of credit is going to fall into that same range of 4% to 9% depending on your personal credit.

All of those types of loans are common, but clearly the lowest-interest loan you can get from a bank these days is for a mortgage on your property. At the time of writing, under normal circumstances you can get a home mortgage in the range of 4% or 5%. Why do the banks choose to lend money at the lowest interest rate when it's a mortgage involved? Why are the interest rates on mortgages lower than any other kind of loan you can get?

It's because the banks realize that they are the lowest-risk form of loan that they can provide. As long as they can get their loan attached to a piece of solid real estate that has value, it's very difficult for them to lose their money.

This is the exact reason why I believe that investing in mortgages, when you do it properly, is one of the greatest investment strategies that is available to Canadians. All that we're doing here is lending our money out on a very well-secured piece of property in exchange for somebody paying us interest on that loan.

The single most important part of investing in mortgages is making sure that you recognize the value of the real estate that you're lending on. Let me give you a simple example of what a mortgage loan looks like just to make sure you understand the process.

Let's pretend that you're going to buy your first home. You have been pre-approved for a $350,000 mortgage and have $80,000 in cash to put down. You find a house on the market that's listed for $410,000 and your offer at $400,000 is accepted. The $80,000 equates to a 20% down payment. The bank has agreed to lend you up to $350,000 on the house on the condition that the bank's valuation of the property meets that threshold. So the bank arranges for a professional to assess the current market value of the house. The appraisal determines the property is worth $415,000, so the bank agrees to go ahead.

When it's time to close on the property and get the keys, you would typically provide your lawyer the $80,000 down payment, and sign off on the mortgage documents that say that you're borrowing $320,000 from the bank—money that you promise to pay back according to the terms in the mortgage that you're signing. Once you've got your mortgage signed off, the lawyer registers that mortgage against the property title of the house, takes the $80,000 down payment and the mortgage proceeds of $320,000 from the bank, and sends the $400,000 to the lawyer representing the seller. You're now the proud owner of a $400,000 house after having put $80,000 down and getting a $320,000 mortgage. The mortgage appears on the title of your property, which means that in order for you to sell your property down the road or refinance it, that mortgage has to be paid off first, because no one will want to buy your property with an existing mortgage registered against it.

This is a very simple transaction that happens literally thousands of times every week across the country. If you step back and you look at this transaction, you can see how a basic mortgage works and what security the lender has in this transaction.

The reason the lender insists on an appraisal in this process is that the lender knows that the main security that protects its investment is the property itself. The lender wants to make sure that the property is worth more than what it is lending on the property, so that if you stop making your mortgage payments, the lender can take back your property, sell it and recover all of its financing (including its costs). This is all possible because the mortgage gives the lender the right to foreclose and take your property back. As long as the property is worth more than the balance of the loan, the lender is protected from loss. There is a very good likelihood that, if you default on payments and the lender needs to foreclose, the lender would be able to sell your house for at least $320,000, which is the amount of the mortgage. The difference between the value of the house, and the balance of the mortgage, is the "safety margin" the lender has if things go wrong.

However, if the market shifts significantly and house prices go down 20% all of a sudden, or if the lender doesn't carry out proper due diligence and loan enough money against the value of the house, the lender is going to face the risk of not being able to recoup all of its money out of the proceeds of the sale. As a mortgage investor, the absolute single most important thing you need to be aware of is the underlying value of the property, because that's going to be the primary way you protect yourself when you lend money to someone on a mortgage.

I often have people come up to me and say, "Oh, I lent money on a mortgage a few years ago and I lost money," or they have a friend or a relative who did, and one thing that I can almost guarantee you is this: whoever lent the money *probably didn't take all of the steps to fully protect themselves* in making that investment.

The whole purpose of this book is to teach you not only about the massive opportunity in mortgages, but also to show you how to ensure that you're protected against any loss. I cannot stress this point enough: as long as you're very clear on what the underlying value of the property is, it's very difficult to lose money. In addition, as we go through this process in the pages ahead, I'll be outlining the steps you need to take in order to reduce your risk.

MORTGAGES AND RRSPS

Bank advertisements repeatedly tell you about all of the great RRSP-eligible things that you can invest in like mutual funds, stocks, bonds and GICs. Most people are aware of this because of the hundreds of millions of dollars spent by the banks on marketing. And I think you know my general feeling on most of those investments. But banks usually fail to mention that one of the eligible investments for an RRSP or a registered account is what is called a "debt obligation"—a vehicle that includes mortgages! Because there's no commission paid to the financial industry when you lend money against the mortgage, the financial industry really has no interest in telling you about it. That's why this is such a little-known investment strategy that you can do with your RRSP and other types of registered accounts, and very few people are aware of them.

There are a number of different types of mortgages, but I'm going to focus on a very specific type that is eligible for registered accounts: the arm's length mortgage.

Using the Arm's Length Mortgage

First of all, it's important to understand that an arm's length mortgage is simply a loan secured by real estate. It's really no different than any typical mortgage where you lend money and in return have that mortgage registered on title. If your borrower fails to make his payments or return your money to you, you can sue and go after the property to recover your money.

However, what distinguishes an arm's length mortgage is that it's registered against property that is owned by someone who is at arm's length to you. In other words, it's intended to be an independent, third-party mortgage, and not a financial transaction between two parties that are somehow related.

Even though the *Income Tax Act* doesn't specifically define "arm's length," the Canada Revenue Agency (CRA) has published an interpretive bulletin that goes into detail regarding its view of "arm's length." To save you the pain of printing the entire bulletin here, let me give you a simple overview of what arm's length means. (You'll also find a link to the entire interpretive bulletin and several other useful documents at our website, www.rrspSecret.com or you can go to the CRA website and search for "*IT419R2*," which is the name of the document that provides the definition of arm's length.)

According to the CRA, someone is arm's length to you if they're *not* related to you by blood, marriage or adoption. So, you would not be considered at arm's length from your parents, your siblings or your children. You would not be considered arm's length from your spouse or common-law partner, or his or her parents or children.

Note that an aunt, uncle, niece or nephew would not be considered related under the CRA definition, and neither would cousins or further distant relatives. Divorce generally disconnects the relationship according to the CRA, so an ex-spouse you've divorced generally would not be considered related to you in the future, and neither would their siblings or children.

There are a number of other exceptions, and I would highly recommend that you refer to the CRA bulletin I mentioned before (*IT419R2*) if you're trying to determine whether a specific relationship is considered arm's length or not.

Now, why is this important? The simple answer is because CRA wants to make sure that when you're lending money from your RRSP or other registered account, you're doing it in an arm's length way. The CRA doesn't want you to lend money to people who are related to you, because the CRA knows that you're not always going to keep that loan agreement *commercially reasonable*.

Put simply, the CRA does not want you to lend money to yourself or your relatives. It wants to ensure that the transaction is made between parties at arm's length. And if it's not obvious enough at this point, let me confirm it—you can't lend money to yourself.

A lot of people get creative and think, "Oh well, if I can't lend money to my brother or my sister, what can I do? How about I create a corporation and have it borrow money from my RRSP, because technically that's not me borrowing the money, it's my corporation, and I'm not really related to that corporation."

That doesn't work, either. Unfortunately, the Canada Revenue Agency is a little smarter than that, and it will determine the ownership and control of the corporation and apply the very same thinking as above. If you create a corporation and have any degree of ownership in that corporation, or if anyone who would be considered related to you holds any interest in the corporation (whether you do or not), then you cannot use RRSP funds from anyone that would be considered related to you.

Remember that this is just a general overview of the concept of arm's length because the topic is important to understand when we're talking about lending money. I strongly encourage you to review the CRA bulletin I referenced above and get an opinion if there's any question about the relationship in question.

The point that I want you to take away from this is that you can't have RRSP funds lent against a property that's owned or partly owned by anybody related to you and vice versa. That means that when you're borrowing RRSP funds, it has to be from an arm's length person. So again, arm's length is critical because in an RRSP or a registered account, the types of mortgages that I'm going to talk about have to be arm's length.

Case in Point

Let me give you a really simple, real-life example of an arm's length mortgage that I transacted. This will help bring home the points I'm making. A few years ago I had a family friend I knew who wanted to buy a house.

YOU CAN'T RUN ON FAITH

As an aside, one of the problems with lending money to friends or family is quite often that we don't document the loan properly—we just do it out of good faith or good intention. We lend the money and we don't put good paperwork in place and inevitably, there's some kind of argument or problem down the road and the lack of paperwork makes the argument even more difficult.

One of the great advantages of using arm's length mortgages, especially with an RRSP, is that by law the documents have to be set up properly and recorded in order for the mortgage to be an eligible investment in your RRSP. You're essentially forced to document the loan properly so that it meets the requirements of the *Income Tax Act*, and this ensures that you don't have undocumented agreements in the future.

I knew that he hadn't saved up enough for a down payment. At the time, I had some extra capital in my RRSP, and was already a fan of arm's length mortgages. So what I agreed to do was provide him with an arm's length mortgage out of my RRSP to help him buy his house. He went and found a house that had financing that could be assumed (in other words, he was able to take over existing financing from the previous owner), and I agreed to lend him a portion of the down payment he needed from my personal RRSP account.

I set up an arm's length mortgage as a second mortgage (because it was registered behind the existing first mortgage held by the bank) and I structured it as 10% interest rate payable annually. This way, he didn't have to make payments every single month; he could get settled into the house, pay for the renovations that he wanted to complete and he wouldn't have to worry about making payments to my RRSP right away. (This is what I refer to as the Deferred Interest Strategy, which I'll detail later in the book.)

After the first year, he was able to make the payments because the interest simply accrued, and by that time he had been able to save additional funds and pay the interest. In the second year, because he had renovated the property and the value had increased, he was able to refinance his original loan and get a higher loan amount.

When he did that, his new mortgage paid off his original mortgage and also paid out the balance on my mortgage. I got my original loan amount back plus the interest from the second year that hadn't been paid yet. I was able to take those funds and reinvest them into another mortgage with someone who wanted to borrow some capital against the equity in their property.

The difference between a first mortgage and a second mortgage has nothing to do with how much is owed on the property. All it means is that there are two different mortgages registered against that property title. The terms "first" and "second" refer to the priority they hold in terms of security. All things being equal, a first mortgage is a more secure mortgage on that property simply because if something goes wrong then the first mortgage holder has a preferred right to try to get their money back. Contrary to what many believe, however, this doesn't necessarily mean that second mortgages are risky. As long as you understand how they work and you know how to manage your risk, investing in second mortgages doesn't have to be high risk.

From my borrower's perspective, he was able to find a flexible lender who was willing to lend him some of his down payment and pay 10% interest on it. To him, this was very fair, because for him, paying 10% was the difference between being able to buy a house and not able to buy a house. On the other side of the table, I benefited because I had a very secure place to put my money where I could make a 10% return. I knew that if something went wrong, there would be a piece of property that I could go after to recover my funds. Not only was I creating a double-digit return in my RRSP, but I was helping someone who normally wouldn't have had the ability to buy a home.

Using the Non-Arm's Length Mortgage

There is such a thing as a non-arm's length mortgage, and you may have heard about this strategy of holding your own mortgage inside your RRSP. The theory goes that rather than having a $200,000 mortgage with one of the big banks, if you have $200,000 in your RRSP you could become your own banker and hold your own mortgage. You would borrow the $200,000 from your RRSP instead of the bank, and make interest payments to yourself rather than to the banking system. On paper this sounds good, but the challenge is that very rarely does it make sense to hold a non-arm's length mortgage in your RRSP.

The main reason is that the fees make it relatively expensive to do this, as you are required to fully insure the mortgage with mortgage insurance (i.e., with Canada Mortgage and Housing Corporation [CMHC]). This can add thousands of dollars onto your mortgage balance, increasing the cost of executing this strategy. Additionally, your goal in your RRSP should be to maximize your returns but if you're charging yourself interest on your own mortgage, that means you're paying a high mortgage interest rate, which doesn't make a lot of sense.

Except in rare circumstances, holding your own mortgage in an RRSP is not a good idea. For the purposes of this book, I'm not going to be talking about non-arm's length mortgages beyond this, because I don't think they're very applicable to most people. We're going to focus on arm's length mortgages from this point forward, because that's where the real opportunity is.

As I said before, I think it's important in this book to give you the view from both the borrower's and the lender's perspectives, because you might be interested in lending your RRSPs to others to create a safe, double-digit return, whereas other readers might be interested in the strategy of borrowing money for their real estate investing, and want to show others how to create that safe return for themselves.

Recognizing the Benefits to the Lender

Let's look at how this strategy will benefit a person who has $30,000, $50,000 or $100,000 or more in his or her RRSP account. First, *the investment is secured by a hard asset—real estate*. It's not like putting your RRSPs into the stock market and hoping and praying that the stocks go up. The benefit to using RRSPs in lending on arm's length mortgages is that you're getting a defined interest rate, with a hard asset backing it up.

Second, in this kind of environment, let me ask you a question. If you've ever gone to get a mortgage, who pays your legal fees when you get a mortgage? You do. Who pays the bank's legal fees? You do. You may not know it, but for the most part, when you get a mortgage you usually pay your legal fees, the bank's legal fees and a lot of the other fees.

As borrowers we've been conditioned to accept that whoever has the gold makes the rules. The banks get us to pay for a lot of the fees. It's kind of crazy if you think about it, but we pay the banks to hold our money for us. We pay $15 or $20 per month in fees to have a chequing account; we're paying the bank to hold onto our money. Again, this is the way the financial system is able to create billions of dollars in profits, and that's how Canadians have been conditioned. The great news is that when you become a lender, suddenly all of those rules now work in your favour! You get to benefit from a lot of these unofficial rules that the banking system has set up.

One of those unofficial rules, which is the second benefit to lenders, is that, generally speaking, *the borrower pays all the fees associated with setting up the loan.* So if you're an RRSP investor with money in your RRSP and you find someone who's interested in borrowing money from you as an investor, typically the borrower will pay for the appraisal and administration fees and quite often the legal fees because, again, you've got the money and the power. You get to make the rules. That's a huge benefit to the investor because it means that when we talk about 10% or 12% or 14% returns into your RRSP, we're talking about ***net returns***—that's *after* expenses, because with the borrower paying all the expenses, the returns that flow to you are net (and tax deferred as well!).

Third, *as the lender, you are in complete control.* You get to decide all the terms on which you are willing to lend. It's up to you to decide how much you're going to lend, the length of time that you're willing to lend it, the interest rate that you're going to charge, and all the other terms of the agreement.

For example, if one of your concerns is that you don't want to have your money lent out for a long period of time because you're concerned that you can't predict the real estate market, you can solve that challenge by setting a loan term of only six months or a year. You tell your borrower that "I'm going to give you a one-year term for your loan, and at the end of the year I'm going to want my money back." The good thing about that is that if you want to lend on a property, and you only lend up to about 80% of the value of that property, what's the likelihood that the property value is going to decline close to 20% or less in a year?

Even in today's environment, where real estate values have declined in some markets, this is one of the powerful aspects of this strategy. You still have strong security. In 2008, I had a lot of family and friends who were invested in mortgages because they listened to me (and did it properly). My in-laws had some capital invested in mortgages and they have since told me they're the only people of all their friends who actually *made* money in 2008.

That's the wonderful thing about lending money to be put in mortgages; as long as you do your research properly, you aren't taking massive risks. You can make money even when everyone around you is losing 40% or 50%, like what has happened to most people in the last few years. You've got that ability to make money in no matter what kind of market you find yourself, and this is a very powerful place to be.

Another benefit is that it's *as close to a hands-off investment as you're going to find*, considering the returns that you get. This is because of the way that a mortgage is set up (and I'm going to teach you exactly how to do this). The payments from the borrower *automatically* go back into your RRSP account. In fact, they're deducted and withdrawn from the borrower's bank account every month or every quarter or whenever they're due by the trustee. You, as the RRSP investor, don't have to do anything at all once the transaction is set up, and the payments *automatically* go back into your account.

If something does go wrong, such as a payment gets missed, then whichever trustee you've chosen to manage your RRSP account will let you know that there's been a problem. If that happens, there's a simple process that you start in order to protect your money, which we'll discuss later.

For the most part, you don't have to do anything at all. You just sit back and wait for the mortgage payments to be made and watch your balance increase. Eventually the mortgage matures and you get your money back. Or, if you're like a lot of our lenders, you don't want your principal back and you simply want to continue on with this hands-free investment.

In our real estate company, we use RRSP mortgages extensively through our portfolio. What usually happens is we put an investor in one of these investments and, by the end of the term of the mortgage, he or she is calling to say, "I want to renew! I'm getting used to this idea of having regular consistent payments being made with no headaches!" This is really about as hands-off as you can get when you look at various investment strategies.

Yet another benefit to the lender is that *the monthly payments are not contributions to the RRSP*, but rather they're *returns*. This is an important distinction, and is often a confusing point that a lot of people don't understand. A lot of people think, "Well, I'm going to lend you my RRSP money, but every time you make a payment back to me, that's a contribution to my RRSP and it's going to reduce how much I'm allowed to contribute each year."

That's not it at all! When you lend money on a mortgage, the payments that are made back into your RRSP are considered as returns on your investment. In other words, they're not contributions. If you have $50,000 in your RRSP and you lend it out on a mortgage, and let's say over the next year you generate $5,000 of income that is paid back into your RRSP, the $5,000 interest that you earned is not going to affect your contribution room. It's no different than if you had bought a stock at the beginning of the year, and then a year later the value of the stock went up by $5,000. The $5,000 profit you made on the stock wasn't an additional contribution but simply a return on your investment. All the payments being made by the borrower are going back into your RRSP account, and they're accumulating without tax consequences.

Finally, and I cannot reiterate this enough, you get double-digit returns and significant security, all packaged into a very simple strategy. Getting double-digit returns is a huge benefit to a lot of investors out there right now who hold RRSP accounts, because they're scared—they don't know how they can possibly make double-digit returns without taking massive risks.

As we've seen, I don't care who you are, the stock market by and large is a very risky place to have your money, especially if you don't understand what you're doing (which describes most investors in the market).

These are just some of the benefits to the lender, and that's why I'm always swamped at conferences and seminars I speak at by a group of people who are looking for a better way to invest. I've been involved personally in dozens of RRSP mortgages; I've done them in my own account, my parents have done them, my in-laws have done them and a lot of my friends and family have done them. When you see how to do this simple transaction properly, you'll realize that it's a fantastic strategy to get you the best of both worlds: high interest and low risk.

Recognizing the Benefits to the Borrower

Let's turn the tables here for a minute, and look at arm's length mortgages from the other side. What are the benefits to a borrower? In other words, if you're the owner (or buyer) of real estate and you're looking for ways to reduce the amount of cash that you have tied up in the property, what are the benefits to the borrower?

As we've discussed, most RRSP lenders are concerned primarily about the value of the property because that's the primary security. For example, let's say you're a real estate investor and you're not able to qualify for a mortgage because you've got a bit of a credit issue. Let's also say that you're looking for a first mortgage on a property. The property you're trying to purchase is a $200,000 property, and you've got $50,000 or $60,000 as a down payment. Your challenge is that you can't find a lender that'll give you a traditional first mortgage. If you're able to find somebody with $150,000 in their RRSP, you could approach them to put a first mortgage on your property, just as a bank would do. You'd buy the property with your $50,000 or $60,000 down payment, and $150,000 from the RRSP would be a first mortgage, which is as good a security as possible and, in this case, the loan would represent about 75% of the value of the property.

The RRSP investor in this scenario has the security of knowing that as long as the property doesn't decline 25% or more during the term of the mortgage, the position is relatively secure. For you as the borrower, you've been able to deal with a lender that has the money and who is not going to put you through all the qualifications and hoops that a normal bank would. As a general rule, it's much easier to work with a private investor or private lender than it is with a traditional bank; however, since most RRSP holders aren't really familiar with this strategy, this is where you're able to create a win-win situation. If you can show them that you can make a secure double-digit return on their money—while holding good security on their investment so their risk is low—you can interest a lot of people with RRSPs. Again, because of how an arm's length mortgage is defined by the CRA, your rich uncle can become one of your lenders (because he wouldn't be considered "related" to you). You could go to him, or any unrelated person, and have them lend some of their RRSP funds against the property that you're buying.

Another big benefit to a borrower (the property owner or investor), is that the terms on the mortgage can be structured and negotiated to meet the specific needs that you have for a property. Let's pretend that you're a "rehab" investor, where you buy houses that need work, fix them up and flip them to a homeowner. You're able to find a property that is significantly below market value; it's kind of an ugly house and you're going to buy it, but you're going to renovate it, flip it and make your profit that way.

A lot of traditional lenders aren't going to want to lend on a house like that, because the banks generally don't like lending money on houses that are in need of major repairs. Finding a source of financing for this kind of property can be an uphill battle. However, what you might find is somebody who is willing to lend some RRSP money to allow you to buy that property. They might charge you 15% or 18% interest, but the important thing to remember is that it's only for a short period of time while you hold the property, renovate it and flip it. As soon as you flip it, you're able to pay off your investor, and the interest you pay is relatively minor compared to the profits you're able to make on the project.

The benefit of working with private investors, if they've got RRSPs, is that you can have them structure the payments so they still help you out as the investor. Think about the fact that if you buy a property, rehab it and flip it, one of your major problems is that you have no income being generated by the property during that whole time. Obviously, if you were able to defer making any payments on your financing until you were able to fix it up and sell, that might come in handy!

You might be able to find a lender who is willing to accept no payments for six months, and when you sell the property you would pay them out the principal amount plus the balance of interest that's accrued. The benefit for you is it improves your cash flow while still giving you access to the capital, and the benefit to the investor is that you can afford to pay them a slightly higher interest rate for the flexibility they're providing in the loan. Again, a win-win situation that helps both parties get what they're looking for.

There's a lot of benefit to the borrower in this situation, and the biggest one is that with credit tightening up over the past couple of years, lenders are being more and more cautious and getting difficult to deal with. Private lenders, such as those who use RRSP funds, represent literally a trillion-dollar market where there's money looking for a place to get a decent investment return. Once you understand how to sell this concept to somebody with RRSP funds, it's amazing how much money you can unlock.

• • •

In this chapter we lifted the curtain and the most powerful investment strategy that's at your fingertips. The strategies are tried and proven, and it's a win-win arrangement—the benefits accrue to both the lender and borrower. In addition, many options exist for using RRSP funds for mortgage transactions—something for everyone—as we will address in the next chapter.

6

The Power of Flexibility

*It is not the strongest of the species that survive,
nor the most intelligent, but the one most responsive
to change.*
—Charles Darwin

What I love about RRSP mortgages is that they're so flexible. First of all, RRSP funds can't be spent by the person who owns the RRSP (withdrawing funds incurs a huge withholding tax hit). If I have an RRSP that contains, say, $50,000, not only can I not spend that money, but if I do invest it into something that generates a monthly income, the monthly payments go back into my RRSP. I cannot spend that money, either. Therefore, there's less motivation to get a monthly payment back into my RRSP because I can't benefit from the monthly payments like I could if I were receiving the monthly income payments in my personal hands (which I could turn around and spend or reinvest).

However, if you're investing in mortgages for a retirement income stream, then you likely would want to invest your mortgages in non-RRSP loans, because that way you can structure the transaction so that you're going to receive a monthly payment from your borrower, which you can spend if you wish. Remember that everything I discuss about investing in mortgages also can be done outside your RRSP or registered account with cash you have available. This is a fantastic income-generating strategy because of the higher returns and lower risk.

Let's return to the notion of monthly payments. I lend $50,000 from my RRSP at 12% interest, which generates a monthly return of $500. After the first month I put back $500 into my RRSP. The problem for me is what am I going to do with that $500? I can't withdraw it. It's going to just sit in my account, as will the second payment, and the third and so on.

The reality is that I probably can't use that money until the balance grows back into a decent amount so that I can go and do something with it. So getting monthly payments as an RRSP lender really doesn't have much advantage to it.

One of the flexibilities of RRSPs is that I know as the lender that I'm likely not going to use those monthly payments. I could talk to my borrower and say, "Here's what I'll do for you. If you make monthly payments to me, I'll charge you 12% interest; however, if you'd like to make quarterly payments or maybe even just one payment per year, I'll allow you to do that but I want 14%."

The real estate investor who's borrowing the money looks at it and thinks, "well, if I have to make payments every month into your RRSP, that's going to affect my cash flow every month, but if I defer payments until the end of the first year—which means I can buy the property, renovate it, increase the rents and get better cash flow—this option gives me more of a chance to stabilize my cash flow before I have to start making payments. That gives me flexibility, so the modest extra interest that I'll pay is outweighed by the convenience of deferring the payments and helping my cash flow."

Hopefully you can see how this strategy truly can create win-win scenarios for all the parties involved!

The second key benefit for you as the borrower is that the mortgage can be structured to create optimum cash flow for the property, which of course is to the delight of the borrower. The interest rate, the length of mortgage and the amount all are completely negotiable. You can even be creative and set the loan up such that the interest rate payable on the mortgage is lower in the first year and steps up to a higher rate in the second year, again to help maximize the cash flow on the property. Since all of the terms of the mortgage are negotiable, you're able to find middle ground that gives you both what you're looking for.

Another benefit is that, assuming you structure the deal yourself, no commissions are paid to the financial industry for setting them up. This cuts out the middleman, and allows the borrower to save a little bit of money because there aren't extra fees associated with commission. For the RRSP lender, you end up making more money because there isn't someone standing over you, taking a cut of all of the investments that you make.

What's more, RRSP mortgages can be provided as first mortgages, second mortgages or third mortgages on virtually any legally registered property, including residential and commercial property, in Canada. In other words, generally speaking, you can use RRSP funds against any property that's registered at any land titles office in Canada.

You also can use RRSP funds for new purchases or to refinance existing equity. Let me describe a common strategy that our company has used several times. Let's assume that I'm buying a small commercial property for $300,000, and the bank will only lend me 60% loan-to-value. This means that I'm going to be able to borrow $180,000 from the bank to buy that $300,000 property. But I still have the problem of coming up with $120,000 in closing cash so that I've got enough funds to buy it.

Let's say that I find someone who has RRSPs, who's looking to make a decent return with solid security. I approach her and propose that I borrow $60,000, which is 20% of the purchase price. In exchange for lending me this money, I'm willing to pay her 12% interest on her money. I then would have a first mortgage of 60% on the property, and the RRSP investor would have a second mortgage of 20%, which means that the total debt on the property is 80% compared to its value—leaving a margin of 20%. In other words, the property value could decline by up to $60,000 and her money would still be reasonably secure.

Commercial property purchase price:	$ 300,000
First mortgage (60% loan-to-value):	$ 180,000
Second mortgage (20% of the purchase price):	$ 60,000
Total debt on property ($180,000 + $60,000):	($ 240,000)
Cash to close (20% down payment):	$ 60,000
Total equity in property:	$ 60,000

Keep in mind that this simple example does not factor in some of the potential costs that the lender might incur to take the property back and sell it—for example, the legal fees and the real estate commissions if a real estate agent were used. However, the point is that the primary protection the lender would have is the equity that exists in the property.

It's important that the holder of the first mortgage knows I'm arranging a second mortgage in a case like this. In other words, the primary lender needs to be okay with the fact I'm borrowing some of the down payment. Most banks are, as long as you disclose this to them up front. However, there are banks that will not allow you to borrow any of your down payment. Each bank has different criteria for lending, so this is something you would need to check with the lender you're planning to arrange the first mortgage with.

The point I want to make very clear is that I'm not suggesting that you don't tell the bank where the money's coming from—that's definitely a bad idea. As I said, my personal experience is that most banks don't have a problem with it *as long as you disclose it up front* and as long as you're putting down a reasonable amount of your own capital. In this case, I would still be putting down 20% cash, and that's generally a reasonable amount. It would be taking a lot of risk if I went out and found someone to lend me all of the down payment as a second mortgage, because I would have nothing invested in the deal. The bank would assume I'd be more willing to walk away from that scenario, so my loan would be considered high risk.

In fact, the idea of borrowing your entire down payment using somebody's RRSP as a mortgage is not going to fly. The banks won't allow it, and it's also not a good idea for the RRSP investor because it puts him or her at risk should the property go down in value.

EQUITY REFINANCING

In addition to the ability to use RRSP arm's length mortgages to fund new purchases in many cases, another way to use RRSPs is to refinance some equity. In fact, I think this is the most powerful use of RRSP mortgages.

Let's assume you've got an investment property that you bought a few years ago, and it's gone up in value. You've been paying down your first mortgage and you've accumulated a fair amount of equity. As an example, let's say you originally bought the property for $250,000 several years ago and now the house is worth $400,000 in the market. You've never refinanced it; you've still got that original first mortgage on the property. If you had gotten a traditional conventional mortgage on the $250,000 property with an 80% loan, then your original mortgage balance was $200,000, and you had put $50,000 down.

Fast-forward to the present, where the property is worth $400,000. To keep things simple let's assume that your mortgage balance is still $200,000 and you've now got $200,000 of equity in that property. (In actuality, your mortgage balance would be lower today, because you've been slowly paying down the principal each time you've made a payment.) You want to tap into some of that $200,000 equity, but maybe the first mortgage you've got in place is at a very low interest rate, which you'd lose if you refinanced the mortgage.

Since we've been in a period with some of the lowest interest rates in history, there are a lot of loans out there with very attractive interest rates. For example, I have some mortgages on my investment properties that are in the range of 3.5% to 4.0% fixed. If I were to refinance those properties, I wouldn't be able to get such a low interest rate again, so I'm hesitant to interrupt that first mortgage. However, I still want to access some of that equity, so what can I do?

Instead of refinancing the first mortgage, I would just leave that first mortgage in place and find someone who will lend me a second mortgage on the property, based on all the equity I have (and of course, lots of equity means lots of security to a lender).

Back to our house example . . . it goes up in value from $250,000 to $400,000, so you have $200,000 equity in the property and a $200,000 mortgage. You come to me, because I'm an investor with RRSP funds. You say to me, "Greg, I've got this house worth $400,000, and I've got an existing mortgage on it of only $200,000 so I've got $200,000 of equity. What I'd like to do is borrow $100,000 from your RRSP, which means that I'll have a total of $300,000 of debt on the property, which is 75% loan-to-value (and in today's environment, a 75% loan-to-value would be considered fairly secure). I'll pay you 12% on your money if you lend me $100,000."

Because there is a significant amount of security, I'd say that looks like a pretty good investment, so through my RRSP I would lend you the $100,000 you're looking for. The term of the mortgage is agreed to be one year. We would record a mortgage on your property for $100,000, and you would get access to that $100,000. With the mortgage registered, you would start making payments into my RRSP account.

At the end of the year, we would either renegotiate and I would extend the terms of the loan for another year, or you could decide you're going to sell your property or refinance it with a new first mortgage. If you sell it, you pay off the first mortgage, pay me off and get whatever profit is left over. If you decide instead to refinance the property, your new loan would pay off both the old mortgage as well as my second mortgage. In either case, I get my money back with my 12% return, and I'm able to reinvest the capital.

This is a great example of how you can use RRSP funds to refinance out some of the equity you've got trapped in a property. This has become a common transaction, now that mortgages have been more difficult to get from the traditional lenders. Sometimes you don't really want to pay off that first mortgage, because it's such a great rate. With banks becoming very conservative when it comes to rental properties, we're seeing banks cancel rental property financing programs that they've had in the past. This adds up to fewer options for the borrower and more opportunities for the RRSP investor/lender.

You may be in a situation where you've got an equity-rich property but you can't figure out a way to access some of that equity. Doing a second mortgage through an RRSP may be your answer. The reality is that you're going to pay a little bit more interest for it, and you'd be better off if you could get a 5% first mortgage and refinance; however, if that's not an option for you and you'd rather access some of that equity—and the numbers makes sense to borrow the money at a double-digit interest rate—then this gives you a tremendous alternative.

IT'S NOT ALL ABOUT THE INTEREST RATE

A mistake that many borrowers make is focusing too much on the interest rate and not looking at the entire deal as a financial transaction. They get stuck on what they think is a high interest rate, and don't do a deal that would have made them a lot of money. Do the math on the deal, and you may find out that what seems like a high interest rate allows you to create a significant profit! Be careful that you don't pass up a deal on which you could have made great money, simply because it seemed like the interest rate you'd have to pay for the money was too high.

THIS IS WHAT THE BANKS DO

One of the most common responses I get when I'm dealing with somebody who doesn't really understand real estate, or is used to a 5% return in their investing, is the following: "Greg, why on earth would anyone pay 12% or 14% to borrow money? That's craziness!"

The answer is that for most real estate investors, it's simply the cost of doing business. I can tell you that I've borrowed millions and millions of dollars at 10% or 12% or 13%, but I've taken that money and I've made *several hundred percent* on that money.

What I'm really doing is using the same kind of thinking as the banks do. I might borrow money at 12%, but I can take that money and go and make 100% or 200% on it through my other investing strategies. For me, it's literally just the cost of doing business, no different than when the bank pays us 1% or 2% for our GICs or our savings accounts, and goes out and makes 6% or 8% or 10% or 12% on our money (or, in the case of credit cards, 25% or 30%!).

The other reason why paying 12% interest or more for a real estate investor makes sense is that quite often it's for a short term. If a borrower had to get a traditional mortgage, he or she would have to jump through all the hoops and pay all the fees up front, and even pay penalties if he or she wanted to pay back the loan before it was due to be paid back. Once the bank has lent you the money, the bank doesn't really want to get it back. It wants to see the regular payments made, receive the interest on the loan and get the principal back. If you only borrow the money from the bank for three months and then pay it all back, it's not worth the hassle of setting up the mortgage to begin with. That's why the banks charge a prepayment penalty.

When you're dealing with private investors, if you borrow money on a second mortgage, you can normally pay that money back any time you like; in other words, you usually don't face a prepayment penalty. If your investment goes better than you expected and you can repay the funds faster than you had anticipated, you have the flexibility of repaying the loan and you don't end up paying a bunch of fees and penalties.

While on the surface it may sound expensive to be paying 12%, using traditional bank lending for things like rehabs, flips and renovation projects tends to be more expensive. And of course the banks do a good job burying the real cost. As I mentioned earlier, the banks shy away from lending money on creative real estate deals. They'd prefer to stick with the bread-and-butter, homeowner mortgages that they understand best.

At the end of the day, real estate investors are happy to pay a premium for the speed and the convenience they enjoy when working with private investors. That's why when I've lent out money for mortgages, one of the reasons why people like working with me is that I'm flexible and I can move quickly. Assuming that your RRSP funds are sitting in the account, you can issue a mortgage in a matter of days. It can take as little as seven to fourteen days as long as everything is in place. That's the great thing about lending RRSPs or just lending private money in general, and that's why people are willing to pay a higher premium.

As well, keep in mind that we're dealing in a different credit and lending environment than we were a few years ago. The credit crisis of 2008 and 2009 removed a lot of the lending alternatives that used to be out there. We've seen at least a dozen banks in Canada shut down, and a lot of the banks that still exist have tightened up their lending. Simply put, there are fewer options out there for the creative real estate investor.

During the boom, when everyone seemed to believe real estate could never decline in value, you may have been able to get loans for less than 12%, because there were a number of foolish lenders willing to lend money with very little security. The lending environment has dramatically shifted, so borrowing money at 12% or 14% is not that uncommon. Once you're in the real estate game for a while, you'll realize that this is standard practice in the business.

Now, if you're someone who is simply looking at this as a way of investing your RRSPs, you're probably thinking, "What kind of high-risk deal would somebody have to take in order to make a 12% or 14% annual return?" I believe that as long as you do your due diligence and structure the deal properly, you're taking far less risk than investing in any kind of stock market investment or many other choices that you have.

What are the typical rates that RRSP borrowers or lenders can expect in this business? First of all, there's no such thing as "standard rates"; the rate paid—the interest rate—is always entirely negotiable. Having said that, it also depends on the type of property that you're lending against, on the loan-to-value, and on the quality of the borrower.

LOAN-TO-VALUE LOGISTICS

The term "loan-to-value" is critical to understand when you're looking at mortgage investing. Let me give you an example of what loan-to-value really means.

Assume you've got a property worth $200,000 and I want to borrow $150,000 against that property. The loan-to-value, or LTV, is calculated as 75% (the $150,000 loan divided by the $200,000 value of the property). This means that the $150,000 represents 75% of the value of the property.

Typically, 75% is considered a reasonably conservative loan-to-value ratio. That's why in Canada, the conventional loan limit that the banks are allowed to lend against used to be 75%. As you probably know, a few years ago the Bank of Canada changed the definition of a conventional loan to 80%, which is what it has been in the United States for a very long time.

In today's world, when you go to the bank, the bank will typically lend you up to 80%, the conservative loan-to-value ratio, of the value of the property without requiring you to get mortgage insurance. As long as you're not lending above 75% or 80%, you're considered to have very good security. If you want to borrow more than 80% of the value, you're required to get mortgage insurance, since going above 80% is perceived to be higher risk—and the banks therefore require insurance against the potential of a default.

Compare that to some of these "no money down" deals that we saw in the U.S. We saw lenders that were literally lending 107% of the value of the property! If you had a $200,000 property, these lenders were willing to lend you $214,000, which was every cent you needed to buy the property and pay your closing costs, too! It's not difficult to see what went wrong with the U.S. lending environment and housing market.

As you can expect, the higher the LTV, the higher the perceived risk of a loan. Therefore, typically the interest rate goes up accordingly, and varies with whether the loan is a first mortgage or second mortgage.

It's typical that you see private investors asking for anywhere from about 7% to 11% on a first mortgage. Again, this is different in every case; I don't want to make you think that this is the way it always is, but this is what would be considered typical. In other words, a private first mortgage is typically a bit more expensive than the rates that the big banks charge, but not a lot more expensive. On a second mortgage, depending on the loan-to-value, the rate is typically anywhere from about 9% all the way up to 18%. That's going to vary according to the loan-to-value, since it defines how much risk a lender is taking.

Let's look at another example to illustrate how loan-to-value is calculated.

Assume you've got a property that's worth $200,000 and let's say you've already got a $100,000 first mortgage on it that's a few years old. Your goal is to tap into some of that remaining equity with a second mortgage.

If you wanted to borrow $30,000 from a private investor, that would make the total debt on the property $130,000. Because the property is worth $200,000, that would equate to a 65% loan-to-value ratio. This would be considered a low-risk deal for most investors; you might be able to negotiate an interest rate of 9% or 10% for it. If you have a $100,000 first mortgage and you're looking for a second mortgage of $60,000 or maybe $70,000 on that property, then the total debt on the property is going to be $160,000 or $170,000 out of the $200,000 value; that's a loan-to-value of 80% to 85%. The risk profile is growing and so interest rates are going to increase, typically to the range of 11% to 12% and higher. Again, this all depends on the lender and what their terms are, but these are typical rates you'd see for private first and second mortgages.

Expecting Points and Fees

When you go to a private lender—somebody who is a professional lender or mortgage broker—often the lender will quote you an interest rate and charge you something that they call "points." Many sophisticated RRSP investors charge these extra fees.

A point is simply 1% of the loan amount, and it's charged up front, almost like a fee for arranging the loan. For example, if you have arranged for a loan amount of $100,000 and the lender is charging you three points, that would be 3% of the loan amount, or $3,000. A more sophisticated lender knows that if they tackle all of the due diligence and make a loan, and the borrower keeps out the money for a month before paying back the loan, then it's really worth the hassle of doing the due diligence and setting up the loan. By charging this upfront fee, the lender will realize a minimum return on his money, plus the monthly interest that accrues.

Using our example above, the lender knows that no matter how long the borrowing period, he or she will realize a $3,000 profit on the investment, plus the interest. Charging points is very common in the U.S., even by traditional lenders on homeowner mortgages. In Canada the practice is less popular, especially with traditional loans for homeowners, but be aware of it and don't be surprised if points are charged when borrowing private money. Also, if you decide to use a mortgage broker to help facilitate a private loan for you, you'll find that mortgage brokers charge points on the loan, and this is how they generate an income from being involved in the loan.

I don't look at the fees a mortgage broker charges quite the same as I do the commissions and fees charged by the financial industry. For one thing, the fee is a one-time cost to the borrower, so it's not an ongoing commission that continues to get charged once the loan is arranged. Similarly, if you're using a good mortgage broker, he's going to save you time with respect to sourcing the lender (or who to lend to, if you're lending money), and he should be able to fast-track the due diligence process and save you time there as well. You certainly don't have to use a mortgage broker if you want to arrange a mortgage yourself, but this is an option we'll discuss later.

Usually, when someone does charge you points up front, there is no penalty for paying the loan off early. Again, this will depend on the sophistication and terms of the lender, but it's much less common to have a steep payoff penalty for a private loan than for a traditional mortgage from a big bank. You're unlikely to run into someone charging points if you're dealing directly with RRSP lenders and individual investors.

Most individual investors are thrilled to get a double-digit return on their money and aren't that concerned about trying to charge fees and points. For most investors, the opportunity to make 10% or 12% on their money, especially when it's a net return and there are no commissions, is a dream.

• • •

In this chapter, I've introduced you to the concept of arm's length mortgages, and using them in conjunction with a registered account like an RRSP. I truly believe this is one of the most powerful strategies available to the RRSP investor today. In the chapters that follow, I'm going to lay out this strategy step by step, so that you can begin harnessing the wealth-building power of this approach.

Don't forget that my website, www.rrspSecret.com, has a number of free resources that will help you learn this strategy, and answer any questions that you might have. Be sure to visit the site and register for your free account so you can access the videos, tutorials, articles and documents and get started on this strategy right away.

Mortgage Investing, Step by Step

Life is really simple, but we insist on making it complicated.
—Confucius

This chapter is going to focus on two major topics. First, I'm going to give you specific step-by-step instructions on how to set up a self-directed RRSP or other type of registered account that allows you to invest in arm's length mortgages. Then, we're going to talk about the steps that are involved in creating an arm's length mortgage investment.

Again, I'm going to look at this from both sides of the table—not only from the perspective of the person with the RRSP account, but also from the view of a real estate investor looking to attract other people's money into the opportunity.

> Remember that when I mention setting up RRSP accounts, I'm also talking about RESPs, TFSAs, Locked-In accounts and RRIFs. I use "RRSP" as a generic term, but you can do this with other types of accounts as well.

In chapter 4 I provided an overview of registered accounts and introduced the concept of a trustee, sometimes called an administrator. This is a third party that acts as the go-between, separating you from direct access to the funds and assets in your registered account. For the purposes of this book, I'll be using the term "trustee," but remember that this is interchangeable with "administrator," as you'll sometimes see them referred to in the industry.

Not all trustees are created equal, and in fact, you may find it difficult to find a trustee who will work with you. As you might expect, because the arm's length mortgage strategy is relatively unknown, and because the transaction doesn't create massive commissions and fees for the industry, most trustees ignore them altogether, choosing instead to focus on high-margin, high-profit investments and services.

Fortunately for us, there are several trustees that have decided to specialize in this kind of alternative investment strategy, and that's who I will be suggesting you consider when you create a new self-directed registered account.

SELF-DIRECTED RRSP SETUP

Step 1: Choose a Trustee

The first thing you need to do is make sure you're dealing with a trustee that allows arm's length mortgages as an investment. Here's the problem: most RRSP trustees *do not allow* arm's length mortgages. For example, a lot of the big banks in their normal online trading RRSP accounts don't allow this. You can forget about trying to hold arm's length mortgages in most brokerage accounts. Even if you already have a self-directed RRSP account set up somewhere, that in itself doesn't mean that you can invest in these kinds of investments. It's important to make sure that you're dealing with a trustee or an administrator that will allow you to hold arm's length mortgages in your account.

There are generally four trustees in Canada that are set up to help you with arm's length mortgages and have a track record of reliably providing this service. The following trust companies specifically allow arm's length mortgages:

- Olympia Trust

- Canadian Western Trust

- B2B Trust (a division of Laurentian Bank)

- TD Waterhouse

This list may not be exhaustive of all the trustees who are willing to administer arm's length mortgages, but these are the four largest administrators that do the lion's share of this type of investment, and that have a proven track record of serving this particular niche.

On my website at www.rrspSecret.com, you'll find links to the website for each of these trustees and copies of all the current documents you need to set up a self-directed account at each of these institutions. I've also provided a comparison of the four trustees based on their fees and the services they provided, along with my own personal experiences and those of many of my students and clients.

What I'd recommend is that you go to each of the sites, check into them, look at their fees and try to decide for yourself which one is going to provide you the best customer service. Don't be too concerned about where the trustees are located, because you'll never need to visit an office or branch. It's such a simple business that location is not a major factor in selecting your trustee. In fact, I've been involved with more than one hundred RRSP loans, and I've never been required to visit any of the trust companies.

Step 2: Open a Self-Directed Account

If you don't already have one set up with them, you'll want to open a new self-directed registered account. To do this, you simply complete an application form (which you can download by going to my site at www. rrspSecret.com. We have links to applications for all the trustees mentioned above.). Send the filled-in application form into the trustee by mail or by fax. It typically takes a week or two to get your account set up.

Whether you decide to set up a self-directed RRSP, RESP, TFSA or RRIF account is going to depend on your specific situation. Again, the goal of this book is not to offer you tax-planning advice, so I can't tell you which account you need to open. Most people will open a self-directed RRSP account, but you need to ensure that's the account that makes the most sense for you, based on your particular situation.

Step 3: "Fund" Your Account

When you're setting up your self-directed account, you should also think about funding that account at the same time. When I say "fund" the account, I'm simply talking about the actual funds that you are going to put into the account that can be lent out as an investment.

There are a couple of ways that you can fund your account. One is to simply contribute new cash (i.e., not already in your registered account), which would be an RRSP (or other registered account) contribution. For example, this might be extra money that came in as a bonus, or that you've accumulated in your savings account. You write a cheque for $10,000 into your new registered account, and it goes into the account to be available for your investing. If you contribute to an RRSP, you'll likely get a tax deduction for that contribution. If you contributed to an RESP or TFSA, you won't get a tax deduction. If you have a RRIF, you cannot make any additional contributions. Again, each account is different and you need to make sure you're setting up the right type of account for your situation.

In addition to funding your account by putting new cash into the account, you can transfer existing funds from another institution where you've already got a registered account. As an example of this, my wife decided to set up a new self-directed RRSP account for herself at one of the trustees I mentioned above. She also happens to have an existing self-directed trading account at an online brokerage with one of the big banks. She filled out the paperwork, opened the new account and directed the new trustee to retrieve the assets she held in the old brokerage account. She did this by completing a form called a Transfer Form, which enables your new trustee to request that the old trustee transfer the funds into the new account; the old trustee must comply. It's important to note here that she did not take the money out of the old account and write a cheque back into the new account. That would be considered a withdrawal and you want to avoid withdrawals because by "deregistering your funds" you trigger tax consequences.

I just want to make sure you understand that if you have assets in an RRSP or a registered account, transfer those funds or assets within the RRSP rather than touching the money yourself. You can see examples of Transfer Forms on the website at www.rrspSecret.com.

> When you fund your account from another RRSP, you *transfer* the money—you do not withdraw the money and redeposit it. If you withdraw and then deposit, you'll risk triggering tax consequences.

Another stumbling block can potentially emerge here, as you can probably appreciate. The brokerage or financial institution that receives a request to transfer funds isn't going to be too happy, because it is losing business. It may take action to preserve its business with you.

This happened to my business partner, Kourosh, when he decided to move his money into a self-directed account so that he could invest in arm's length mortgages. He had a fairly sizable investment account at one of the big bank's brokerage firms. He had a broker—in other words, a salesperson—who managed his portfolio, which was an RRSP account. Kourosh was tired of losing money in his RRSP and I had finally convinced him to take a different approach and take control of his own money by using this strategy.

He filled out the paperwork (albeit sheepishly, not knowing what his broker was going to say), and avoided telling his broker what he was doing. He just filled out the paperwork and sent it in to the new trustee. About three weeks later, he got a call from . . . guess who? . . . his broker, of course, who proceeded to tell him that there must have been some mistake, because it looked like a transfer had been requested. Kourosh told him that it wasn't a mistake and that he had in fact submitted the transfer request.

The broker went on and on about how risky it was to do what he was doing, and how he was getting out at the worst time, the market was going to improve, and all of these things about why Kourosh was being foolish moving his money out of the market.

Kourosh quietly listened to everything he said, and then came to me, saying, "I don't know if I can do this anymore because I feel so bad." I looked at Kourosh and said point blank, "Whose money is this? Is it *his* money or is it *your* money? It's up to *you* to make the decision."

His broker had tried to guilt him into leaving the money where it was, where it wasn't making money, but Kourosh held firm. I can tell you now that it was one of the best financial decisions that Kourosh has ever made, because he's never lost a dime and has consistently made 12% to 14% in his RRSP for several years, including during one of the worst investment periods in history!

I can almost guarantee that this will happen to you if you have a managed account with an advisor, planner or broker. You can expect that you're going to get a phone call, and your advisor is going to tell you nineteen reasons why it's a bad idea for you to do what you're doing. You'll be told that mortgages are risky, that the market's about to move, that you're forfeiting new strategies to grow your returns. The advisor may even become angry and tell you pointedly that you don't know what you're getting into.

The bottom line is that you have to resist the pressure. If you're the real estate investor who's trying to convince an RRSP investor to engage this strategy, you will definitely need to warn him or her about this, too. Explain that this *is exactly* what they're going to hear from the broker or account manager. The self-interest for the sales rep is obvious; if you move that money away, that's less money that the rep has to manage so he or she will see fewer fees and commissions. It's in the rep's best interest to keep you and your money where it is, but don't listen to false arguments.

Everyone, *every single person* that I've talked to who has gone through this situation, who moves forward despite feeling that they are betraying a trusted advisor, has been grateful they did. Kourosh thought his advisor was his friend, but when he moved his money he found out the truth.

Remember, one of the greatest challenges you'll face in creating wealth for yourself is your own mindset. You'll need to be firm and focused in this process if you're trying to move money out of someone else's management. Just remember that as I told Kourosh, it's *your* money and *your* decision. Don't let anyone tell you otherwise!

The Question of Liquidating

Another question people have at this stage goes something like this: "Greg, I have a bunch of mutual funds in that other institution. I want to sell them and use the money to invest in mortgages. Do I have to liquidate them or can I just transfer the mutual funds over into the trustee into my new account?"

Generally speaking, the easiest approach is first to liquidate the assets in the old account and then transfer over the cash into your new account. This is because it's possible that whatever assets you hold in the old account may not be acceptable to the new trustee. You certainly can transfer the assets over to the new account (assuming the new trustee considers them eligible investments) if you prefer. But understand that what you're really trying to do is invest in mortgages, which means you need to have liquid cash available inside your account anyway. Transferring the mutual funds over doesn't really do you a lot of good until you liquidate them and have access to the cash. One of the decisions that you have to make is whether or not it makes sense to liquidate your mutual funds or your shares or your GICs or whatever you might be currently invested in.

Again, I want to be clear about this: I'm not telling you to sell your mutual funds or any assets that you might hold in your account. I am not a financial planner or advisor, and I have no idea what assets you might hold or what the potential ramifications would be of selling or liquidating your assets.

What you absolutely have to do is a cost-benefit analysis of what it looks like if you liquidate your assets. For example, if you hold mutual funds in your current RRSP account and are restricted from using funds for arm's length mortgages, and you're looking to transfer those funds so you can start investing in mortgages, one of the things you've got to look at is what happens if you sell those mutual funds. This is one of the reasons why I dislike the financial industry so much.

One of the problems with having mutual funds is they often have some kind of back-end load attached to them. For example, you may have been told that on the purchase of a mutual fund there was no upfront commission. That may be true, but what the salesperson prob-ably *didn't* tell you was that you have to hold that mutual fund for a period of time of, say, five to seven years. If you don't hold it for that period of time, for every year you withdraw early you'll be assessed a penalty.

As an example, let's say you own a certain mutual fund and you cannot withdraw or transfer the funds for at least seven years. If you sell your shares after just two years, you could be penalized 5% or 7% of your original investment just to get your money out!

For this reason, I do not suggest that you liquidate all of your invest-ments and move them to a cash position. You need to do an assessment of that beforehand so you know what such action will cost you. You should consider the actual performance and return of the investment you have as well, not just the cost of liquidating.

Consider that you have a mutual fund that you've owned for a few years, and you're trying to decide whether it makes sense to liquidate it and pay the costs in order to move that money into an arm's length mortgage. Let's say that for you to liquidate today you're going to have to pay a 5% penalty, and that for the past two years, that mutual fund has generated net gains of 5% in each of those years for you.

Now let's look at the other side of the coin to decide if it makes financial sense to take that 5% penalty and liquidate. Let's assume you've decided that arm's length mortgages make sense, and you're going to target mortgage investments that pay 12%, which is not a difficult number to find in the arm's length mortgage business. If you liquidate your mutual fund, it's going to cost you 5%, but you'd be able to increase the return on your money from 5% annually to 12% annually. If you liquidate and move your money, it's likely you'll increase your annual returns by 7% each year, but you'll have to pay a 5% fee to do it.

How long does it take you to get your money back and make it worthwhile to go ahead and liquidate your funds? If you liquidate, you'll take the 5% penalty, but you're going to make an additional 7% per year on your money. The reality is, you'll make back that 5% penalty in less than a year, and then be making 7% more every year thereafter. And remember, this assumes the mutual fund would consistently continue to make 5%, which cannot be guaranteed to happen. On the other hand, if you place your funds into an arm's length mortgage, your return is going to be very predictable.

It's very important to look at not just the penalties that you're going to incur if you liquidate the assets in your RRSP, but also at the potential upside of liquidating and how long it'll take you to recover any penalties you might pay. Typically what you'll find is that it's not going to take you more than several months or maybe a year to recover the fees. Plus, you'll have the benefit of not paying ongoing commissions thereafter, and you'll have a very solid sense of what your returns will be going forward, not to mention having a physical asset backing your investment as opposed to just a piece of paper that's worth nothing!

The other argument you'll hear against liquidating goes something like this: "It's a terrible time to sell out of the stock market, because stocks are at lows. With the market, your mutual funds may have lost 40% in value, so you're selling at the bottom." Should you leave the money in the funds, let it ride, and hope the market comes back up and see if you can get your money back? There are a couple of issues with that premise.

Nobody knows where the stock market is going. I don't care who you are, you simply cannot predict with consistent accuracy what's going to happen. The second problem is that financial turbulence is here to stay, and it's quite possible that the stock market will continue to gyrate into the future. The governments are not doing anything productive to reduce the amount of volatility and swings in the stock market—so you can bet we'll continue to see drops in the market, just as much as there will be moves up. If you stay in a specific stock or a mutual fund, there's no guarantee that it's going to turn around any time soon, much less get you back to where you started if you're in a loss position right now.

As I covered in chapter 1, you need to be careful of the biases that are wired into you as a human being. It's not an intelligent investment choice to hold an investment because it's going to "come back." Unless you have sound reason to believe that the investment will increase again, you're simply gambling and letting your emotions drive the show. Getting real about this is one of the hardest parts of being an intelligent investor, but it's really the only way if you plan to become financially free.

If you move your money into arm's length mortgages and you invest intelligently by doing your due diligence and picking solid mortgages to invest in, there is a very strong likelihood that you're going to generate a 10% to 14% return on your money. There are no guarantees, just like anything else, but you're in a much more secure position than investing in the stock market. And perhaps the best part is that you're not going to have to get up every morning and look in the newspaper to see if you've lost more money.

In some cases, there may be investments you've made where the penalty to liquidate it is as high as 20% or 30%. If that's the case, you might want to think carefully about whether or not liquidating makes sense. For the most part, what you'll find is that the consistency and predictability of the income and the interest that's generated from arm's length mortgages offsets the penalty.

You need to sit down and really think this through. This isn't just a quick decision to make because I'd hate to hear that somebody went and sold off a bunch of assets and got penalized because they hadn't thought about it in advance. So again, check out your account, check out your specific investments, and make sure you understand what penalties there are. Do a cost/benefit analysis of whether or not it makes sense to liquidate and move into a cash position so that you can transfer the cash over to a self-directed account.

Once you've made that decision and assuming that you've either moved money from an existing registered account or you've contributed new capital into your account, it's time to start investing in mortgages. Naturally, looking for potential investments is the next step.

Step 4: Find a Mortgage Opportunity

You're now in a position where you can lend money on mortgages. At this point many of you are probably thinking, "Where on earth am I going to find a mortgage to invest in?" Don't worry, I'm going to devote an entire chapter to telling you where to find mortgage opportunities, or if you're the real estate investor, where to find the people who have RRSPs to invest. For now, let's just focus on the process to make sure that you understand the big picture. We want to get the fundamentals in place first, and we'll talk about how to create opportunities later.

The first thing you need to do is identify the property on which you're going to lend money. Once it's identified, you would complete your due diligence on that property and the investment. (I'll discuss the due diligence process thoroughly in a later chapter so that you feel confident in verifying an investment opportunity and are able to protect yourself. At this point, I simply want to give you the high-level view of the process.)

Let's assume that you're the RRSP holder and you've come across a real estate investor who owns an investment property appraised at $200,000. He has an existing mortgage of $90,000 on the property. That means he's got $110,000 of existing equity in the property. He says to you, "I'm interested in borrowing some money from you, and if you lend me some money against my property I will pay you a 12% return." That sounds fair so you ask how much he's interested in borrowing. He says, "I'd like to borrow $40,000."

If he already has a $90,000 mortgage on the property and you're going to lend him $40,000, that would be a total of $130,000 of debt on that property. If you look at this in terms of the loan-to-value, you take the $130,000 of debt against the property divided by the appraised value of the property, which is $200,000. That equals a 65% loan-to-value. Essentially the property's resale value would have to drop by close to 35%, or $70,000, before your money is at serious risk. As an investor, I would say that's a pretty safe investment.

Even today where property values in some markets are flat or declining, you have to figure out what the likelihood is that the values are going to decline by 20% or 30%. If you're picking the right kinds of properties in the right kinds of markets, it's pretty unlikely that that's going to occur.

Back to the scenario: you agree to lend this investor the $40,000 out of your RRSP for twenty-four months and he's agreed to pay you 12% interest. Since there's $40,000 being lent, 12% on a monthly basis is a $400 per month payment. Twelve percent annually is the same as 1% per month; that's why 12% is so common in second mortgages—it's easy to calculate. *Remember that second mortgages are almost always interest-only, because we're dealing with simple interest and it's easy for everyone to calculate.*

The next step is finalizing and negotiating the terms and the conditions of the mortgage with the borrower. You're going to need to talk about the amount of the mortgage (in this case, $40,000), the interest rate payable (12%), the term of the mortgage (twenty-four months), and anything else that you might want to add to the terms of the mortgage. Later you'll learn about some advanced things that you can do, but for the purpose of this example that's really all you need.

Let's say that of the $40,000 second mortgage, the investor intends to use $10,000 to renovate that property, and he's going to take the other $30,000 and use it as a down payment on another property. You as the RRSP investor really don't care too much about where he's going to spend that money. What's most important to you is what the value of the property is and how much debt is going to be held on that property, because the property is your security.

The Mortgage Direction and Undertaking Document

Once you've completed your due diligence and verified all of the information, you'll summarize the basic terms of your agreement and provide those details to your real estate lawyer, who will draft the agreements for you. The main document that will outline the terms of the agreement is what's referred as a Mortgage Direction and Undertaking Document, and it provides a summary of the mortgage details such as the amount being loaned, interest rate, term of the loan, and all other important details. There is an example of a Mortgage Direction and Undertaking Document on page 108. (You can find a sample template of this form on www.rrspSecret.com.)

SAMPLE MORTGAGE DIRECTION AND UNDERTAKING DOCUMENT

Mortgage Direction & Undertaking
Regarding Arms-Length Mortgages as Investments in
Self-Directed RRSP/RRIF/LIF/LRIF/LRSP

TO: ABC Trust Company ("ABC Trust")

Further to the Declaration of Trust made with respect to my Plan # _____ ("my Plan"), I hereby authorize and direct ABC Trust to invest funds held by my Plan in a new mortgage selected by me and described below (the "Mortgage").

I understand that ABC Trust is not obligated to accept my investment in an arms-length mortgage.

In consideration of ABC Trust accepting the Mortgage as an asset of my Plan, I hereby agree to the following terms and conditions:

1. I understand and acknowledge that it is my sole and entire responsibility to verify that:

    (a) the Mortgage is an "Arms-Length" transaction as defined in the *Income Tax Act(Canada);*

    (b) the Mortgage is a qualified investment as governed by the *Income Tax Act(Canada);*

    (c) the Mortgage is a proper charge against the Land therein described and is adequately secured;

    (d) all payments due on the Mortgage are made on the specified date as outlined in the mortgage document;

    (e) all mortgage payments are paid directly to ABC Trust; and

    (f) there is adequate fire / property insurance in place.

2. I acknowledge that I do not rely and have not relied upon any representation made by ABC Trust in deciding to invest funds in the Mortgage. **Without limiting the generality of the foregoing, I ALSO SPECIFICALLY UNDERSTAND AND REPRESENT TO ABC TRUST that I have not and cannot look to ABC Trust or any of their employees for advice as to:**

    (a) whether or not interest in the Mortgage constitute qualified investment for my Plan;

    (b) whether or not the underlying properties securing the Mortgage are adequate or will always be adequate; and

    (c) whether or not the interest in the Mortgage otherwise constitute a suitable investment for my Plan.

I understand and acknowledge that ABC Trust does not authorize their employees or any other person to make such representations or give such advice on their behalf and I hereby release and exonerate ABC Trust from any liability and agree to indemnify and hold them harmless of all losses, expenses, liabilities, damages and claims of any kind or nature whatsoever which arises or may arise by reason of the choice of this investment.

3. I understand and acknowledge that I shall be solely and entirely responsible for the

---

collection of all arrears of mortgage payments to my Plan. Without limiting the generality of the foregoing:

(a) I shall be solely and entirely responsible for instituting and pursuing any necessary legal proceeding in the event of a default by the mortgagor, including all direct and indirect decisions, legal fees, costs (including all fees, costs, expenses and charges of ABC Trust if any) pertaining to such action;

(b) I understand that I require ABC Trust's authorization before I institute or respond to legal proceedings in connection with the mortgage. I further understand that ABC Trust may refuse its authorization, at its sole discretion, and require that the mortgage be withdrawn from my Plan and assigned to another party before commencing legal action;

(c) I understand and accept that as a result of ABC Trust agreeing to be named as a party in any necessary legal proceeding, the Trustee shall be entitled to intervene, at its sole discretion, in any decision to be made with respect to the conduct of the proceeding (including the choice of legal counsel);

(d) ABC Trust shall deposit all funds received as the result of such proceeding in my Plan;

(e) ABC Trust shall forward by registered mail to my last address for such purpose copies of any legal proceeding received by the Trustee from a third party;

(f) I shall be solely and entirely responsible for any tax consequences resulting form such proceeding or from my decision not to institute any proceeding.

4. Except for the gross negligence on their part, I hereby release and exonerate ABC Trust from any liability and agree to indemnify them and save them harmless against all losses, liabilities, damages, and claims of any kind or nature whatsoever which arises or may arise by reason of their having acted in connection with the Mortgage.

5. ABC Trust's obligation to me is limited to accounting to me from time to time for the amounts received by them in respect of the Mortgage. I agree that for each and every cheque remitted to ABC Trust by the Mortgagor which is not honoured for any reason, a charge (in accordance with the current fee schedule) shall be payable by me.

6. I acknowledge that the mortgage fees charged by ABC Trust are not pro-rated and are not based on the amount of activity, value, quality or standing of a mortgage.

7. I have received a copy of ABC Trust's current fee schedule.

8. Postponements and partial discharges will only be provided upon confirmation of current property value, based on the Canada Revenue Agency definition of a qualified investment.

Having read and accepted the foregoing, I hereby direct ABC Trust to advance the amount of **$80,000** to: **Lawyer:**   Lawyer Firm LLP   in trust
   Address: 200, 999 – 9th Street S.W., Calgary, AB T2T 2T2
   Phone: 555-555-9999   Fax: 555-555-8888

Face Value of Mortgage: *(if different from amount advanced):*	**CAN $ 80,630.00 (includes Fees of $630)**
Discount Amount:	N/A
Is this discount amount prepaid interest?	N/A
Legal Description	Plan 1234A Lot(s) 1 & 2
Mortgagor / Debtor:	John Borrower
Interest Rate:	3% base annual simple interest rate plus bonus rate of 12% annual interest paid out at end of term (see Terms and details below)
Interest Calculation Method:	Interest only
Term of Mortgage	36 Months
Amortization Period:	N/A
Payment Frequency: Annual	Annual Payment Amount: $2,418.90 (plus bonus payment at mortgage payout; see below)
First Payment Date: June 1, 2010	Maturity Date: June 1, 2012
Mortgage Position: 2nd Position behind existing ABC Bank 1st mortgage	

Additional Terms To Be Included In Mortgage:
A minimum base rate per annum of 3% simple interest shall be paid to the mortgagee. Upon the mortgage becoming due and payable – either at maturity date or by the decision of the Mortgagor, the Mortgagor shall pay to the Mortgagee an additional payment equivalent to 12% annualized interest per year, calculated yearly and not in advance on the face value of the mortgage, from the interest adjustment date to the date of the mortgage was paid in full. The net effect shall be for the Mortgagee to receive an annualized interest rate of 15% for the duration of the mortgage. The lender is agreeing that the mortgage can be subordinated to allow a first mortgage finance, provided that the new loan-to-value does not exceed 85% at any time.

I hereby confirm that I am perfectly aware of the nature of the Mortgage and its terms and conditions.

I acknowledge that I have been advised to seek independent legal or other professional advice before deciding to invest funds held in my Plan in the Mortgage and before signing this Direction and Undertaking.

Dated at _____, _____ this _____ day of _____, _____.

_____
Witness Signature

_____
Annuitant Signature

_____
Witness Name

_____
Annuitant Name

Let me point out that the paperwork required by the trustee is designed to ensure that the trustee is not liable should the mortgage investment go sideways. The typical intent of an agreement is something like "Hey, if this mortgage goes bad, don't come back to the trustee! We'll administer the account and do what we're required to do as the trustee, but we're not making any representations about whether this is a good or bad investment. That's up to you to determine."

In other words, the trustee will take no responsibility as to whether the mortgage you're investing in is a good one or bad one. It's up to you to ensure that you are making a good investment, and you do that by completing the proper due diligence (and we'll look carefully at the due diligence process in chapter 8).

I also should point out that the sample mortgages I'm including are actual mortgage documents that we've used in Alberta; however, each province has its own standard form of document and agreement, and even if you're from Alberta, you absolutely should not attempt to use these sample documents without advice and direction from a lawyer. I'm providing them simply as examples of the information I'm sharing with you, but it's essential that you have your own legal representative involved in reviewing and drafting any documents you intend to use.

Fees

If you're going to lend money at 12%, your goal should really be to make 12% **net** in your account. However, the reality is that most financial institutions charge fees for providing the self-directed account services to you, and those fees eat away at your overall return. Typically there's an annual administration fee, a set-up fee for a mortgage, a monthly management fee for that mortgage, and so on. They're all very small fees, but the point is that they exist and they have to be paid. The way that trustees collect their fees from you is to simply deduct them from your RRSP account.

So, how do we avoid having to pay those fees ourselves as the account holder, so that we can generate a net return instead of letting the fees eat away at our return?

As I discussed previously, when someone is borrowing money on a mortgage, the standard is that the borrower pays most, if not all, the fees and costs. In this case, with you being the lender, my advice is that you pass those fees onto the borrower as a cost of doing business, because that's what the banks do and you're acting like a bank in this scenario.

If you're going to lend RRSP funds, I suggest you add up your trustee's fees that you're going to incur as the RRSP account holder. Calculate out what the fees are going to be if the mortgage stays in place until the end of the term, and add that total amount of fees to the face value of the mortgage.

Registered Amount vs. Advanced Amount

The amount that ends up registered as a mortgage on a property doesn't necessarily reflect exactly what a borrower ended up receiving as cash. The registered amount is the dollar amount shown in the mortgage and registered on title that the borrower has to pay back. The advanced amount is the net amount that is given to the borrower, after fees and expenses are deducted as allowed by the mortgage. This is the mechanism that we use to recover the fees and expenses as the lender, to ensure that we end up getting a net return and don't have to pay the expenses out of our account.

If we go back to the example I was using previously on page 106, we were looking at lending $40,000 for twenty-four months at 12% interest. When we set up that loan through the trustee, we will be exposed to several modest fees. Let's assume in this case that we're going to incur a $100 mortgage set-up fee, a monthly account admin fee of $10, and a mortgage discharge/payout fee of $50. Assuming that the mortgage goes for the full term and is paid back after twenty-four months, our total fees would be $100 + ($10 × 24) + $50 = $390.

Knowing this, we would detail in the Mortgage Direction and Undertaking Document that the mortgage amount to be registered is going to be $40,390, but the advanced amount is going to be $40,000. That difference, which is $390, is referred to as a "discount" because it's not going to be advanced to the borrower. The borrower will receive exactly $40,000, but when it comes time to pay off the mortgage, he or she will have to pay off $40,390 because that's the amount registered on title. This is when you recover all of your fees for setting up that mortgage in your account. This means you truly get a 12% net return on your money. (In fact, it's slightly higher, because you earn interest on that extra $390 during the term of the mortgage as well!)

If you refer back to the sample Mortgage Direction and Undertaking Document on page 108 (where the details of the loan are outlined), you'll see that the Registered Amount in that case was $80,630, but the Advanced Amount was $80,000. That difference of $630 is the calculation of what the fees would have been in that situation, and this is how the lender is able to recover the costs they incur, ensuring their return is truly "net."

Structuring your loans this way is a very powerful strategy for the RRSP investor, and most borrowers don't really care because it's not a significant amount of money; in their mind, it's just the cost of doing business. That's a secret that a lot of people don't know about how you capture the net return as the RRSP lender. When we say a 12% net return in the mortgage, this is how you ensure that's what you are really getting.

Also note that if the lender pays you off earlier than planned, you still keep all of those fees, and that increases your net return. For example, in our scenario, if the borrower pays you back in twelve months instead of twenty-four, you end up making a profit of $120 because some of the upfront fees are not realized because the loan was paid off early.

Once the details of the mortgage are agreed upon and the Mortgage Direction and Undertaking Document is completed, the lawyer draws up a mortgage that will secure the RRSP investment. He or she takes the details of the transactions and inserts them into a typical and standardized mortgage document. If you refer to Sample Mortgage #1 (Simple Interest) on page 114, you'll see a typical second mortgage using RRSP funds where the borrower is to make monthly payments.[*]

Cash Flow Management: The Deferred Interest Payment Strategy

Here's another idea that allows you to potentially increase the interest rate you're charging on your mortgage as a lender. I've touched on this before, but it's worth repeating because it's something most investors never think about.

Instead of requiring the borrower to pay you every month or every quarter, why not let the borrower defer as much of the payment as possible and so incur a higher interest rate as a result? If you think about it as a borrower, would you rather pay 12% every month or would you rather pay 13% but just make one payment once a year? If you're a real estate investor and you own property, cash flow is likely important to you. If you buy a property and use some RRSP funds, but your cash flow is tight, one of the things that can help your cash flow is to defer the first year's interest payments until the end of the year. This allows you to do your renovations and get the rents up, without having to make the money payments when cash flow is low. Then, once you've increased the revenue on the property, you're in a better position to be able to make the payments.

---

[*]Please note that for the sake of our trees, I've only reproduced the first page of the mortgage document so that you can see the mortgage payment details. However, you can download several complete sample mortgage documents at my website, www.rrspSecret.com.

SAMPLE MORTGAGE #1: SIMPLE INTEREST MORTGAGE, SINGLE LENDER

Land Titles Act

MORTGAGE

PROPERTY OWNER of 123 MAIN STREET, CALGARY, AB, T2T 0T2

(the "Mortgagor"), being the registered owners of an estate in fee simple in possession of all and singular those parcels of land situate in the Province of Alberta and being described as:

PLAN 1234AB
BLOCK 1
LOT 99
EXCEPTING THEREOUT ALL MINES AND MINERALS

(sometimes referred to as the "Lands" or the "Mortgaged Premises"), in consideration of the receipt of $100,000.00 ("Principal Sum") from OLYMPIA TRUST COMPANY (in trust for RRSP #12345) (the "Mortgagee") of 2300, 125 - 9 Avenue SE, Calgary, AB, T2G 0P6, and for other good and valuable consideration, the receipt and sufficiency of which is acknowledged, covenants and agrees with the Mortgagee:

1. The Mortgagor will pay to the Mortgagee in Canadian Dollars, at 2300, 125 - 9 Avenue SE, Calgary, AB, T2G 0P6, the Principal Sum $100,000.00) in trust for RRSP #12345), plus interest calculated in the following manner:

    (a) Interest on the Principal Sum, calculated thereon at the rate of 12.00% per annum from June 1, 2009, in monthly payments of $1,000.00 on June 1, 2010 and continuing thereafter on the 1st day of each month up to and including June 1, 2012; and

    (b) on June 1, 2012 repayment of the Principal Sum plus accrued interest on the Principal Sum;

    with payments to be applied firstly in reduction of all costs, expenses, or charges, insurance premiums, or taxes, which the Mortgagor has failed to pay, and secondly in payment of any interest due herein, and lastly in payment of the Principal Sum; and

2. The Mortgagor agrees to pay interest from the June 1, 2009 on the Principal Sum outstanding in the manner aforesaid calculated annually and payable annually; all interest in arrears to become principal, and to bear interest at the rate stated above, payable at the times, in the manner, and at the place provided for, from the date the same becomes due and payable, such interest to be payable on the Principal Sum, and any interest in arrears, both before and after default and/or judgment.

    When not in default hereunder, the Mortgagor shall have the right to pay all or part of Principal Sum remaining at any time.

    (only page 1 shown of the document)

For you as the real estate investor, this can be a huge cash flow management tool. On the other hand, the RRSP investor ends up getting a higher interest return on her money because getting paid money monthly or even quarterly doesn't really present much of a benefit. As I discussed previously, those monthly interest payments going into the registered account are exposed to market volatility. So why not leave the money invested at a higher interest rate?

Most trustees require a mortgage to have a minimum interest rate payable per year and the reason they do that is because they have to get their fees from somewhere. If you lend all of your money out of your RRSP in one five-year interest deferred loan, then the trustee would have nowhere to recover their ongoing fees. A minimum interest rate is mandated by the Canada Revenue Agency, and each trustee has its own guidelines as to what the minimum annual interest rate must be. It is typically in the range of 2% to 4%, depending on the trustee. That means you have to pay at least that amount per year in interest.

As long as you make the minimum interest amount required each year, the rest of the interest can be deferred until the end of the mortgage. To give you a simple example of how this works in practice, refer to Sample Mortgage #2 (Deferred Interest) on page 116.* You'll note under the repayment terms in Clause #1 that the borrower will make a reduced interest payment during the term of the mortgage and a "bonus" interest payment when the mortgage expires and is paid off.

In Sample Mortgage #2, there is a 15% interest rate applicable, but it's using the deferred interest strategy and requires only 3% annual interest payment, with the remaining 12% to be accrued until the end of the mortgage. The mortgage is for three years (thirty-six months).

The borrower would make a payment of 3% at the end of the first and second years, and at the end of the third year would "catch up" all the accrued interest. This would mean that, at the end of year three, a total of 39% interest would be paid: 12% from the first year that was deferred, 12% from the second year, and the full 15% from the third year. That still averages out to 15% per year, so the lender is getting the 15% interest. But

---

*Please note that for the sake of our trees, I've only reproduced the first page of the mortgage document so that you can see the mortgage payment details. However, you can download several complete sample mortgage documents at my website, www.rrspSecret.com.

SAMPLE MORTGAGE #2: DEFERRED INTEREST MORTGAGE, SINGLE LENDER

Land Titles Act

MORTGAGE

PROPERTY OWNER of 123 MAIN STREET, CALGARY, AB, T2T 0T2

(the "Mortgagor"), being the registered owners of an estate in fee simple in possession of all and singular those parcels of land situate in the Province of Alberta and being described as:

PLAN 1234AB
BLOCK 1
LOT 99
EXCEPTING THEREOUT ALL MINES AND MINERALS

(sometimes referred to as the "Lands" or the "Mortgaged Premises"), in consideration of the receipt of $80,630.00 ("Principal Sum") from OLYMPIA TRUST COMPANY (in trust for RRSP #12345) (the "Mortgagee") of 2300, 125 - 9 Avenue SE, Calgary, AB, T2G 0P6, and for other good and valuable consideration, the receipt and sufficiency of which is acknowledged, covenants and agrees with the Mortgagee:

1. The Mortgagor will pay to the Mortgagee in Canadian Dollars, at 2300, 125 - 9 Avenue SE, Calgary, AB, T2G 0P6, the Principal Sum $80,630.00) in trust for RRSP #12345), plus interest calculated in the following manner:

    (a) Interest on the Principal Sum, calculated thereon at the rate of 3.00% per annum from June 1, 2009, in annual payments of $2,418.90 on June 1, 2010, June 1, 2011 and June 1, 2012; and

    (b) on June 1, 2012 the Principal Sum plus additional interest on the Principal Sum, calculated thereon at the rate of 12.00% per annum from June 1, 2009 to June 1, 2012;

    with payments to be applied firstly in reduction of all costs, expenses, or charges, insurance premiums, or taxes, which the Mortgagor has failed to pay, and secondly in payment of any interest due herein, and lastly in payment of the Principal Sum; and

2. The Mortgagor agrees to pay interest from the June 1, 2009 on the Principal Sum outstanding in the manner aforesaid calculated annually and payable annually; all interest in arrears to become principal, and to bear interest at the rate stated above, payable at the times, in the manner, and at the place provided for, from the date the same becomes due and payable, such interest to be payable on the Principal Sum, and any interest in arrears, both before and after default and/or judgment.

    When not in default hereunder, the Mortgagor shall have the right to pay all or part of Principal Sum remaining at any time.

    (only page 1 shown of the document)

the borrower has been able to defer that big payment for almost three years, giving him the opportunity to renovate and increase the rents.

The great thing about RRSP mortgages is that they can be very flexible depending on the property. This is important for a real estate investor, especially when buying a property that's going to produce initially negative cash flow because of renovations. In the first year, you might not want to incur full financing costs and add to your expenses, so by structuring a second mortgage with a lender this way, you reduce your initial costs in the first year and the RRSP investor benefits from getting a higher interest rate return. It's a win-win situation, and again you can build mortgage arrangements according to each situation so that they benefit not only the RRSP investor but also the real estate investor.

If you refer to the Sample Mortgage Direction and Undertaking that relates to Sample Mortgage #2 on page 116, you'll see that the "interest calculation method" is interest-only. The "term of the mortgage" is thirty-six months. There is no "amortization period" because it's interest-only, so that's not applicable. The "payment frequency" you see is on an annual basis, so the annual interest payment is $2,418.90 and you have to add the bonus payment at the payout. The "first payment date" is June 1, 2010, and the maturity date is June 1, 2012. "Mortgage position" in this case suggests second position, acknowledging that there's an existing first mortgage in place by a traditional bank.

Solicitor's Certificate of Disclosure and Undertaking

As the property investor, if you were looking to have other people lend you RRSP funds, here is another critical piece of the process. Most trustees will require that you provide what's called a Solicitor's Certificate of Disclosure and Undertaking (often referred to simply as the "Solicitor's Certificate"). You can see a sample Solicitor's Certificate on the website at www.rrspSecret.com.

This is a document that your lawyer or solicitor fills out, and the purpose is to confirm that a legal representative (solicitor or lawyer) was involved in the process. It outlines the solicitor's role and responsibilities in the transaction. The trustee requires this to ensure that the lawyer discloses any important facts that might affect the mortgage and its registration. For example, the solicitor must confirm that he doesn't have any interest in the property, and that he will not use the funds until the mortgage is registered properly.

Trustees take this due diligence step to ensure that proper legal advice and supervision has been provided on the transaction. Each trustee has a different Solicitor's Certificate or similar form that they require you to complete, so you should review the appropriate form depending on which trustee you choose. I'll emphasize that you *should not* attempt to set up these kinds of mortgages without the help of a lawyer.

I cannot reiterate this enough: whether you're the RRSP borrower or the RRSP investor, you want to have a lawyer involved in the process. The lawyer prepares the undertaking, prepares the disclosure and the terms sheet, and sends them to your chosen trustee. The lawyer also draws up the mortgage itself and receives the funds in trust from your trustee. He'll register the mortgage against the property, and release the funds to the borrower. Throughout the process, you want to make sure that you are represented properly, and that everything is done correctly. That's the reason to have a lawyer involved in the process. Don't try to cut out this step!

Because there are a few documents involved, I've created a simple checklist of the documents that you can download from my website at www.rrspSecret.com.

Mortgage Payments

Trustees want to make life as simple as they can for themselves and for everybody else. At the time that you complete the mortgage document, you must deliver a signed authorization form through your lawyer for pre-authorized payments. In other words, you give your trustee access to a chequing account and the trustee will automatically deduct your mortgage payments every month, every quarter or every year—whatever's applicable based on the payment schedule you structured in the mortgage.

For both parties, this is a big benefit because the real estate owner doesn't have to write out a bunch of cheques or deliver payments to the lender every month. The RRSP investor has the peace of mind of knowing that the money is going to directly flow back into their account on a regular basis.

It's important to remember that the trustee accepts and administers the payments, and if a payment gets missed, the trustee will notify the lender about that missed payment. As the lender, you have to decide what you're going to do to try and solve the problem. Anything related to defaults or other problems that may arise will be covered later in the book, but what I can tell you is that we've done dozens of these kinds of mortgages and I've only ever had one problem where payments weren't being made in a timely fashion. In that case, a simple conversation with the borrower cleared it all up. Defaults are not a common occurrence, provided you do the proper due diligence on your borrower to begin with!

Property Valuation

You are not allowed to "over-leverage" a property beyond its value. You cannot put an RRSP mortgage onto a property where the total debt exceeds its market value. One of the steps that all trustees take is to verify the value of the underlying property by asking you for proof of the market value. This is not only to protect themselves from being involved in a foreclosure, but also because the *Income Tax Act* specifically says that a property that is over-leveraged is not an eligible RRSP investment.

Most trustees are happy if you can provide them the current year's property tax assessment demonstrating that the property value exceeds the total amount of debt you are proposing to register against the property. Alternatively, you can obtain a current professional appraisal (generally it cannot be more than six months old). Technically, you can borrow up to the full amount of the property on a current appraisal using an RRSP mortgage, but I strongly recommend against doing this because it massively increases the risk to the lender. In fact, some trustees have a policy where they will not allow you to lend beyond 90% of the property value, because they consider anything beyond that too risky for the lender.

THE POWER OF MULTIPLE INVESTORS

One of the concerns I hear often from people is that they can't find anyone who has enough money in their RRSP to fund the size of mortgage they need. I'd like now to touch on a twist to this strategy that will create even more options for you, whether you're the RRSP lender or the borrower.

If need be, you can pool multiple registered funds together from more than one investor and register one large mortgage. When I say multiple, I'm talking two or maybe three people. We've used this strategy success-fully many times in the past when the loan amount we were looking for was higher than what most investors had available in their accounts. Let me tell you about one of these situations that worked out well.

We were looking for some financing on a property that we had, and we knew two investors—complete strangers to each other—who were both interested in lending some funds. One happened to be a friend of mine who had bought property with me in the past. He hadn't been contributing to his RRSP for a while and recently had caught up several years of available contribution room. He had decided to put about $40,000 or $50,000 into his RRSP at the time, so the cash was available for immediate use.

At the same time, one of the lawyers that I worked with who for many years had watched what I do finally said to me, "Look, how do I get involved in this? I know that your investors are making 12% on their money. If you need some money for a loan I've got some RRSP funds that are looking for some action." Again, this was a very successful lawyer who was asking me if he could participate! When I say that a lot of successful and wealthy people are using this strategy to build wealth, I'm not kidding.

The problem we had was that the property we were looking to borrow on required $80,000, which was more than each of these two individual investors had available individually. To create a solution, we combined both of their investments into one mortgage, and both of them were registered on title as co-sharing this mortgage. That way, we were able to get one second mortgage registered for $80,000 and paid each investor half.

Just to be clear: I'm not talking about setting up a big investment pool or anything like that. I'm simply talking about getting two or three additional investors involved in a single mortgage that's registered on title, and it's really not that complicated.

This is a great strategy when you have two investors who both want to participate. Doing it this way is more effective than having each register their own mortgage on the property title. That's because if we were to have registered the two investors we had as individual mortgages, one of them would have gotten a second mortgage and the other one would have gotten a third—there would be no way around this, because we would have to register two different mortgages. However, by pooling them together, both investors have equal security in the investment and both get to participate in a mortgage that neither could have done on their own.

If you refer to Sample Mortgage #3 (Multiple Lenders)* you'll see that it outlines that there are three different lenders involved, each with a self-directed RRSP account with Olympia Trust. This single mortgage document is registered against the property title, and each of the three investors has a pro-rata interest in the mortgage.

---

*Please note that for the sake of our trees, I've only reproduced the First page of the mortgage document so that you can see the mortgage payment details. However, you can download several complete sample mortgage documents at my website, www.rrspSecret.com.

SAMPLE MORTGAGE #3: DEFERRED INTEREST MORTGAGE, MULTIPLE LENDERS

Land Titles Act
MORTGAGE

PROPERTY OWNER of 123 MAIN STREET NW, CALGARY, AB, T2T 0T2

(the "Mortgagor"), being the registered owners of an estate in fee simple in possession of all and singular those parcels of land situate in the Province of Alberta and being described as:

PLAN 1234AB
BLOCK 1
LOT 99
EXCEPTING THEREOUT ALL MINES AND MINERALS

(sometimes referred to as the "Lands" or the "Mortgaged Premises"), in consideration of the receipt of $150,730.00 ("Principal Sum") from OLYMPIA TRUST COMPANY (in trust for RRSP #11111, RRSP #22222 and RRSP #33333) (the "Mortgagee") of 2300, 125 - 9 Avenue SE, Calgary, AB, T2G 0P6, and for other good and valuable consideration, the receipt and sufficiency of which is acknowledged, covenants and agrees with the Mortgagee:

1. The Mortgagor will pay to the Mortgagee in Canadian Dollars, at 2300, 125 - 9 Avenue SE, Calgary, AB, T2G 0P6, the Principal Sum ($65,365.00 in trust for RRSP #11111, $32,000.00 in trust for RRSP #22222 and $53,365.00 in trust for RRSP #33333), plus interest calculated in the following manner:

    (a) Interest on the Principal Sum, calculated thereon at the rate of 4.00% per annum from June 1, 2009, in annual payments of $6,029.20 ($2,614.60 for RRSP #11111, $2,134.60 for RRSP #22222 and $1,280.00 for RRSP #33333) on June 1, 2010 and June 1, 2011; and

    (b) on June 1, 2011 the Principal Sum plus additional interest on the Principal Sum, calculated thereon at the rate of 9% per annum from June 1, 2009 to June 1, 2011;

    with payments to be applied firstly in reduction of all costs, expenses, or charges, insurance premiums, or taxes, which the Mortgagor has failed to pay, and secondly in payment of any interest due herein, and lastly in payment of the Principal Sum; and

2. The Mortgagor agrees to pay interest from the June 1, 2009 on the Principal Sum outstanding in the manner aforesaid calculated annually and payable annually; all interest in arrears to become principal, and to bear interest at the rate stated above, payable at the times, in the manner, and at the place provided for, from the date the same becomes due and payable, such interest to be payable on the Principal Sum, and any interest in arrears, both before and after default and/or judgment.

    When not in default hereunder, the Mortgagor shall have the right to pay all or part of Principal Sum remaining at any time.

(only page 1 shown of the document)

Keep in mind that the examples I'm providing here are primarily to give you an idea of how the process works, and the specific documents and language will vary according to the province in which you are undertaking a transaction.

For example, in B.C. there's an extra declaration that needs to be signed along with the mortgage.

If you go to my website at www.rrspSecret.com, you'll find a summary for each province, including specific exceptions and unique elements required in each province.

* * *

To set up the mortgage, first you start out by identifying the property that you're going to lend it against and do all of the due diligence on the property. Second, you negotiate and finalize the terms and conditions of the mortgage. Consider the amount, the interest rate, the terms, whether there will be deferred interest or not, etc. Third, you provide the final details that you've agreed on to your lawyer, who drafts all of the documents including the mortgage itself, the Mortgage Direction and Undertaking Document and the Solicitor's Certificate. Finally, you sign off on the mortgage documents and have your lawyer register the mortgage on title.

The borrower obviously has to sign the mortgage itself because he or she is mortgaging the property to the benefit of your RRSP account. The money transfers to the borrower's lawyer, who releases the money to the real estate investor. Finally, you get the automatic payments made into your account. When the mortgage term ends, the loan comes up for renewal and it either gets paid off by the borrower or is renewed by both parties to continue into the future for another term. The reality is that if the property investor has been making his payments in a timely fashion, most RRSP investors are fine with simply renewing the mortgage for another year or two, because they've grown accustomed to the hands-off strategy that seems to be working just fine.

You can imagine what it's like these days when these RRSP investors go to a family reunion or cocktail party and they talk to others about RRSPs. When most people have lost 30% or 40% or 50% in their RRSPs, these savvy RRSP mortgage investors are making 10%, 12% or 14% like clockwork.

Once you understand how this process works, you'll see it's very simple. And after completing a couple of these deals (whether it's as the borrower or as the lender), you're going to want to do more of them.

If you're the real estate investor, one of the things you'll want to do is make sure that you understand how this system works well enough that you can explain it to a potential investor who has RRSP funds and doesn't know what to do with them. I can guarantee you that as you learn to ask the right questions of people and bring real estate investing up as a topic in conversation, you're going to have a lot of people asking for more information on what it is you do. As a real estate investor, you need to turn every conversation you have into a discussion about real estate if you can. There are a lot of people out there with RRSPs who don't know what to do with them, and if you can show them a safe and secure way of making a double-digit return without the volatility of the stock market, they're going to be interested.

If you're the RRSP lender, there are no shortage of real estate buyers, owners and investors that are eager to borrow your funds. In the next chapter, I'll discuss specifically how you can easily find these borrowers and do the necessary due diligence on them.

8

How to Find and Evaluate Opportunities

The opportunities are all around you . . . you just need to believe they're waiting for you to find them.
—Kourosh Assef

This chapter is going to answer some of the most common questions I get about the strategy of investing in mortgages. I'm going to cover two specific areas.

First, I'm going to talk about where it's possible to find solid-gold opportunities for RRSP mortgages, from the perspective of both the investor who wishes to put his or her RRSP funds to work, and the real estate investor who is seeking RRSP funds. One of the great aspects about employing arm's length mortgages is that the strategy is dually effective (1) for the person who has the funds sitting in a registered account and (2) for the real estate investor.

Second, I'll outline the process you can follow to research and analyze the opportunities you'll come across, to make sure you end up investing in a solid opportunity.

Previously, we walked through the specific steps involved in setting up a self-directed arm's length registered account. Then we went through the process of what happens when you create an arm's length mortgage transaction. Let's turn now to the specifics of where to find these opportunities.

FOUR SOURCES FOR FUNDS

Whether you're the investor with funds or you're looking to borrow funds, there are four excellent sources that make the most sense for you when trying to find opportunities.

Source #1: Investment Groups and Clubs

Let me start by talking from the perspective of someone who has registered funds to invest and would like to find people interested in borrowing those funds. If we think of this as a marketing challenge, ask yourself this question: *Where could you go where you'd find a whole bunch of real estate investors in one place so that you could easily tell them that you have funds that you are looking to lend on quality properties?*

The simple answer to this question is that in almost every city or decent-size town in Canada there is at least one real estate investment club or group that gets together on a regular basis. The largest and most successful investment group in Canada by far is called REIN Canada, which stands for the Real Estate Investment Network.

I've been a member of REIN for several years. It's the largest and most successful real estate network in the country, and every one of its 3,500 members is a potential investor looking to borrow money for their investing purposes. REIN holds regularly scheduled meetings and events in Canadian cities including Vancouver, Calgary, Edmonton and Toronto, so if you're looking for real estate investors who would be interested in mortgage funding, that's a great place to start. You can go to www.reincanada.com for more information and to www.myreinspace.com for public discussion forums. There you'll be able to start connecting with real estate investors right away. (I've posted these links on www.rrspSecret.com.)

Aside from REIN Canada, there are several other local and regional investment clubs that operate in various towns and cities across the country. The simplest way to find out about them is to talk to local real estate investors in your area and find out if they attend any local investment meetings. You also might want to watch the local newspaper and community bulletin boards for ads promoting upcoming meetings. Real estate investment groups are a great source of potential mortgage investments because real estate investors are always looking to borrow money in order to build their portfolio and their net worth.

Of course, if you're a real estate investor, you should already be a member of a real estate investing group like REIN or a local program. You'll likely find investors in the club that have funds that they're looking to invest as well. Another action you can take is to simply Google "real estate investment club" and the name of your city or town. See what comes up.

You won't be left empty-handed, because there are clubs operating across the country.

'Source #2: Local Classifieds

The local classifieds can be a great source of opportunities both for the real estate investor and the lender. If you're a real estate investor, you'll often come across ads from individuals looking to lend their money out to generate a secure return. If you're a lender, you'll see ads from real estate investors seeking funds for a specific project.

When you do look at the ads in the newspaper, you'll notice that a lot of the ads are run by professionals in the business (i.e., mortgage brokers or "hard money" lenders—people who are in the business of lending money). Generally speaking, for you as a borrower, those are not going to be the best kinds of loans to arrange, simply because you're going to have to end up paying fees to whomever it is that's doing the marketing. Ideally, what you want to do if you're the borrower is connect directly with an individual who has some money to loan—someone who's not a professional lender, but simply a person who has some registered funds and is looking to make a secure, predictable investment.

You can place your own ad that specifically details what you're looking for. For example, let's assume you have funds in a registered account ready to lend, and you've already got them in a self-directed account with a trustee that allows arm's length mortgages. You could run a simple classified ad that says something like the following:

PRIVATE INVESTOR LOOKING TO LEND FUNDS ON SECURE QUALITY REAL ESTATE. Flexible terms and rates depending on the situation. Willing to lend up to $100,000, maximum 75% LTV. Call John at 555-555-1212.

I assure you that if you were to place that little ad in the classifieds section, you'd start getting phone calls from investors looking to borrow funds on different kinds of property. You're also likely to get calls from homeowners who are looking to take equity out of their property. It's up to you if you're willing to consider lending to a homeowner or not. One advantage is that a homeowner is less likely to default on a mortgage for fear of losing his or her principal residence. On the other hand, homeowners are generally not that familiar with private lending and may not understand how it works. Or, when you tell them that you're looking for a 12% or 13% interest rate, they may not understand that these are pretty common rates in the private mortgage world.

Notice in the above example that I gave specific details, such as said "willing to lend up to $100,000" and "maximum 75% LTV." Most people may not know what "LTV" means, but any seasoned real estate investor is going to know exactly what that is. By placing your basic criteria right into the ad, you're going to reduce the number of calls you get from people who don't have a suitable deal for you to lend money against. It's completely up to you who you decide to work with and what kind of deals you'll consider lending on because it's completely up to you to set your own rules.

On the other hand, let's say that you're the real estate investor looking to borrow funds on a specific property. There's no reason that you couldn't run a small ad that says something like the following:

TIRED OF LOSING MONEY IN YOUR RRSPS? Local investor looking to borrow up to $80,000 for a two-year term on a mortgage secured by quality real estate. Will pay 12% interest and all of your costs. Finally a double-digit RRSP return with good security! Call John at 555-555-1212.

AN IMPORTANT NOTE ON ADVERTISING FOR MONEY

When you're placing ads related to borrowing money, you need to advertise a *specific* opportunity that you have on a property that you own or that you're in the process of purchasing. Or, in the case of being a lender, you need to advertise specifics about your own funds and that you wish to lend directly to a borrower. The reason for this is because you're not allowed to just broadly advertise that you're looking to borrow or lend money, as this starts to cross into the type of advertising and marketing that would require a licence. For example, you can't advertise that you're looking to borrow money and, when a person responds, connect them to another investor and get paid a referral fee. That's against the law, because you have to be licensed to do things like that. However, as long as you're advertising a specific opportunity in which you're the owner of the property or it's your money that you're lending, there's nothing wrong with doing this.

Also, you cannot say that the return is "guaranteed" because that's a word that carries a lot of liability in the world of securities. Almost any investment where the claim is made "guaranteed" can cause some trouble with the local regulators. You want to be careful about how you word your ads. If you're going to advertise for lenders, I would strongly recommend that you speak to someone familiar with the law and the rules, such as a securities lawyer, just to make sure you're not falsely representing yourself where you're seen as making an offer of a security.

Small classified ads in the local newspapers, community newsletters or online advertising sites that have local content like Craigslist or Kijiji and similar types of marketing will begin generating deals for you to look at almost immediately once you place the ads.

Source #3: A Mortgage Agent or Broker

If you're already attending local investment meetings and working with classified ads—or maybe you're not—but those seem like too much work for you, then you'll like this option.

Speak with a reputable mortgage agent or broker who works in your area. If you think about it, mortgage brokers are in the business of financing—bringing borrowers and lenders together—so it stands to reason that they're constantly being contacted by people interested in borrowing funds. Quite often a mortgage broker receives a call from a borrower who doesn't meet the standard lending criteria of the banks, but instead of just turning him away, the broker may be able to connect him to a private investor who can provide a solution.

The mortgage agent or broker's job is to match borrowers with lenders, and he gets paid a fee for providing this service. The type of mortgage agent or broker you want to work with is somebody who is reputable and has at least a couple of years experience in the business. I would suggest that you work with a mortgage agent or broker who has experience dealing with investors in particular, because that's where you're going to find most of your opportunities as a private lender. I mentioned this before: homeowners typically are looking for first mortgages and are not willing to pay the higher interest rates that investors recognize as the cost of doing business. For this reason, working with seasoned investors is slightly easier, because they understand that higher rates are part of the business.

Working with mortgage agents or brokers has a few key advantages. To start with, they usually have the background and the knowledge to help you do the due diligence on the mortgage investment opportunity. They have existing relationships with appraisal firms, and more often than not they know the market well enough to help you determine the value of the property. As I'll cover later in this chapter, you will absolutely want to get a proper professional appraisal done on any property that you're thinking about lending funds on.

Another benefit is that they always have a number of people who are looking to borrow funds for various types of real estate projects, so it's possible that they can show you several deals to consider based on your criteria, allowing you to focus on the ones that you're most comfortable with. This can save you a lot of time, because they're able to filter a lot of potential deals so that you're only looking at the ones you would most likely be interested in.

Yet another advantage of working with a mortgage agent or broker is that it adds a layer of separation between you and the other party. Now, in some cases you may see this as a disadvantage if, for example, you'd like to meet the person who is borrowing from you. However, for many people, they don't really want to meet the other party. They simply want a solution to their problem, and allowing the mortgage broker to do the negotiation saves them from being involved in that process.

But What About Paying the Commission and Fees?

If you work with a mortgage agent or broker, doesn't that mean a commission will be due? The short answer to this question is yes, but it doesn't necessarily have to be *you* who pays the commission if you're the lender. In the real estate financing world, it's typically the borrower who pays the expenses. If your mortgage broker arranges to lend your money to an investor, then you can normally pass on the related costs to your borrower. In a traditional deal where you're buying a house to live in, for instance, your mortgage broker typically gets paid his or her commission by the bank, because the residential mortgage market is pretty competitive. However, when the lender is not one of the big banks, the commission often will get charged to the borrower because second-ary banks and private lenders don't generally pay the commission—they expect the borrower to pay it.

One issue to keep in mind is that there's a certain threshold in terms of what a borrower is willing to pay. For example, if you're doing a second mortgage that is typically in the area of 12%, but your broker wants to charge the borrower a 3% fee, that means the borrower is going to have to agree to pay 15% total in the first year. For some borrowers, that's going to be too high and they'll choose to find another investor that isn't working through a broker.

The only alternative that you have as the lender in this situation is to make it more attractive to the borrower by reducing your interest rate. In this way, when you add the broker's fee, the total fee the borrower is pay-ing is within the typical range. The downside is that now you're getting a reduced return on your investment, plus you have to assume the fees because the borrower is still only paying 12%. In most cases, I would not be reducing what I make on the deal just to make it affordable for your borrower. *There is nothing wrong with charging market value for the service of providing a private loan to somebody.*

The truth is if one borrower isn't willing to pay what the market will bear, then you'll find another who is happy to do business with you. The key is to know what the market rates are and ensure that you're expecting a rate that reflects the type of deal, risk and profile of the borrower. Your costs still have to fall within the reasonable range of what the market will bear for that type of mortgage.

The more motivated the borrower, the more power you're going to have as a lender. Usually, significantly motivated borrowers have a good reason for their motivation, meaning there is likely higher risk in the deal, so you want to be careful to do all of your research. This is especially true when you're dealing with a borrower who seems to be in a major rush and willing to pay you anything.

Keep all of these issues in mind when you're deciding whether or not to use a mortgage broker to help you find and evaluate your deals. While it can certainly make sense to use a mortgage agent or broker on your first couple of deals to benefit from their knowledge and expertise and learn the ropes, I do believe that as you become accustomed to how the process works, it makes more sense to do the work on your own and keep all of the returns for yourself.

If you're a borrower looking for funds, you also can go to a mortgage broker, but you can expect that you'll be paying commissions and fees to the broker for their services. That's why, when you're looking to borrow funds, it makes sense to find individual investors who are willing to lend their money to you. This prevents you from having to go down that road of negotiating commissions or fees, and your ultimate cost of doing business will be lower. Most private lenders won't even think about trying to charge upfront fees, but that's a standard in the mortgage industry that you need to be aware of. Private lenders are just happy to have an investment strategy that allows them to generate an attractive return with good security backing up the investment.

This Book as Education

Most people don't even realize the opportunities that exist to lend their funds out on a mortgage so they can earn double-digit returns and have great security. I think that this kind of information is going to be the missing link for the many investors who would love to borrow RRSP funds from other investors and give them a safe, solid return. But there is still the fear factor that comes with not really understanding how this all works. If you're trying to find people that you can borrow money from but you're not comfortable with the idea of trying to educate them on the idea of lending you money, simply hand them a copy of this book and let me do the educating for you. Once they've read this book, they'll come back to you and be interested in what you have to say and it won't be up to you to explain the process.

The Relationship Between Lender and Borrower

The other reason why I like doing deals without a broker involved is that, as I said before, I like to get to know who it is I'm working with on the other side. In other words, if I'm the borrower I like to know who it is I'm borrowing the funds from. I like to let them know more about me and I usually want to meet them so they can find out what I'm all about and learn more about my business. Doing this allows them to gain confidence in me as a real estate investor, while giving me the opportunity to demonstrate my credibility and experience. I think it's important to build this relationship because as long as you take care of your lenders, chances are they'll continue to re-lend their funds to you once you've shown them that you can be trusted. I can't emphasize this point enough. If you're a borrower, make sure that you make your payments on time and ensure that the process is seamless and worry-free for your lender. This will pay off hugely in the future for you, because you'll help create a long-term lender that you can return to over and over in the future. Let's face it, most people are looking for safe, consistent returns on their RRSPs, so as long as you do your part and you make sure that your lender gets paid on time, it's very likely that when your mortgage expires and it's time for you to either pay in full or renew the loan, the lender will happily renew with you. By then they will have grown accustomed to this simple cash flow machine that you've created.

It's no different when I'm lending funds. I like to meet the borrower so I can get a better sense of what they're about and understand their investment model. Obviously I'm in a position where I can evaluate an investor pretty well, so for me it makes sense to meet the borrower to ensure they know what they're doing and that they're going to represent a low-risk investment for me.

Source #4: Your Personal Network of Friends and Contacts

I've saved the biggest source of opportunities for last. The fourth place to look is everyone that you know! What's great about this strategy is that if you're looking to borrow funds, you're literally doing someone a favour by showing them how to invest with a safe, predictable, double-digit return. I have several of my friends that I've gotten involved in lending money on mortgages, because I truly think that it's one of the greatest hassle-free investment strategies that there is. If you want to start uncovering potential lenders who might be willing to invest in a mortgage with you, it's simply a matter of making sure everybody you know is aware that you're a real estate investor. If you're looking to lend funds, you won't have too many conversations before someone says, "Oh, I have a friend who's a real estate investor and is always looking for financing," or perhaps the person you're speaking to is an investor herself.

Try and turn every conversation that you have with friends, family, co-workers and associates into a real estate conversation. For example, if you go to your kid's soccer game and talk to other parents during the game, it won't be difficult to bring up real estate as a topic of conversation since it's on a lot of people's minds these days. For some people, the idea of trying to educate someone on investing in mortgages is a scary idea. A lot of people don't like to sell or even talk about financial or investing topics. Again, this is one of the reasons I decided to write this book. If people show some interest in the idea and you're looking to borrow funds, you can simply lend them a copy of my book and let them learn on their own. You'll be in a position where you can provide them a powerful resource where they can learn about the strategy. Of course, if they're interested in learning more, you're the first person they will contact.

I'm a big believer in letting people put up their hand to ask for more information instead of chasing people around, trying to knock them over the head to buy something. That's truly a fundamental of marketing, as it allows people to seek out what they want to buy instead of you having to sell it. At the end of the day, most people with RRSPs are simply looking for a safe, predictable return, and that's exactly what this strategy enables you to provide.

Once you become more comfortable with the process, and you begin raising the concept in conversation with friends and family, you'll be shocked at how many people are interested in what you have to offer. As you continue to gain knowledge and confidence, you'll be able to easily explain the process and answer any of the questions that people might have without having to think much about it.

If you're going to be discussing the idea with friends and family, you absolutely, positively have to make sure that you structure it as a professional arrangement, because you can get into trouble doing business with friends and family. One of the reasons why I like mortgage investing is that by law everything has to be registered properly and clearly, so the messiness that often comes with being in business with loved ones can't happen so easily. The trustee of the self-directed RRSP account, for example, is going to require you to get all of the proper documentation in place. You always want to be careful when money is involved and you're dealing with friends and family. With respect to lending registered funds, we've already talked about the fact that you cannot lend to your immediate family, so that removes the risk of getting into a fight with your parent or child about a loan that goes bad.

CASH IS OKAY, TOO!

I want to remind you that everything I'm teaching you in this program works not just for registered funds, using RRSPs, RESPs, RRIFs, TFSAs, LIRAs and so on, but also can be done with good old-fashioned cash.

For example, consider the situation if you have investment capital or a savings account, or let's say your sibling or a parent has cash sitting in an account and it's not registered money. You can do everything I'm talking about here, and in fact it's much easier because you don't even need to use a trustee or have any kind of special account. There are very few restrictions on what you can do with cash in terms of investing it, and you may want to use liquid cash for building equity as opposed to generating income. I would still recommend that you follow the processes that I discuss such as the due diligence and making sure you use a lawyer, but the point is that a trustee isn't required if non-registered money is being used for the mortgage. And there's no restriction from lending cash to anyone, including your immediate family.

That's what investing comes down to at the end of the day. You need to understand your objectives and your needs. Some people don't have a lot of capital and they're looking to build their equity whereas other people have capital, registered or not, and they want to convert that cash into cash flow. It all depends on what you're trying to do.

There are very few strategies that exist where you can generate such a consistent, predictable double-digit return while really taking a measured small amount of risk, all the while having control over so many elements of the investment at the same time. If you run into somebody with cash, and maybe it's sitting in a GIC or a savings account, he or she can invest that money in a mortgage with you, and generate the safe consistent returns we've been talking about all along. However, as I've emphasized, I do think that people with registered accounts are prime for this strategy because I know of no other strategy that offers such solid returns coupled with the managed risk and control.

According to Statistics Canada, there is approximately $700 billion held in registered accounts, and that's just in RRSPs. There's more than $400 billion of unused contribution room. Translation: people are not taking full advantage of their RRSPs and other registered accounts. If you think about it, that's not really a surprise because why put your money into RRSPs and get killed in the stock market?

I think that's how most people look at it, especially in the last couple of years. I believe that one of the best things brought about by the recent economic volatility we've seen will be that more people will decide that they're simply not going to leave their financial futures to other people and they're going to start taking more of an interest in their own finances.

It's a bit of a silver lining from all of the damage and carnage we've seen in the last couple of years. Once you start becoming more active, whether you're a borrower or a lender, you'll find this huge world of opportunity that you've never seen before, and after reading this book, you'll know how to take advantage of those opportunities.

ADVANCED STRATEGY: PURCHASING AN EXISTING MORTGAGE

While everything I've covered to this point assumes that you are involved in setting up a new mortgage, there's another approach you can take that can be very profitable: buying a mortgage that already exists.

At any given time, there are literally billions of private loans and mortgages that are currently held by investors who, at some point, agreed to lend money against a property and earn interest, waiting for their principal to be returned to them at some point in the future. As you become more familiar with private mortgages, you'll discover that there is an active market of private mortgage holders out there who hold existing mortgages that they want to liquidate right now but cannot, because the mortgages have not expired yet.

In real estate investing, one of the most important fundamentals you can learn is to deal only with sellers that have some level of motivation— what we call "motivated sellers." For example, if you find a seller who has to sell their property, either because they're behind on their payments, or they're moving out of the country, or for whatever other reason they might have, they're going to be more flexible to deal with and you're more likely to negotiate a better deal for yourself.

As I teach my students, you want to deal with "have to" sellers instead of "want to" sellers. The higher their motivation to "get out" of the property, the more likely it is that you'll get a great deal.

In the mortgage world, there's a similar idea from the perspective of buying existing mortgages. There are always lenders out there that are willing to sell their mortgage at a "discount" because their circumstances have changed and they need the money back instead of waiting for the mortgage to mature.

These lenders become what we call a "motivated lender," and in much the same way a motivated seller often is willing to sell their property below the market value, a motivated lender will sometimes consider selling their mortgage at a lower "yield" than what it is really worth because they need or want the cash immediately.

As a mortgage investor, if you're able to find someone that is willing to sell you their mortgage at a discount to the face value or return of the mortgage, you've put yourself into a position to create attractive returns for yourself.

Most of the mortgages that are owned by motivated lenders are not originally set up as mortgage investments by the lender. Instead, the lender may have agreed to carry a mortgage on a property that they sold at some point in the past, in the hopes of increasing the number of potential buyers by offering some amount of "seller financing."

In a slow market it might be difficult for the lender to sell the property, so if the lender was willing to "carry" some of the purchase price for a buyer, and allow the buyer to pay them some of the balance in the future, that would reduce the amount of cash they need to come up with today and the lender would instead carry that unpaid balance as a mortgage against the property.

Let's use some real numbers so that I can illustrate the concept.

Suppose you're trying to sell a house that's worth $200,000. For a typical buyer that's getting an 80% mortgage, this would mean that they would need a down payment of $40,000. Obviously, the higher the down payment required, the fewer buyers there are that can buy that house, so you might get creative and decide that you're going to help a buyer by "carrying" 10% of the purchase price ($20,000) as a second mortgage on the property.

This means the buyer would arrange for a $160,000 first mortgage (which would be an 80% mortgage), they would put down $20,000 cash as a down payment, and you would take the second mortgage of $20,000. Let's assume that mortgage is for a three-year term, and that it pays an interest rate of 10% per year.

The main reason you would do this is to increase the pool of potential buyers for your house and to speed up the process of selling it. You would simply forgo getting all of the cash today, and you would agree to wait for that $20,000 to be paid back, based on the terms of the mortgage you reach with the buyer.

Depending on your motivation and need to sell, this is a scenario that might make sense to you—and it has for thousands of Canadians who are currently holding these types of mortgages. They never really intended to be mortgage investors, but they did this in order to get their property sold faster.

But there's the challenge: most of these lenders would much rather have the cash instead of holding the mortgage, and in some cases their motivation to sell that mortgage is high. Perhaps a medical problem surfaces for them or a family member, requiring them to quickly come up with cash. Maybe it's another investment they could make that offers high returns for them. Or, maybe they are moving away and they don't want to keep holding this mortgage because they need the money to buy a new house.

Mortgages Can Be Bought and Sold

Like most other investment instruments, an existing mortgage can be sold to, or purchased from, another investor. If you're able to find someone that holds a good mortgage that they're interested in selling, you could pay them whatever is owing on the mortgage and step into their shoes and collect the payments on the mortgage until the mortgage expires, and then you'd received the principal back.

Let's look back at the example I just gave you to demonstrate this. I said that you had taken back a mortgage of $20,000 on the home that you sold, because you wanted to get it sold quickly. The mortgage had a three-year term on it, meaning that you would receive payments for three years and the borrower would have to pay you off.

Suppose I decide that I want to invest in mortgages, and I decide that I like the mortgage that you currently hold, so I'm willing to purchase it from you. I would agree to pay you the $20,000 that you are owed on it, you would assign or transfer the mortgage to me. I would step in and begin collecting the monthly mortgage payments.

You've sold it to me at full face value, which means I've paid you the full amount that the borrower must repay when it expires. You're happy because you've been able to get your $20,000 out without having to wait for it, and I've found an existing, secure mortgage investment for my $20,000.

This would allow me to save myself some of the hassle of finding a borrower and doing all the paperwork to initially set up the mortgage. In this case, I would still want to do the due diligence on the property, the borrower and the mortgage that already exists, but this might be a way of reducing the amount of work for me to get into mortgage lending. When you're buying an existing mortgage, the due diligence process is really no different than when you are setting up a new mortgage, so be sure to do all of your research and get the facts.

The Real Secret of Profiting When You Buy Mortgages

I'll let you in on a secret about buying mortgages. The truth is, most sophisticated investors would never buy an existing mortgage for the full face value, because there's really very little reason to do so. There are a lot of "accidental" mortgage lenders out there who thought it was a good idea at the time, but didn't know what they were doing. As a result, they become a motivated lender and are looking to get their cash out—and often they're willing to give you a great deal to help them out.

Let's go back to the example above, where you're holding a $20,000 mortgage that pays a 10% annual interest rate. It's been a few months and you've been receiving your payments on that mortgage, but you stumble across an incredible investment opportunity and you believe that you can make a 50% return on your money—if only you had some liquid cash to invest right now.

You need $15,000 to invest in a start-up company that your cousin is creating (he has a track record of several business successes). You realize that if you can raise the $15,000 you'll make a lot of money, but you just don't have $15,000 cash readily available.

You remember that you have this $20,000 mortgage you're holding, but it's going to be more than two years before you can get that capital back. You decide that if you sell that mortgage, even at a discount, it would be worth it, because then you could invest the money and make a lot more than just 10% interest the mortgage is currently paying you.

You approach me, and offer to sell me your mortgage for $15,000. In other words, you offer to sell me the mortgage at a discount. The mortgage has a face value of $20,000, which means the borrower has to pay off the full $20,000, regardless of what I pay you for it.

What would be my return on investment if I were to purchase this mortgage at a discount from you?

Here's what we know about the mortgage:

Principal amount:	$20,000
Annual interest rate:	10%
Annual interest payments:	$2,000

Let's assume I buy this $20,000 mortgage from you at a discount for $15,000, and the borrower makes two years worth of payments, and then decides to pay the mortgage off early because they sell the property.

Here's what my total return would look like:

Amount that I invested to begin with:	$15,000
Interest payments of $2,000 for year 1:	$2,000
Interest payments of $2,000 for year 2:	$2,000
Return of capital at end of year 2:	$20,000
Total amounts received:	$24,000

I've received $24,000 on an investment of $15,000 over a two-year period. This is an annual return of $4,500 per year, which is 30% per year!

Hopefully now you can see how powerful it can be to invest in discounted mortgages from others who hold mortgages they want to sell.

Why Would Someone Sell a Mortgage at a Discount?

When I teach this strategy, a lot of people challenge me on the idea because they don't understand why it is that someone would take a discount on a mortgage they hold.

As I said before, the main reason is because circumstances change for them and they must get the money out of the mortgage. They're no longer interested in the monthly interest payments—they need the cash and they're willing to negotiate a discount in order to get it quickly.

In fact, as a real-life example, here is a classified ad (name and contact details changed for obvious reasons) that I found running in the *Calgary Herald* newspaper in December 2009:

MORTGAGE FOR SALE ON PRIME ALBERTA REAL ESTATE. Must sell to look after other commitments. Will discount to show 35% return. $2,050,000 . . . LTV 40%. John Smith, 555-555-1003.

This is a real ad where what appears to be an investor is willing to discount the mortgage so that the return to a buyer would be 35%. Why would they do this? Who knows. They hint that they need the money for other commitments. The point is that buying discounted mortgages can be very attractive.

And remember that if you had the cash in your RRSP, you could buy this mortgage and earn 35% in your RRSP!

Not only will you see mortgages for sale in newspapers and online, but if you wanted to attract people with existing mortgages to sell, you could place a simple classified ad such as the following:

ARE YOU HOLDING A PRIVATE MORTGAGE YOU WANT TO SELL?

I'm a private investor with cash, looking to buy mortgages. Must have current appraisal, maximum of 70% LTV. Contact Joe at 555-555-1100.

The important point I'm trying to make is that you don't have to create your own mortgages for investment—you can find existing mortgages and purchase them (preferably at a discount).

HOW TO EVALUATE YOUR OPPORTUNITIES

Now let's talk about how to evaluate the opportunities that are coming across your desk, so to speak. This is obviously going to apply primarily to those who are looking to be lenders, but if you're looking to borrow funds from other investors, I want you to pay close attention here as well. I'm about to explain the due diligence and research that a lender should go through in evaluating an opportunity. This means that if you're a borrower, I'm going to give you a blueprint for structuring and presenting your deal to make it more attractive to a lender. If you're trying to raise money from investors, this is the due diligence that any intelligent investor is going to do on *you*. If you're prepared in advance and you have this information readily available for them when they ask for it, you'll impress them and be ahead of the game.

Doing Your Due Diligence in Three Steps

In the mortgage investing world, doing your due diligence really comes down to three key principles:

1. You need to **assess the property** that is going to be pledged as security for your loan—the property on which you're going to hold the mortgage as collateral.

2. You need to **assess the borrower**—the investor or group of investors who are borrowing the funds.

3. You need to **assess the actual deal itself**—what the investment looks like (i.e., the terms of the LTV, the interest rate, the length of the mortgage, and all of the details of the investment).

It's really no more complicated than that. As long as you research the property, your borrower and the deal, you'll put yourself in a powerful position to make an educated decision on the investment. Let's go into each of these in a little more detail.

Step 1: Research the Property

I put researching the property as number one because it truly is the most important part of the due diligence process. If something goes wrong with your investment, it's the property that's going to matter most in terms of getting your money back, and that's the primary way that you protect yourself. Someone who has lost money lending on mortgages usually has made a mistake in this critical step. In fact, if you do this step correctly, and you make sure that you determine the value of the property and you're not overlending on its value, it's very unlikely you will take a loss on your investment.

I'm not saying that it's 100% impossible. You'll never hear me say that, because nothing is guaranteed, whether it's investing or anything else! However, you have to work pretty hard to lose your money if you know what you're doing, because the property is what gives you protection in this strategy.

How do you do the due diligence on the property? You've heard me repeat this many times already, but it's worth saying again: *Above all else, you must have an independently verified value for the property.* This may be the single most important piece of advice that I can offer you in this entire program. You should not lend money against a property when you are not totally clear on the real value of the property. If you don't do anything else but you never break that rule, you'll probably be okay in the mortgage business. Of course this begs the question, "How can I know what a property is really worth?"

Use an Appraiser

The best way to establish the value of a property is to have a professional appraiser complete an appraisal of the property. Appraisers are certified professionals, and they have a specific process to determine the market value of any given property. The primary method they use is looking at recent sales in the marketplace of properties that are comparable to properties they are valuing. Once they have examined the characteristics and selling prices for comparable properties, they make adjustments to account for different features so that they're truly comparing apples to apples. This allows them to back-test their calculations in a number of ways.

For example, if you're trying to evaluate a house that has three bedrooms, two bathrooms and a single garage, you'll want to compare it with a similar property. If you compare it with another house that recently sold on the same street with the same features but perhaps the garage is bigger, then you'll have to adjust your price accordingly to reflect that difference. In this case you might determine that the house with the double garage is worth perhaps $5,000 to $10,000 more than the house with the single garage, enabling you to estimate the single-garage home's price.

This is exactly the process that appraisers go through in making adjustments to arrive at a market appraisal value. They'll take several of the most recent sales and line them up side by side, compare all of their similarities and make notes of where they're different in terms of square footage, number of bedrooms, garage size and so on. They make adjustments to come up with what they really believe is the true market value. I'm not saying that appraisers are perfect. There will always be a certain amount of subjectivity involved in placing a value on a piece of real estate, and when choosing which comparables to include in the evaluation, but most appraisers will come to a similar value within about 5% as long as they know what they're doing.

The step that you want to take to mitigate your risk is to make sure you use a certified appraiser. In a similar way to accountants who have to stand behind the financial statements they produce, appraisers must sign off on their appraisal, and by doing so they have a level of liability and responsibility if those numbers turn out to be fraudulent or a complete misrepresentation. There is a legal context; lenders need to be able to rely on the opinion of appraisers so there's no room for manipulation.

Remember that when you are investing in mortgages, you are literally acting like the bank in the transaction. If you've ever purchased a home, you're aware that getting a third-party-certified appraisal was part of the transaction. Our goal here is to model what the banks do, because it helps us reduce our risk and potential of loss.

A professional appraisal on a single-family home is going to cost somewhere in the range of $300 to $400. This will depend quite a bit on your market and on the specific appraiser that you pick, but an appraisal usually doesn't cost you more than about $400. The cost of having other types of properties appraised is going to vary depending on the size and complexity of the appraisal. If you're lending on a commercial property, for example, then the appraisal cost is likely going to be higher. Our investment firm has paid $15,000 or more for appraisals on commercial property, depending on the complexity and type. My advice would be that you focus on lower-density residential real estate to keep your due diligence simple, at least initially so that you're not complicating the process. There are far fewer potential problems and complexities to consider in the low-density residential world, which includes condos, townhouses, single-family homes and duplexes. These are the easiest properties to understand and evaluate. If you're going to work with larger properties, just recognize that the appraisal and other costs will be quite a bit higher, and you're likely going to want to bring in other types of professionals to evaluate the property, such as structural engineers, environmental consultants and other specialized professions.

Also remember that the borrower typically pays for the cost of the appraisal. What I recommend is that you as the lender choose the appraiser. This gives you the assurance that the borrower doesn't have a relationship with the appraiser that might give them some influence over the value. Let me put this another way. A lot of people who are looking to borrow money already have an appraisal done on the property so they can move a lot faster when a potential lender is found. In most cases, if you're the lender, I would strongly caution you not to take an appraisal that's already been done by the borrower and use it for your own purposes. For one thing, there are several reasons that an appraisal can be ordered and there are a lot of different assumptions that an appraiser can make within the appraisal. If you don't hire the appraiser yourself, you can't be completely sure what the intention or purpose of the appraisal is when it was ordered. Even if there is an existing appraisal on the property, you should arrange for a new one yourself and make it part of your arrangement with the borrower. This is particularly true if the appraisal is not current.

If the borrower has an appraisal that's less than six months old, you might choose instead to have that appraisal updated and re-certified. In this case, the appraiser who did the original report is asked to re-certify the appraisal and confirm all of the assumptions that were made at the time the original was done. Rather than having to do all the research again from scratch, an update takes a fraction of the time for the appraiser to complete. This can save some money and time getting the appraisal done, and you can ensure during the re-certification that the appraiser is signing off on the appraisal for the specific purpose of determining the market value of the property. I'll say this one more time: the security that you hold as the lender is based primarily on ensuring that you know what the value of the property is, so it's up to you how you want to deal with the appraisal. I strongly recommend not taking any shortcuts in this step.

In terms of timelines, an appraisal may take anywhere from a couple of days to a couple of weeks. It depends largely on how busy the appraiser is. You want to get the appraisal completed before you ever think about sending money to your lawyer or engaging your lawyer, so the clock is ticking. Do not waste time starting to arrange the mortgage with your lawyer until you're certain that the value of the property has been confirmed. To protect yourself as the lender, arrange the appraisal but have the borrower pay for it up front.

If you agree to do a mortgage for someone and you order an appraisal and pay for it, what happens when the appraisal comes back way lower than what you thought the property was worth? It likely means that you as the lender are going to second guess whether you should be lending that money at all, because your security or equity in the property is lower than what you thought it was. The lower the value, the less security you ultimately have with your mortgage.

In this case you might not want to proceed to loan the funds, because the loan-to-value ratio takes you out of your comfort zone. This also indicates that your borrower tried to steer you in the wrong direction, telling you that the value of the property was substantially higher in the hopes he could get a mortgage from you at a higher LTV. Obviously, a business relationship where your money's at risk isn't one that you'd want to be involved in. If the value does come back substantially lower and you decide not to proceed with the loan, the problem remains that you've paid for this appraisal. You then call the borrower and tell him you're not proceeding, but what's the likelihood you're going to be able to convince him to pay you back for the appraisal? Not only will your borrower not offer to reimburse you, but he won't want the appraisal at all because it's proof that his property is worth less than what he told you.

The key take-away here is to get the appraisal paid for by the borrower so that you're never out of pocket or at risk of having money spent that you can't recover. If you haven't figured it out yet, I'm big on putting yourself in a situation where you cannot lose and that's what I'm trying to teach you right now.

Let's say that the appraisal comes back fine, which is often the case. In other words, the value is approximately what the borrower said or maybe it's even higher. However, let's say that the borrower, for whatever reason, changes his mind after you've ordered the appraisal and he doesn't want to follow through with the mortgage. Perhaps he's found a different lender who's willing to provide funds at a lower cost than you are. If you've already paid for that appraisal, congratulations! You're the proud new owner of an appraisal that's completely worthless to you. This is why you do not want to pay for the appraisal up front and take the risk that you're not going to get the cost covered. Many appraisers take credit cards, so it's usually a simple process to get the borrower to pay for the appraisal. Ask that a copy of the appraisal be sent directly to you by the appraiser. By doing it this way, you can be 100% sure that what you receive is exactly what the appraiser generates; it's been known to happen where a borrower edits or alters the appraisal to make it more appealing to the lender, which clearly puts the lender at a higher risk. If you have any questions about the appraisal and you've been provided a copy directly by the appraiser, then contact them directly.

You should also verify the land use and the zoning of the property. Make sure that the use of the property conforms to whatever rules and regulations are in effect with the local municipality. If, for example, you do a mortgage on a property that's being used for commercial purposes, but it's not supposed to be used as such, the city or town can shut it down. The value of that asset could decline quite a bit because it's no longer valued for commercial use. The appraisal should state the allowed use of the property, and whether the current use conforms to the zoning of the property. Make sure you verify this, if necessary, with the appraiser and/or the zoning authority.

In summary, getting an appraisal is *the* critical step that you have to do and you should never ever *ever* skip this step. If you'd like to see a sample appraisal, so that you know what to expect, you can download one from my website at www.rrspSecret.com.

Examine the Property in Person

Aside from getting an appraisal, there are a couple of other things you can do in terms of due diligence to try and reduce your risk. An important step I strongly recommend that you take is to go and physically see the property. At the very least, you should be driving by it and if possible, getting a peek inside of it so you know what you're dealing with. If it's a rental property, ask the borrower (who is presumably the landlord) to arrange with the tenant for you to have a walkthrough of the interior. In most situations, it's an acceptable reason to enter a rental property for purposes of inspection, so your borrower shouldn't have a problem arranging this for you. If your borrower shows any resistance to you seeing the inside of the property, I would consider that a red flag and you need to be cautious. What is he trying to hide?

The reason it's so important for you to physically visit the property is because you want to see where the property is located, the condition it's in and the general desirability of it. Here are the types of questions you should be asking yourself:

- What if I end up owning this property?

- What's the marketability of it?

- Who would want to buy this property if I am trying to sell it?

You want to make sure that if something happens and your borrower cannot or does not make his payments, you'll be willing to take that property over so that you can sell it and recover your money. Make no mistake, while the likelihood of taking back a property is relatively low (especially if you follow the steps I'm laying out for you), **there is always the chance that you'll have to take back a property to recover your funds**. And you don't want to get stuck with a lousy property that you can't resell to recover your funds!

The key is to ensure that if you were to take back this property, you'd be able to resell it at a value that recovers all of your investment capital, plus any expenses that you may incur during the foreclosure or take-back process.

Step 2: Research the Borrower

Assuming that the property checks out in terms of the condition, value and security, the second piece of due diligence is research on the borrower.

Remember that when you're lending funds on a mortgage the number one piece of security that you've got is the property itself. As long as you research the property very well and have good security, you're likely to recover your money from the property. I also think it's a good idea to get an understanding of who it is you're lending money to. I'm not talking about doing the full due diligence that banks typically do when they receive an application for a new loan. Remember, part of the reason you're able to charge a double-digit interest rate is that borrowing from you is more convenient for the borrower than from a traditional lender. It's reasonable to complete a decent amount of due diligence on your borrower because of course you want to make sure he is going to make his payments and that he has the capacity of paying. At the same time, remember that you don't want to make it so difficult that he stops wanting to work with you and finds another lender.

Review the Borrower's Credit Report

The easiest way to do research on prospective borrowers is to obtain a copy of their credit report. If you're only lending funds once or twice a year, it probably doesn't make sense for you to become a member of a credit reporting agency. The easiest way to get a copy of a borrower's credit report is to have the person arrange to obtain a copy for you. In Canada, everybody has the right to receive a free copy of their credit report once per year by mail. At a minimum, your borrower can submit a request for a free copy of their credit report from the credit bureau, which typically arrives by mail about six to eight weeks from the time of the request. If you go this route, I recommend you tell the borrower that you'd like him or her to provide you the credit report when it comes in the mail, unopened in the original envelope. That way, you know that the report was not opened, altered, fabricated or tampered with. The downside to requesting the free report by mail is that it takes a fair amount of time to receive it.

The other approach, which is much faster but has a small cost associated with it, is for the borrower to go online to one of the credit bureau websites and request an electronic copy of the report that can be downloaded instantly. In Canada, Equifax and TransUnion are the two major credit bureaus and both provide the option to instantly download a credit report. You must register on their website (for Equifax, www.equifax.ca, and for TransUnion, www.tuc.ca) and answer a series of questions to verify your identity, after which you'll be able to pull your own credit. If your borrower is willing to register and pay for their credit report, it's typically going to cost somewhere around $20, and most people can get theirs within a matter of minutes. (*Note: there used to be a third credit reporting company in Canada called Experian. However, it discontinued consumer credit reporting in April 2009, leaving only Equifax and TransUnion as the credit reporting companies operating in Canada.*)

> I strongly recommend that you pull your own credit report at least once a year so you can make sure that there isn't erroneous information that's hurting you without you even knowing it. In fact, I pull my own credit at least three or four times per year to ensure that I'm managing my credit and catching any potential problems where information is not being reported accurately. Being proactive with your credit also allows you to quickly become aware if someone tampers with or steals your identity.

Of the two primary credit bureau websites in Canada I find that Equifax is used more commonly, so if you're going to ask your borrower to pull from one of the sites, that's probably the one I'd recommend. Of course, you could ask him or her to pull a copy from both bureaus if you want to. Each bureau's report will look a little bit different because not all creditors report to both of them, so for example you might find a bank that only sends information to one credit bureau and not the other. In addition, each of the companies has their own reporting format, and they use different scoring methods, so don't expect them to reflect identical information or ratings.

Getting a copy of your borrower's credit report is a pretty efficient way to do basic research. What you're looking for is to ensure in general that the borrower is responsible with his or her money and does not have a pattern of late or delinquent payments. Having several late payments, delinquent accounts or perhaps a bankruptcy or foreclosure on record is a danger sign about irresponsibility. From the credit industry's perspective, past behaviour is a strong indicator of future performance. Be concerned if there are numerous indicators on the bureau's report that the borrower has not met his or her financial responsibilities in the past.

On the other hand, if someone has one blemish on his or her credit report and is able to explain why—for example, sudden loss of job or a move to a new city and the bill didn't catch up and went to collections without their knowledge—in those cases you can use your discretion.

This exercise is not about having perfect credit. Some people look to private investors because they do have issues with their credit and can't get a traditional bank loan. That shouldn't immediately disqualify them from your consideration. The point is to take this into account along with the security you have in the property. Don't expect someone looking to you for a loan to have perfect credit and remember, the more steps and hoops that you make the borrower jump through, the more likely it is that they're just going to throw up their hands and go find another lender. The purpose of them coming to you is partly because of that convenience. While you want to make sure that you do your basic research, you don't want to make the process too painful for the borrower. As long as you've got great security on the property, the borrower is secondary to that security. Any time you lend money and there is a default, your first step will be to go after the property.

Step 3: Research the Deal Itself

The third and final piece is evaluating the actual deal itself. Quite simply, this is looking at all of the aspects of the deal and making sure that as a whole the deal makes sense for you to do. For example, once you have the appraisal back and you understand a little bit more about your borrower, you can determine whether the interest rate that you discussed with the borrower makes sense or not. Let's say that the appraisal comes back and it's a little bit lower than what you understood the value was going to be, which means that you would be lending at a slightly higher loan-to-value ratio. Once you know that information, and you've researched your borrower and found out that he or she has a good credit standing and appears to be a good credit risk, then you might decide to ask for a little bit extra in the interest rate to offset the fact that it will be a higher LTV.

The interest rate is always completely open to negotiation between the lender and the borrower. It depends on a number of factors, including

- the security

- the relationship between the borrower and the lender

- the current interest rates in the marketplace

- how motivated the lender is to lend and the borrower to borrow

- many other things as well, which I'll cover in detail in the next chapter

Keeping in mind that these are only general ranges and not always the rule, first mortgages are typically arranged somewhere between 7% and 11%, and second mortgages anywhere from 9% to 18% and sometimes higher, depending on the LTV or the motivation of the borrower. When somebody absolutely must come up with funds to close on a deal, for example, sometimes he or she will be willing to pay 20% or even more. But for the most part you'll find that rates are typically in the range of 12% to 16% for second mortgages, which is a very attractive return for most investors, considering the security you receive on your investment.

• • •

I've presented to you the three key elements of doing research on a potential mortgage investment opportunity, and I gave them to you in order of importance. Without question, the property itself is the most important part of this process, because it's what provides the security if your borrower fails to meet their obligations under the mortgage.

Once you've properly researched the property, you need to consider the borrower and think through the details of the proposed investment.

In the next chapter, I'm going to continue the discussion about "the deal" and the elements that you need to think of when you're structuring a win-win deal for all parties involved.

9

The Terms of the Deal

The ability to create win/win agreements with others is a key to building good relationships.
—Dr. Stephen R. Covey

Mortgage lending is more than just "x" amount of dollars being lent at "y"% interest for a specific period of time. You can get a lot more creative than that, and that's what I'll cover in this chapter. I'll also go over a few critical mistakes I see investors making when they're structuring their deals that can create very serious problems down the line if they're not addressed.

There are several key components of a mortgage investment that you need to think about. Let me first review the key elements that you need to make decisions about, and then we'll look at some creative ideas and strategies on how you can structure win-win deals with the other party.

COLLATERAL

As I outlined in the previous chapter, you've got to do your due diligence, and that starts with the property itself—it represents the collateral you're going to receive in turn for lending your money. Sometimes, you may feel like you want more security than just the mortgage on that particular property. If you decided you wanted additional security, you can require that the mortgage be registered not only against the property that the investor is offering, but against other properties they own. This is called a "blanket mortgage." A blanket mortgage is exactly what it sounds like; it's a mortgage that blankets more than one property. Here's how it works.

Let's say that I'm a real estate investor with several properties. I want to borrow some RRSP funds from you on a brand new property I'm about to buy. This property is a bit beat up and needs a ton of work, but I can get a really good deal on it. The condition of the property makes you a little nervous and reluctant to lend money because you really don't want to take that property back if I don't make the payments. I really want to make this deal happen, though, and I have another property that's much more enticing. This other property that I've owned for a couple of years has got great tenants and cash flow. In order to make you more comfortable, I agree with you that I'm going to allow you to "blanket" both the property I'm buying to renovate and the cash flow property that I already own.

All this means is that the mortgage gets registered not only on the new property I'm buying, but against my existing property as well. This restricts me from refinancing or selling either one of the properties until you get paid off. I'm essentially pledging the equity in the other house as collateral to make sure that you get paid. In the worst-case scenario, if I defaulted and you got a blanket mortgage, you now have the legal right to go after both properties to get your money back.

I've used blanket mortgages in the past to protect myself when I wanted to be sure that I had a lot of security. In some cases I've granted blanket mortgages when a lender I was working with was a little nervous about one of the properties I had for whatever reason—either because of condition or location, or maybe it was a turnaround project.

If you're the one borrowing, be careful about offering blanket mortgages. You don't want to encumber all of your properties to get one loan. Once they are tied up together in the blanket, you can't refinance or sell anything until you pay off that mortgage. Each situation will be different and it's up to negotiating each deal to determine whether a blanket mortgage is something that makes sense, whether you're the lender or the borrower. Obviously if you're the borrower and you're dealing with somebody who doesn't bring up the blanket mortgage, neither should you.

Also keep in mind that the more complicated you make it as the lender, and the more security you demand, the more likely it is your borrower is going to find it too difficult to work with you, and they'll go and find a different lender.

Your job is to find a balance so that as the lender you have sufficient security or collateral, while still allowing the borrower to feel like the transaction is in their best interest and isn't going to be too difficult or complicated.

INTEREST RATES

The biggest question I get when teaching about mortgage investing concerns interest rates. A lot of people ask, "Does the interest rate depend on what the prevailing interest rates are in the economy?"

The simple answer to this question is no. Generally speaking, private investors do not peg their rates to the prime rate, mirroring its changes. While it would make sense that the interest rate expected by private investors would follow the movement of the prime rate, that doesn't tend to happen. For example, when interest rates rise or fall, you don't see a corresponding increase or decrease in the interest rates that private investors are asking for.

This doesn't mean that if you're a borrower, you can't try to negotiate a little more aggressively if interest rates are low or are declining. However, the prevailing interest rates at the bank usually don't have a lot of impact on interest rates being sought by private lenders.

Commonly, interest rates in the private lending business stay fairly static, regardless of what's happening with interest rates in the country. Even though interest rates may be lower right now, lending is a lot more difficult to access, and if you're a real estate investor you know this to be true. It's simply more difficult to get access to capital today than it was a year or two ago. That's partially why interest rates are kept low; the central bank hopes to motivate people to go and borrow money. But while the central bank may continue to drop interest rates, the country's financial institutions are not softening their criteria for borrowers when it comes to qualifying for lending. Access to capital is still difficult, thus allowing private lenders to continue charging the same interest rates that they've been able to charge for the past few years. There's a premium for accessing private capital, so there is no direct correlation between the mortgage rates that the banks are offering and the private lending business.

Contrary to what you might be thinking, there is no actual interest rate standard in the private lending industry. As I've outlined before, there are general ranges that you often will see for certain types of mortgages, but the interest rate will be affected by a number of things, including the property, the security, the buyer's motivation to borrow, and the seller's motivation to lend money. As an example, let's assume you sign a deal to buy a property with a $25,000 non-refundable deposit and you think that you've got financing. A week before the deal is supposed to close, your bank backs out of the mortgage commitment. You're facing the prospect of losing your $25,000 if you don't come up with the financing in a week. On top of that, you may be sued for not performing if you're not able to close on time. In that circumstance, what interest rate would you be willing to pay on a short-term basis in order to get the money in time to close on that deal and save your $25,000? The answer should be "almost anything," because if you can go and borrow money on a short-term basis—even if it's really painful and it costs you $15,000 to borrow it—you may end up still further ahead because you didn't lose your $25,000.

In this case, the motivation to borrow money is extremely high. A borrower who is in that position is unlikely to negotiate over one or two percentage points in the interest rate. The same holds true with lenders. If you're looking at a whole bunch of different deals and you can hand-pick which deals you're going to do, you can hold out for a higher interest rate. But if you've got money sitting in the bank earning you nothing, and you're only looking at one deal that's offering 10%, you may be better off taking that deal at 10% at least for a year. This will give you more time to fill your pipeline and find other opportunities that may be more worthwhile.

Charging Minimum Interest Rates

Although there is no standard interest rate, there is a minimum rate that you must charge on an RRSP mortgage, and it's determined both by the *Income Tax Act* and the policies of the trustee. Usually, the minimum rate you must charge on an arm's length mortgage in a registered account is 2% to 3%. No matter which company you use as your trustee, it will require that at least a certain amount of interest be paid back into the account every year, because that's how the company gets its fees.

This is a simple question you can ask the trustee you choose to work with when you open your account. Ask them what the minimum required interest rate is that must be charged on a mortgage each year.

Charging Maximum Interest Rates

At the high end, the maximum that most trustees will allow you to charge is in the area of 30% per year. Trustees must ensure that any mortgages or investments they are administering fall within the rules of both the *Income Tax Act* from the CRA and the *Criminal Code of Canada*. They don't ever want to get into a situation where a mortgage investment starts to get close to "usury rates," which are considered a criminal act. Usury is an exorbitant or unlawful rate of interest. In other words, in Canada you're only allowed to charge a certain amount of interest on a loan before it becomes illegal. The purpose of this is to protect people against predatory lenders. In Canada it's against the law to charge more than a 60% annual interest rate on a loan, so the trustees set their maximums well below that rate to make sure they don't run into trouble.

Depending on who your trustee is, you need to determine the minimum interest that must be paid into an account each year and the absolute maximum interest rate that's allowed to be charged. Knowing those two parameters will give you your range. For many investors, that range is somewhere between 3% and 30% a year.

Keep in mind that the mortgage also will need to be reasonable from a market perspective. In other words, if you lent money to someone at 95% loan-to-value on a property and only charged them 3%, is that a market value deal? No, because lending at 95% loan-to-value is very high risk and only charging 3% to offset that risk is totally unreasonable. In a circumstance like this, you're going to face the risk that the CRA will analyze the deal, and deem it a non-arm's length transaction. Their view would be that it's unreasonable to lend money at 95% loan-to-value for only 3%, assume it isn't a "commercially reasonable" deal, and may deem it ineligible, in which case it would be treated as though the investor had taken that money out of their RRSP. They'd be subjected to tax consequences and penalties. Common sense is going to prevail; as long as you're lending within reasonable limits, this should never pose a problem for you. As well, the trustees have policies in place that are intended to protect you from getting into trouble with the interest rates you are setting up in your transactions.

Working Within Reasonable Limits

In private lending agreements, you'll typically see first mortgages of anywhere from 7% to 11%, and they're usually at least a couple of points higher than the current going mortgage rates at the big banks. In a low-interest-rate environment, you could probably negotiate a little bit lower first mortgage with somebody that's a private lender simply because interest rates are so low. But remember that just because interest rates are so low in the marketplace doesn't necessarily affect the private lending business. Remember, too, that interest rates also will depend on the property, the motivation of the lender, the LTV and so on.

Second mortgages typically range anywhere from 8% or 9% all the way up to 18% or more. It directly depends on the risk in the deal, specifically the loan-to-value ratio. It's also affected by the borrower, and the type of property. For example, raw land is considered much higher risk from a lending perspective than an apartment building. Because the raw land doesn't generate any income or cash flow, it's harder for a borrower to pay the mortgage. On the other hand, if you own a 50-unit apartment building, then chances are pretty good that mortgage payments won't be a problem with the positive cash flow coming in from tenants.

Most private lending including RRSP mortgages are "interest only" agreements, and that's primarily because it makes it very simple for everyone to calculate the interest on the loan. For example, it's relatively common to see a 12% second mortgage interest rate in the marketplace. I've lent money at 12% and we've got loans where we're paying 12%. The reason for this is simple: 12% per year is equal to 1% per month, which is very easy to quickly calculate in your head.

Let's say you have a $100,000 loan at 12% and you're trying to calculate the monthly interest-only payment. All you do is figure out what 1% of the principal amount is. In this case, it's $1,000 ($100,000 loan × 12% per year / 12 months per year). You'll almost never see secondary lending (such as RRSP mortgages) amortized, because it just complicates the process for everybody involved.

Using the Delayed Payment Interest Strategy

I briefly covered this strategy earlier, but I wanted to mention it again because I think it's a very powerful tool you can use to create win-win transactions for everyone involved.

Every lender wants to get as high an interest rate as possible, but consider what happens from a lender's perspective when you get those interest payments. Each month when you get a payment from the borrower back into your account, you can't really spend or reinvest that money right away. The payments simply accumulate in the account month after month until the balance is such that you can go and do something with it. If you think about it, it's really not that beneficial for an RRSP investor to receive monthly payments that can't be reinvested.

To illustrate, let's assume that you're an RRSP investor who wants to lend on mortgages. Would you rather get paid 12% monthly or 13% quarterly? Or what if you could make 14% but you are only going to get one payment per year? If you're like many RRSP investors, you'd rather have the 14% interest even though it's only one annual payment. Whether you get monthly payments, quarterly payments or one annual payment, it really doesn't matter since the money all goes back into your protected account anyway. If you can't spend or invest the money month to month, why not maximize the interest rate and not worry about getting monthly payments? Some investors prefer that monthly or quarterly payments be made back into their account, but this is primarily from an emotional place. They simply feel better seeing the regular payments being made, even though they can't use the payments that are coming in.

If you're a lender using registered funds, my suggestion is that you consider doing the delayed or deferred payments as I've outlined previously, because you'll be able to achieve higher interest rates and maximize your returns.

Case in Point

Let's now look at the other side of the coin—the real estate investor who's looking to borrow funds from someone with a self-directed RRSP account. From this perspective, would you rather make payments to your RRSP investor every month, or would it be better for you only to have to make a quarterly payment or one payment per year? Speaking as an experienced real estate investor, I can tell you I'd much rather make mortgage payments once a year. During the course of that year, I'm able to reduce my outgoing monthly cash payment, which means the property generates better cash flow throughout the year. What's more, instead of having to pay it back to the investor, that money can be used to improve the property and to maintain a reserve fund in the account. This is particularly helpful when you first buy a property and may need extra funds during the year to make improvements and to generate a higher cash flow.

For example, you might buy an abandoned house that needs renovations, and in the beginning it's not going to provide any cash flow at all. It will take you some time to get it fixed up and put tenants into it. Regardless of the reason, most real estate investors would much rather defer some of their payments so they can accumulate more cash to invest in the property. Then they will make a mortgage payment at the end of the year.

With the RRSP investor, who'd rather get the highest interest rate and is not concerned about getting paid every month, and the real estate investor, who's more concerned about cash flow and would be okay with paying a slightly higher interest rate if the payments were deferred, you can see how it's possible to create attractive win-win mortgage situations for both parties.

In this case, a mortgage could be created at 13% interest with one annual payment being due each year. The RRSP lender gets more interest on his investment because instead of charging 12% and getting paid monthly, he's getting 13% paid annually. Meanwhile, the real estate investor is able to improve his cash flow from the property throughout the year because he's not required to make payments every month. This reiterates the benefit that mortgage investments offer to investors, whether borrowers or lenders, because they can be structured to provide whatever each party needs.

Using the Deferred Interest Strategy

The deferred interest strategy, of which I've also given you an overview, is another tool that can be used to create win-win situations for the RRSP lender and borrower.

In this case, the goal is to defer most of the interest to be paid on the loan until the very end of the term of the mortgage. Instead of making the full interest payment at the end of each year, the borrower pays a minimal amount of the interest, and the balance is deferred until the end of the mortgage term. By doing it this way, the RRSP lender still receives his or her full return on their money, but the borrower benefits from reduced burden on making payments until the mortgage expires.

As an example, let's assume that a real estate investor is buying a property that requires renovations and an infusion of cash before the property generates any cash flow. The investor finds an RRSP investor who is willing to invest his funds for a two-year term without being concerned about getting monthly or quarterly payments. This lender is most interested in trying to get a higher interest rate for his money. The deferred interest strategy allows both parties to get what it is they want. Recall that the minimum interest rate you must charge for an RRSP mortgage is typically in the 2% to 3% range, but you're allowed to pay only that minimum 2% to 3% each year, and defer the rest of the interest until the end of the mortgage.

Using the example above, let's assume that the lender agrees that if the borrower pays him a 15% annual interest rate on their money, the lender will allow him to defer most of the interest, as long as he pays the 3% required by the trustee. In other words, the RRSP lender in this case would lend the borrower the money, and at the end of the first year the borrower would make a payment of 3% interest back into the lender's RRSP account. If the interest rate was 15%, the borrower would still owe the lender 12%, but that 12% payment gets deferred.

The second year passes, and because this is a two-year loan, at the end of the second year the real estate investor (the borrower) pays the lender what he is owed, which would be the 12% from the previous year plus the full 15% for the second year. The RRSP lender still ends up making 15% per year on his investment, but the real estate investor benefits because he didn't have to come up with all of the interest payments during the two-year period.

This can be a huge benefit to a real estate investor who would rather have the cash during those two years to put toward improving the property. It's a win-win for both the borrower and the lender. It gets the RRSP investor higher interest and the real estate investor gets better cash flow and lower cash requirements during the investment term.

Using the Stepped Interest Rate Strategy

Another creative example of how you can structure these kinds of deals is called the "stepped interest rate strategy." Similar to the deferred interest strategy, the idea here is to help the investor with cash flow on his property while at the same time generating an attractive return for the RRSP investor. In this case, you would simply come up with a schedule whereby the interest rate starts out lower in the first year and progressively increases throughout the term of the mortgage. In this way, the overall average interest is what the lender is looking to achieve, but it reduces the payments in the first year to help with cash flow and increases the payments in the later years once the property has been renovated and is producing better cash flow.

With the stepped interest strategy, you simply determine an interest rate that you agree that you're going to pay throughout the term. Let's say you're the RRSP lender and you want to earn a 13% interest rate on your money, and you're okay with up to a three-year term. Using the stepped interest strategy, you'd come up with a lower interest rate at the beginning, but each year that the investment goes on, the interest rate goes up so that overall the average remains 13%.

For example, if the borrower suggested that they could manage to pay 5% in the first year, that means that there is 8% that is not paid in that first year. In this case, you could set up the interest rate schedule so that the first year was 5%, the second year was 13%, and the third and final year was 21%. The three-year average is still 13%, but the schedule of payments is such that payments are more convenient for the borrower, based on the cash flow of their property.

One key issue you might be asking here is "What if the real estate investor pays off the mortgage early? Doesn't that mean that the RRSP investor only gets paid the lower interest rate and misses out on the higher rates that they could have received later?"

The answer is no, as long as you draft the mortgage documents properly. You would simply include a clause that says, in effect, "If the mortgage is paid out early, then the interest owing at payout will be adjusted such that the overall interest cost will be 13% for the duration of the loan term." You can see an example of this language in the sample documents at www.rrspSecret.com.

As long as you're making at least one payment per year of the minimum required interest rate imposed by the trustee, you're able to defer the rest of the amount owing if it makes sense for the investor, as I've outlined in the deferred interest strategy. My experience has been that initially most RRSP investors want to receive monthly payments because in their mind, they somehow believe that it must be better to get monthly payments rather than quarterly or annually. But since they can't spend the money anyway, a lot of investors end up liking this arrangement of fewer interest payments, especially since they can command a higher interest rate to justify the less-frequent payments. And it's easier to manage quarterly or annual payments.

THE TERM

Another variable is the length of the mortgage—the term. Keeping in mind that the primary security that an RRSP investor has when lending money on a mortgage is the value of the property itself, I always suggest to people that they never lend funds on an RRSP mortgage for more than a maximum of three years. And I would add that two years is probably the most common time frame. A lot can happen in a real estate market in three years. The market could shift and perhaps the property's value could drop to where you're at risk of losing some of your money.

If you're only lending money for a one- or two-year term and you're keeping your LTV at a reasonable level, it's very unlikely that the market will move quickly enough in that time to put your money in jeopardy. Suppose you're lending at 80% loan-to-value. It would be highly unlikely for the real estate market to correct 20% in a year. It also would be unlikely in two years, but for every additional year that you add to the term, it becomes more difficult to be confident of what's going to happen that far out. That's why the shorter the term of the mortgage, the less risk there is to the lender.

Remember, the property is your primary security, so if you lend on a property that you don't know the real value of, or you're investing in a market where the fundamentals are poor and you don't understand it well, you might be in for a disaster. In this case, the term doesn't really matter too much. If you lend against a property that isn't worth what you've lent, you're in trouble the moment the money gets sent to the borrower.

> Try to keep your term to absolutely no more than three years, and preferably to two. This gives you better control as the lender, and ensures that you are in a position to demand the return of your money without having to wait several years to do so.

OPTION TO RENEW

Another strategy you can use whether you're the RRSP investor or the real estate investor is to include in the document an option to renew the mortgage; for example, a one-year mortgage with an option to renew the mortgage for one more year. If you're the real estate investor, this gives you the ability to extend the mortgage when the first year is up. It's not unusual to see some kind of modest renewal or option fee being charged in this case by the lender. You might, for instance, pay the RRSP investor a $200 option renewal fee for extending the loan another year. If you were talking about a mortgage of $20,000, a $200 fee to renew would be 1% of the mortgage amount, which would seem pretty reasonable. This benefits the RRSP investor of course, because he or she really doesn't have to do a whole lot to get this extra income. The $200 is deposited in the RRSP account, and the mortgage is extended for the additional year (which can be done with a one-page document—see www.rrspSecret.com for an example of a Mortgage Extension Agreement). This is convenient for the borrower, too, because it avoids the need to go out and try to find another lender, to qualify for a loan, and all of the other steps and work involved if they were going to pay off that loan instead of extending it.

My experience as a real estate investor is that once we've worked with someone who lends us money from their RRSP, and we make the payments on time every time for a year or two years, when the mortgage comes up for renewal very rarely does the lender want to get his money back. They've fallen in love with this 12% or 13% consistent return going into their RRSP, while at the same time they're hearing their friends cry about losing 20% or 30% in the stock market.

PREPAYMENT

Another key element of structuring a deal is the topic of prepayment, or paying the mortgage off early. As you're probably aware, when you get a fixed-term closed mortgage with a major bank in Canada, there is generally some kind of prepayment penalty embedded in the mortgage. The reason for this is that the bank commits their funds to you for a certain period of time, say five years. They agree to lend you money at a fixed rate for that period, and by doing this, the bank can calculate what their profit is going to be over that period of time, and they like that predictability.

If you change your mind and you want to pay your loan off early, this isn't good news for the bank. The bank is forced to take its money back, which is fine, but now it has to re-lend it to somebody else in order to keep making money on the money. This process costs the bank money, so in order to offset that cost, the bank builds in a prepayment penalty.

In Canada, the more standard mortgage prepayment penalty is three months of interest. In this case, the bank simply calculates what you would have paid in interest for three months had you continued paying on the loan, and charges that amount to you as a penalty if you paid off the loan early.

Paying the IRD

Aside from the three-month interest penalty, there's another prepayment penalty being used by more banks these days, and it can be very painful.

The IRD, which stands for "interest rate differential," gives the bank the right to charge you a penalty for all of the interest that it *would* have received had you continued paying out the mortgage until the end of the contractual term. The IRD factors in what the interest rates are today compared to what they were like when you signed your mortgage. If interest rates have gone up significantly since you signed your mortgage, then it's likely you will not incur an IRD penalty. If your mortgage rate is low, the bank can take the money and re-lend it at a higher rate, which it will be glad to do. In that case, the IRD will not apply.

However, if the reverse is true—the interest rate on your mortgage is higher than what the going rates are today—it's likely you'll face the IRD penalty. This penalty enables the bank to recoup its losses because it has to lend out the money you've repaid, at a lower interest rate than the rate you've been paying on your loan. That's what the IRD is all about—it helps the bank recoup lost profit if interest rates go down. Many banks will say that you have to pay them either the three-month minimum interest or the IRD, whichever is greater.

Suffice it to say you're going to pay a penalty no matter what you do when you have a mortgage with one of the big banks, unless you have an "open" mortgage that can be paid without penalty (although you pay a small premium for this benefit). Banks build in hefty prepayment penalties for people who pay off their mortgages early, hoping to discourage borrowers from doing so. They want you to keep the mortgage for the full term because that allows them to predict their financials and what their profits are going to be, and helps ensure they don't lose profit because you pay off a lucrative (high interest) mortgage and they can't re-lend that money at similar rates.

In the private mortgage world, most loans are set up as fully open, which basically means that the borrower can pay off the loan anytime he wants during the term of the mortgage. This is one of the big benefits of using RRSP mortgages for a real estate investor. Interest rates may be higher, but an RRSP investor can be more flexible because paying off the loan usually is not restricted or heavily penalized by the lender.

If you're in the market to buy a fixer-upper that you plan to flip in three or four months, you can choose either to go to a bank and get a traditional mortgage or to find an RRSP investor who has the funds you need. If you borrow it from the bank, it's going to be a much more complex approval process and you may have to agree to a prepayment penalty in your agreement. Qualifying for the mortgage also may be complicated by the appraisal, especially if this property is in dire need of repairs. If you do get a mortgage and the bank puts a traditional loan in place, you'll certainly be paying that penalty when you flip it.

On the other hand, if you go to a private lender with RRSP funds, you're likely going to be charged a higher interest rate, but there's not going to be nearly as painful a qualifying process. In addition, as soon as you sell the house you often can pay off the loan without a prepayment penalty. What you've got to do in these circumstances is weigh the pros and cons as a real estate investor. Consider the overall costs, because a lot of people always look at the interest rate and think "that's too expensive" or "what a rip-off," but they fail to calculate in all of the other extra costs that are associated with borrowing money from a bank. Don't make that mistake!

STRATEGIES TO PROTECT YOUR MONEY AS A LENDER

There are a number of "insider" ideas and strategies that you can employ in order to ensure you're maximizing your returns, while at the same time reducing the risk that you're taking with each opportunity. I've touched on a few of these points already, but I want to emphasize these ideas because incorporating them can, when used properly, make a good investment even better.

Charging a Penalty

Even though I just explained that oftentimes, private mortgages do not have prepayment penalties, that doesn't mean that you can't charge a prepayment penalty when *you* lend out your RRSP funds. Always remember, when you're the lender, you get to set your own rules! In fact, I personally build in a prepayment penalty when I lend funds because I want to be assured of some reasonable return on my money. The reality is that if you're doing this business properly, you're taking time to do due diligence on the investment. If you lend money to someone who pays you back almost immediately, that's not good for you.

Let's assume that you lend out $100,000 at 12% interest. You expect that the borrower is going to keep your money for a full year, but in the meantime they shop for cheaper money. Let's say they find someone unsophisticated—maybe a relative who agrees to lend them money for only 5%. They find this person a week after you lend them your money, and they pay you back your $100,000 with interest. If you only charged them 12% for the time your money was lent, that means your $100,000 investment only generated a return of about $250 (remember that 12% is the same as 1% per month). If they only kept your money for a week, that's one quarter of a month, so you're only getting paid a quarter of a percent of interest for the time your money was out. For all of the time you spent doing the research and due diligence and negotiating the deal, obviously this doesn't make a lot of sense. This is why prepayment penalties and upfront fees are regularly charged.

How can you protect yourself from this happening, and how can you build into the agreement some minimum payment that's going to be made regardless of when the loan is paid off? The loan could specify that the borrower agrees that he will pay a minimum of six months of interest on the loan regardless of whether he pays back the loan sooner than the first six months or not. In doing it this way, you're essentially protecting yourself as the lender because you know that you're going to collect at least six months of interest. Even if your borrower only takes the money for two months, to pay off that loan he still has to give you that interest. The bonus is that if he does pay you off early, you increase your yield on the investment because you're going to collect the full six-month interest payment even though your money wasn't lent out for that long. Here's another way to look at it. If you get six months of interest but you only have to lend your money for three months, that means you're going to get back double the interest rate. You've lent the money for half as long.

Charging Points

Another approach you can take to protect your return is to charge the borrower what we refer to in the industry as "points." As I pointed out earlier, a point simply means 1% of the loan amount. On a $100,000 loan, that would be $1,000. In the private lending world, it's not uncommon to see lenders charge upfront points plus the interest rate. For example, a lender might charge three points and 12%. The lender will be paid 3% of the loan amount upfront no matter how long the loan is out for, and he's going to earn 12% per year for however long the money is out. By doing it this way, the lender ensures that he's going to get paid upfront for the time it takes to negotiate the mortgage with the borrower and do the necessary due diligence.

Charging points in the RRSP mortgage world is not a common thing, especially when you're just dealing with private individuals, but it's certainly possible to do so if your borrower is willing to pay it. This underlines again why it can be a more profitable strategy if you're a real estate investor to deal direct with RRSP lenders rather than going through mortgage brokers. Most mortgage brokers add points to deals. That's how they get paid, whereas most individual RRSP investors don't think to try and charge points in the deal.

Calculating Fees in Advance

As I've said before, you're going to incur some modest fees from the RRSP trustee that holds your self-directed account. Each trustee publishes a schedule of fees, so it's really easy to predict what fees you're ultimately going to pay when you open and fund a self-directed RRSP account. The goal of the RRSP investor is to generate a net return on the investment regardless of the fees. In other words, if I'm shooting for a 12% return, I don't want to have to pay any fees out of that 12%. Instead, I'll want to have already factored the fees into the deal, such as the account set-up fee, the mortgage set-up fee, the ongoing administration fee for managing the account, and a "mortgage discharge" fee that's usually charged when the loan gets paid out at the end.

If you move your money to a self-directed account specifically to lend it to someone else, you're incurring all of these fees. If it's my RRSP account, and I'm looking to lend money, I calculate all of these fees in advance and add that total amount to the face value of the mortgage. By doing this I get paid back the full amount of all the fees that I anticipate.

Let's assume that I'm going to lend you $50,000 from my RRSP account. It's money that I've got in a self-directed account right now and I agree that I'm going to lend you a two-year mortgage. I look at the trustee's fee schedule and learn that my total fees to make this deal happen will be $370 during the two years. I agree to lend you $50,000, but I say there's a fee of $370 that applies because that's the cost of my administration. We then set up a mortgage that's registered for $50,370 rather than the flat $50,000. You still get $50,000 when the mortgage proceeds are delivered to you, but you've agreed to pay me back the $50,000 plus the $370—the total face value of the mortgage. I'm going to get the original $50,000 back that I invested, but I'm also going to get the $370 in fees, plus my interest. This works out even better for me as a lender because I'm getting paid interest on the $370 during the mortgage term.

If you pay back the loan earlier than the original two-year term, I get another bonus. You still have to pay me the $370 back because it's part of the mortgage, but I end up getting that money even though I may not have incurred all of those expenses. From the borrower's perspective, agreeing to pay the lender's fee is not a big deal. It's simply the cost of doing business for a real estate investor. Again, if you were to go to a professional lender or a mortgage broker, you're going to pay a lot higher fees than that, which is why most real estate investors don't have a problem covering the fees. It's a relatively minor cost.

RRSP FUNDS AND NEW PROPERTY

You can use RRSP funds not only to take equity out of an existing property (which is a common use of it), but to buy a new property. This leads into some of the landmines and problems that a lot of investors make in their investing.

Assume that you're looking to buy a new investment property. The purchase price is $200,000 and you've been approved for a bank loan of $150,000, so you need $50,000 cash to close. If you can find an RRSP investor who has $20,000, you might be able to get them to lend the $20,000 against the property as a second mortgage, which would mean that you'd have the first mortgage of $150,000 plus the second mortgage. In this case, you'd only have to come up with $30,000 to buy the property. The loan would be at 85% loan-to-value, which in my mind is the upper end of what you should be lending.

On the surface that sounds easy, but it doesn't always work in reality. It especially won't work if you're planning on a traditional first mortgage for the $150,000 with a bank and a second mortgage for the balance ($50,000) with a private lender. The first mortgage lender, typically a bank, in virtually every case will not allow you to do that because they want to make sure you've got something at stake in the purchase. The bank will require that you've got some of your own equity—your own money—going into the deal. And the days of being able to buy a property with no money down are gone, outside of using seller financing or other creative techniques.

A lot of people will tell you that you can't put a second mortgage on a property that you're buying new when you're getting conventional financing. Here's the key (and I've done this several times). Some lenders are completely fine with you using additional funds like a second mortgage to close on a property *as long as you disclose it to the lender*. What you don't want to do is apply for a first mortgage with a bank without having your second mortgage already lined up if it's going to come from a private lender's RRSP account.

Not all lenders will allow you to use an RRSP lender or some other secondary financing to cover some of the closing cash, but I've bought over a dozen properties using a first conventional loan for 75% or 80% of the value and used a second mortgage from someone for an additional 10% or 15% to get us up to about the 85% loan-to-value threshold. As long as the lender knows about it, this strategy is permitted. You're still putting in 15% of your own cash. It's when you hide the secondary financing plans that you hurt your chances of getting that first loan approved.

When in doubt, disclose. The last thing you need to deal with is a claim of mortgage fraud. If you've been told that you cannot use a second mortgage to buy a new property, that's not necessarily true. You may just have to hunt down another lender working with a different set of rules.

Other lenders will not allow you to have any kind of secondary financing whatsoever; you have to come up with the cash to close behind the first mortgage. If you find yourself in that circumstance, you'll need to close on the property first and go back later on to arrange for a second mortgage. At this point you can take out some of your equity. Let's say that you bought a property for $200,000 a few years ago and originally you had a $150,000 loan on it. Over the last few years the property value has gone up to $230,000 and you've paid your first mortgage down to $130,000. Now you've got $100,000 of existing equity sitting in that property.

Let's assume that you can't go and qualify to refinance the first mortgage for whatever reason. So here you are: you've got a property worth $230,000, a $130,000 mortgage, and $100,000 of equity that's sitting there dead. You want to unlock some of that equity so you find an RRSP investor who is interested in lending you funds as a second mortgage against your property. That person lends you $30,000, bringing your total debt to $160,000 (the original $130,000 plus the new $30,000 second mortgage). A total debt of $160,000 on a property worth $230,000 gives you a loan-to-value ratio of about 70%.

Using an RRSP Mortgage to Refinance

RRSP mortgages can be used not only in new purchases but also when refinancing an existing property to get access to equity. Again your options will depend on the lender, and when you begin the refinance process you would do well to disclose your intentions to use RRSP funds to refinance.

If your lender says that they won't allow it, then that's the way it is. And I'll repeat this again: The critical thing for you as the RRSP investor is to make sure that you know the value of the property and that you don't lend too much against it.

OTHER BIG MISTAKES TO AVOID

Let's review a few more of the landmines. Below are some key mistakes I see people make when they're structuring RRSP mortgages.

Failing the Arm's Length Test

Failing to create a true arm's length situation risks having the CRA come in and declare the transaction illegal. A lot of people get creative when they start thinking about how to use their RRSPs in investing, and they may try to sneak around the arm's length rules. Inadvertently, you could be violating the *Income Tax Act* and setting yourself up for serious fines. A neophyte RRSP investor may initially think, "What if I take $30,000 and I lend it to my friend at 12% interest on his property and he turns around and lends me $30,000 at 12% on my property? That would be perfect because it's almost like we're borrowing our own money."

That's exactly the problem. It's almost like borrowing your own money, and it would not be considered a legitimate transaction by the CRA. The CRA will say that the only reason that you lent to your friend is because your friend lent to you, so the two transactions don't stand on their own individually. Therefore, this wouldn't be considered a proper arm's length transaction. The CRA is going to deem that you took the $30,000 that you lent out of your RRSP the day that you lent it. And you'll be charged interest and penalties, and of course you'll have to pay the tax in the year that you took it out of your RRSP.

If you've gotten away with such a transaction in the past, whereby you've lent money out against somebody's house and they've lent you money as well, just recognize that you're open to a potential issue if you're ever audited. When two people lend back and forth to each other, I call it a bilateral lending agreement, and it's a big red flag for the CRA.

Not every bilateral lending agreement is illegal. Some can and do stand on their own. For example, let's say that I lent you $50,000 at 12% interest today for three years. A year later you lend me back $30,000 at 14% for two years. The CRA may not have a problem with that because it would be hard for it to argue that the two transactions didn't stand on their own. Of course, if you lent the money without me immediately lending the money back to you, that seems like a pretty reasonable transaction a lot more than if we do a mirror loan back and forth with the identical terms, in the same time frame. As with most of the *Income Tax Act*, there is a lot of grey area and room for interpretation, so my suggestion is that you don't try to outsmart the CRA, and ensure that your mortgage transactions don't cause red flags to shoot up in Ottawa.

Using Creative "Borrow Your RRSP Funds" Strategies

If it were allowed, a lot of registered account holders would love to be able to borrow their funds out of their account and utilize that money to buy real estate or perhaps personal assets such as a car or personal recreational property. As a result, a few different creative strategies have been developed that suggest it's possible to get your RRSP or other registered account funds out for your use without having to "deregister" those funds and create tax consequences.

For example, there is a company in Canada that promotes the ability for you to essentially "borrow" your own registered funds and use them for whatever purpose you like. Their approach is to have your registered account purchase bonds in a specific corporation that is an eligible investment for registered accounts under the *Income Tax Act*. Then, that company lends money to a separate company, which lends you back your money. Your registered account is paid a modest interest rate, and you pay a higher interest rate on the money you've borrowed out.

Let's put some numbers to this to illustrate the idea. Assuming you have $50,000 in your registered account, you would "buy" $50,000 of bonds from this company. Your $50,000 would go to them, and in exchange, your account would hold the bonds, worth $50,000. If the bonds paid 5% annually, your account would earn a 5% return on the $50,000.

Once your $50,000 had been received by the corporation that issued the bonds, it would lend that money to another (related) corporation under control of the same organization. That $50,000 would be lent back to you personally at perhaps 9% annual interest. This means that your registered account generates a 5% return, but you personally pay a 9% interest rate on the money. However, you now have the $50,000 in your personal hands, and the concept is that you can use that money for anything you want, since it is not registered money and is no different than any other loan you might arrange.

There is the interest cost of that money, plus fees that the company charges to maintain and manage this structure for you, but for many investors this is appealing because it allows them to access their registered money without triggering tax consequences. At least, that's the sales pitch that is offered.

After speaking to a number of experts regarding this and similar strategies, it's clear that there are mixed opinions and views on this strategy; I remain in the camp of being skeptical about whether this structure is guaranteed to stand up to the scrutiny of the CRA. One of the underlying issues (among many) that concern me is that you're not allowed, under the *Income Tax Act*, to use registered account assets as collateral for loans you arrange. In this scenario, it's pretty clear that the bonds held in your account are being used as collateral for the loan to you personally. This increases the risk that the CRA may say that those bonds are ineligible investments, which would mean in our example that you would be deemed to have withdrawn $50,000 from your registered account, creating a series of tax problems including interest, penalties and withholding issues.

These companies that offer these programs are adamant that they've had the top legal firms in Canada help construct them, including those who advise the CRA themselves, and therefore the structure is safe from the scrutiny of the CRA. I should be clear that I am not aware of anyone being audited and attacked on this structure, and I do not believe that this has become a problem—yet. However, I also believe that the government is constantly looking for ways it can increase its revenues, and taxes are the government's source of revenues. Therefore, the CRA is always looking for creative tax strategies that it feels it can unwind.

The reality is that when I can make double-digit returns in my registered account using strategies such as what I'm teaching you here, I don't think it's worth the risk to get too creative with the CRA as they are eager to step in and unwind the brilliant but questionable strategies you might come up with.

Failing to Get the Advice You Need from an Independent Expert

If you are looking at any kind of strategy that essentially allows you access to your registered account funds (directly or indirectly), I strongly recommend that you get advice from an independent tax expert before making any decisions. Remember from Part I of this book that you always have to be careful of the advice you get, especially when it's coming from someone who profits if you accept his or her advice. Do not take the advice from someone offering this strategy; always get a separate, third-party opinion from someone who has the expertise and knowledge to render a proper opinion to you (and that doesn't have a vested interest in your decision).

Whether it's using a creative lending program or anything else, if you're looking to do something that's a little creative, you absolutely need to talk to a lawyer and possibly a tax attorney who's very familiar with the *Income Tax Act*. Find out what they think and whether or not what you're doing is going to cause problems or be open to attack by the CRA. Creativity is a great thing, but when you're dealing with government rules you know that creativity can sometimes get you in trouble—expensive trouble. Be careful of the bilateral lending agreements, and by the same token, watch out for lending at too low of an interest rate or doing anything that wouldn't seem reasonable to the average person.

Not Getting It All in Writing

Another big mistake or landmine that I see people stepping into is not putting all of the terms of the agreement in writing. I don't care whether you're dealing with a long-time friend or trusted co-worker, get everything in writing and don't rely on handshakes or verbal agreements. Make sure that you put all of the terms, conditions and understandings down on paper and make sure that all such documents are registered properly.

This is why it's critical for you to use a lawyer who understands how mortgages work and, specifically, how they work when using RRSP funds. Not all real estate lawyers understand how to work with RRSP mortgages. Even though your trustee will only send money to a registered lawyer, be sure to pick the right lawyer who has experience dealing with arm's length mortgages using RRSP funds.

Failing the Test of Time

Make sure you allow yourself a lot of time for the mortgage proceeds to be generated through the process. This would be especially true if you're either using RRSP funds to help close on a new purchase or if you're trying to refinance a property with an RRSP mortgage. Obviously if you run into a hiccup and it takes an extra week or two to get the funds dispersed, it may be too late to close on that property. And if you're trying to buy a property and the mortgage money doesn't come in, you're going to be a super motivated borrower from somebody else on a short-term basis. And being a motivated borrower or a motivated lender is never a good place to be.

Being Lazy About Solving Problems

Not acting immediately when a problem develops could spell disaster. When I'm lending money, I'm actively monitoring my account. I'm making sure that I'm seeing the payments on a regular basis and I'm keeping tabs on my trustee's responsibilities. Typically you're warned pretty quickly when a default happens, but I watch investors all the time who don't do anything right away about a default because they're trying to be nice and give the person an opportunity to catch up.

Recently one of my new students was telling me about a deal where he lent some money on a property for a rehab, and it was supposed to be sold in four months. It's been seventeen months and he hasn't received a payment on his mortgage in over a year. The borrower keeps calling him and telling him that he's trying to sell it, meanwhile refusing to rent the house out of fear the property will get trashed by tenants. In this situation, I told my student that he needs to consider that the borrower is stealing money from him. The borrower is choosing not to pay the required payments because he is either too lazy or too ridiculous to get a tenant into that property and do what has to be done.

Most problems that happen involving mortgages stem back to the fact that whoever held the mortgage failed to act quickly when they should have. They just waited and hoped and prayed that the problem would fix itself. When someone gets one, two, three, four months behind on a mortgage, rarely does it ever fix itself—it just gets worse.

Act immediately if a problem develops, and if you're a lender you need to be clear to the borrower that that's the way you're going to play the game. You're not a bank, and you can't afford to go month after month after month with no payments. If a default occurs, you're going to be acting very quickly.

• • •

In this chapter, we focused on the various elements that go into constructing a win-win arrangement between a lender and borrower. As you've seen, your deals can be created to benefit everyone involved, and there is definitely no need to take a "one-size-fits-all" approach when creating mortgage investments.

The burning question that you have now might be: "what if things go wrong?" So let's move on and tackle that subject, because it's very important for you to understand how to manage your risks, and deal with a problem if it develops.

10

Managing Risk and Dealing with Defaults

Rule No. 1: Never lose money.
Rule No. 2: Never forget rule No. 1.
—Warren Buffett

At this point, you're probably wondering, "What are the risks and the downsides of investing in mortgages? What are the biggest risks to watch out for, and how can I avoid them? What happens if someone doesn't pay? How does the default process work? How can I lose my money in this strategy?"

Like anything else, when it comes to investing, nothing is truly risk free. The key isn't to try and figure out how never to take any risk, as there is risk in everything you do in life. The perspective you should take is this: how do I *reduce* and *manage* the risk, and set myself up to ensure that I don't lose money in this investment strategy?

A FEW DEFINITIONS

When a borrower fails to follow the terms and conditions that are included in the mortgage they sign, such as by being delinquent on any payments or by violating any of the clauses in the mortgage, they are considered to be in **default**. This is important to understand, because a default generally gives the lender the right to call the loan due, or "accelerate" the mortgage.

An **acceleration clause** is a provision in a contract or a promissory note that allows the lender to demand immediately the entire amount owing, as opposed to waiting for the payments and eventual payback at the end of the term. In other words, rather than waiting the three, five, ten or twenty-five years for the funds loaned, the lender has the right to accelerate the loan and demand that it all be paid off now.

A **due-on-sale clause** is something you'll find in almost every mortgage in Canada. It states that if you transfer, assign or otherwise dispose of that property, and you do not have the lender's permission to do so, they have the right to call the loan due immediately (i.e., the loan is "due" upon a "sale" occurring). As an example of that, if you own a property and cannot make the payments, one option you might think about taking is to sell the property to someone else and let them take over the payments. However, if your mortgage has a due-on-sale clause (which again, virtually all mortgages do), when the lender discovers you've transferred the property with the mortgage still attached—and you didn't get their permission—they're going to call that loan due immediately.

The word **"foreclosure"** is obviously an important one in real estate and it has a lot of interesting connotations to it. In simple terms, a foreclosure is the legal process that is undertaken when someone who has borrowed money and registered a mortgage or lien against the property defaults. Ultimately, the lender or mortgage holder goes after the property as security for their loan, and the borrower's interest in the property is extinguished by the court or by a legal process. The term can mean slightly different things depending on which province you're in, but for the purposes of this book I'm using the term foreclosure generally to refer to the process of taking ownership and/or possession of a property away from the borrower, when they fail to meet the terms of the mortgage or loan. Upon obtaining ownership of the property, the lender would seek to sell the property to recover the money owing to them.

The term **"lis pendens"** is Latin and refers to a specific type of notice that's registered on a property title when there is a legal process affecting that property. In other words, it's like a red flag to anybody who looks at the title of the property to let them know that there's a legal proceeding underway with that property, and to move ahead with caution.

Another term you'll hear in relation to foreclosures is **"redemption period."** During the foreclosure process, usually the borrower is provided some period of time to pay off the debt before their property is taken away. This period of time is normally called the redemption period because the borrower can "redeem" the property—pay what's owed (which may include the loan amount itself, the interest owing and any of the legal costs) and get the mortgage back into good standing.

THE TWO BIGGEST RISKS IN MORTGAGE INVESTING

Every type of investment strategy has a certain degree of risk to it, some higher than others, and most types of strategies have several different types of risks. When we talk about investing in mortgages, there are two primary risks.

> **Risk #1: The underlying value of the property that you've lent money against declines below the amount of the mortgage.**
>
> This scenario would leave you, as the lender, holding security on a property that wouldn't cover the loan you're owed if the property were taken back and sold. For example, if you hold a $200,000 mortgage on a property that can only be sold for $180,000, you're going to take some kind of loss on that investment, because when you sell you'll be unable to get back the entire $200,000 that you loaned against the property. Don't forget also that you'll have legal expenses and other costs that will cause your loss to be even greater.

> **Risk #2: The borrower stops making their payments to you.**
>
> This is always a risk when you are lending money on mortgages; however, as long as you've done your due diligence and the underlying property has solid security, then this risk is more an inconvenience than it is a risk of loss. Ultimately, as long as there's equity remaining in the property, eventually you should be able to recover all of your initial funds, plus expenses, fees and lost interest; that is, assuming there's sufficient proceeds from the sale of the property after you've foreclosed and taken it back.

Now that you're aware of what these two primary risks are, let me go into a little more detail so you can understand how to manage this risk. I'll then discuss the process of going through a foreclosure and of being a mortgage holder who's not getting paid.

Risk #1: When a Property Loses Value

What causes a property to go down in value? There are two primary reasons this occurs: either (1) the real estate market declines, or (2) the owner allows or even causes something to occur to the property to reduce its value. For example, the owner may not keep up the maintenance, thereby allowing the property to deteriorate, or a house is destroyed by fire and the owner didn't have insurance in place. Vandalism is another possibility. If the owner doesn't pay attention to the entire property, or if the property is vacant and vulnerable to vandalism, significant damage can take place and hurt the value of the property.

Ultimately, if the value of the property declines, that's a problem for you as a lender. The property value is the primary protection you have as security for your loan.

Market Value

It's so critical for you to understand how to evaluate a real estate market, because you need to understand what the value of that property is, given that particular real estate market. Again, the best way to do that is to get a professional appraisal done.

As we discussed in the due diligence section, I strongly believe that it's a good idea to physically investigate the property. You should go to the property yourself, or at least have somebody that you trust to do it on your behalf. One of the biggest disconnects that many investors have is they really don't know how to investigate a real estate market. All they do is look at the local real estate board's information and try to gauge whether it's a good or bad market.

In order to help students and investors understand the factors that affect real estate markets and property values, I created a tool I call the "Property Market Matrix," which is a set of fifteen key indicators that help you understand what's going on in a specific real estate market. How healthy or how sick is that particular real estate market? By using these fifteen indicators, you can establish the health of a particular market and start tracking trends. You can access this tool at www.rrspSecret.com under "Resources."

Value Decline Caused by the Owner

How could a seller allow or cause the destruction of property value in some way? Let me give you a few examples. Let's say a seller doesn't replace a roof that desperately needs replacing, perhaps either because he can't afford it or just doesn't care to do so. It might be a property he rents and he's never around to manage it. If that owner is not living in the house and does not know first-hand the effects of the rain on the worn roof, the property can deteriorate rapidly from water damage. Water leaks can quickly create serious damage, even causing structural issues in the property. Every time something like this happens to that property, its value decreases, as does your security.

Let's look at another example. What if a buyer uses a piece of property for illegal or negative uses that cause safety or health problems? A great example of this is what we see quite frequently—especially in British Columbia and Alberta—grow-ops. This is where someone buys or rents a property and then uses the property to grow or manufacture marijuana, crystal meth or other drugs or hazardous materials.

Several years ago, a friend of mine bought a property and rented it out. About six months after buying it, he discovered that the renters had converted it to a grow-op and were stealing electricity from the city. Fortunately for him, he happened to catch it relatively soon into the process, so his property did not incur significant or structural damage. But this risk exists, and is something that you need to think about because again, this type of property abuse will hurt the resale value if you were to take the property back as security.

If you're lending money on a property, you always have to think about what the owner could do to damage the value of the property. Grow-ops aren't a major concern, perhaps happening in one in twenty thousand houses, but you really need to be aware of what can happen.

Another example might be where you lend money on a property that was once zoned to store environmentally dangerous chemicals. Or perhaps the owners were operating a garage and dumping oil on the property rather than properly disposing of it. Or perhaps a gas storage tank is on the property and there's the potential of a leak. Either way, contamination is a risk.

To you as a lender, if an environmental problem develops on the land, the owners are responsible, but they can cause such a problem that the cost of fixing it far outstretches the value of the property. The owners may just throw up their hands, say, "I'm not fixing this," and walk away. You would have to step in, foreclose on the property to try and protect your interest, and take over an environmentally contaminated property. Unfortunately, the law says that you would be responsible for the clean-up costs. In this situation you really can't win, because the alternative is you don't foreclose—you don't enforce your right to take back the property—and you lose all of your money that you lent on the mortgage.

I've heard of legal cases where a court forced a lender to take over the property and then made it responsible for the environmental contamination. Again, I'm not saying these are common happenings and I don't want you to be overly worried about them. I'm simply trying to give you as many examples as I can for your information and awareness.

Let's focus on the important question: how do you protect against this kind of problem?

The reality is, most standard mortgages provide some protection for many of these situations because as you can imagine, lenders have dealt with them in the past. Over the years, the banks and lenders have added language to mortgages that protect against several of these kinds of occurrences. There are a number of clauses that can (and should) be included in a mortgage that will protect you as the lender.

"Act of Waste" Clause

Your mortgage should include a clause that ensures that the borrower cannot do anything that will cause the property to fall into disrepair or do irreparable damage (what's legally referred to as "an act of waste"). If you go to my website at www.rrspSecret.com, you'll find sample mortgages that contain this "Act of Waste" clause, with the following language:

> The mortgagor (borrower) will not commit any act of waste thereon. The mortgagor will at all times during the continuance of this security sustain, repair, maintain, restore, finish, add to and put in order and in the event of any loss or damage thereto or destruction thereof, the mortgagee (lender) may give notice to the mortgagor to repair, rebuild or reinstate the same within a time to be determined by the mortgagee. **The mortgagor failing to do so shall constitute a breach of covenant hereunder.**

What this really says is that the borrower is agreeing to keep up the property, secure it, fix it up and ensure that it remains in a reasonable condition. If there is any kind of damage or loss or any destruction that causes the property value to decline, the lender has the right to give notice to the borrower to say, "I want this fixed, and I require it to be fixed immediately." By doing this, the lender is protecting the value of the property and his interest in it. If the borrower refuses to do the repairs, the lender can call the loan due. If your borrower does anything to create a risk such as an environmental contamination, this clause would enable you to act quickly about it.

In case you're now shivering, afraid that you're going to have to write up legal language like the clause I just gave you, relax—these are boilerplate clauses in most standard mortgages, and your lawyer will be taking care of these details. It's just important that you understand what this language actually means.

Insurance Clause

Another critical clause that you see in most mortgages ensures that the property on which you hold a mortgage has insurance at all times. If you've ever bought a house, you know that before the mortgage company will allow the money to be released, you have to prove that you have a current insurance policy on that property, and once the property is mortgaged, you are required to maintain insurance on it. This is why the ~~insurance~~ mortgage company requires that you add it as an "additional insured" to your home insurance policy. By doing this, it receives all notices about your insurance, including if you cancel the policy or it gets cancelled because of non-payment.

This is a huge thing for those of us looking to lend money as investors, because the only protection that you have if a fire or other major catastrophe occurs is a comprehensive and current insurance policy that covers such a loss. If a fire were to destroy that property, and it turns out that the homeowner doesn't have any insurance on the property, then there's no one for you to go after in order to recover your money. You can sue the owner, but if that person doesn't have any personal assets to repay you, chances are you're not going to get your money back.

Insurance is a critical component. You should insist that you are to be named on the insurance policy as an "additional insured," as I explained above. This essentially flags the insurance company that you have an interest in that property and, if an insurance claim is paid out, that they're going to pay the bank, and then you as the secondary mortgage holder, before they give the money to the owner. They also are required to send you any notices related to the policy, such as cancellation. That's why if you've registered your mortgage and the insurance is about to lapse on the property, the insurance company will send you a notice acknowledging and notifying you that action must be taken. As a lender, you immediately can step in and make sure that the insurance doesn't lapse.

Improvements Become Part of the Mortgaged Property

Another clause that you should include is to clearly state that any improvements on the property become part of the land and the security, because doing this can potentially increase the value of your underlying security as the lender. As an example, assume that you provide a mortgage to somebody and they later add a triple garage to the property. Do you think that the new garage increases the value and security in the property? Of course it does, and you want to ensure that your mortgage covers any of these types of improvements or additions.

Here's an example of language from a mortgage that speaks to this particular issue:

> All erections, buildings, fences and improvements, fixed or otherwise, now on or hereafter put on the said land are and shall in addition to other fixtures thereon be and become fixtures and form part of the realty and of the security and are included in the expression of the said land.

Again, most mortgages already include these fairly standard clauses, but I believe it's important for you to understand the logic of including them and the reasons behind them.

Risk #2: When a Borrower Stops Making Payments

What happens if the borrower stops paying altogether, or only pays a portion of what is due under the mortgage? The foreclosure process can begin after a single missed payment, but it doesn't often happen that way. Most banks and lenders have a grace period for late payments and usually it comes with a fee attached to it, and it typically takes a few months before the lender starts down the foreclosure path.

That's for the big banks, but for you, I would recommend that you take action immediately once you're aware there is a problem looming.

As a lender, it's critical that you act immediately when you find out that you're not getting paid as agreed. If you've lent this money from an RRSP account, one of the things that your trustee will do for you is alert you when a scheduled payment is not received. Then it's up to you to act immediately. To be clear, the trustee's job is not to start a foreclosure or to represent you in the process; the trustee's job is only to administer and manage the payments, and to advise that you have a problem with payments if one develops.

What that means is that if your borrower doesn't make the payments according to the mortgage, you'll get the notice or a phone call from your trustee, and you either have to contact the borrower to try and resolve the problem, or you can call your lawyer to consider the best step to take.

Generally speaking, the best first step to take is to contact the borrower directly and try to find out whether there is a problem or not. You may find that it was a simple oversight on his or her part. Perhaps the borrower changed banks and forgot to update pre-authorized withdrawal information with your trustee. Or the borrower may have been out of town and forgot to deposit the funds to his or her account. Whatever the case may be, you should immediately get in touch with the borrower to ascertain the reason for the missed payment. You'll typically resolve 80% of the problems simply by taking this step, and will let the borrower know that you're taking quick action and paying a lot of attention to the mortgage.

If you are unable to contact the borrower, or the borrower is not responding to you and it appears he or she does not intend to make their payments, you need to start the legal process as quickly as possible. Every day you delay is another day it will take for you to resolve the problem, and more time rarely fixes this kind of a problem.

IF THINGS GO WRONG

While we all hope that dealing with a default is something we never have to do, the reality is that you need to be prepared should this happen with a mortgage that you lend.

For most mortgage actions, the borrower is going to be responsible for any costs, fees and expenses that are incurred in enforcing the mortgage. In other words, if you borrow money from someone and they have a mortgage on your property, and you don't pay them, you're going to end up paying any of the costs that the lender incurs to protect their money and go after you. You as the borrower will not only have to pay your own legal fees defending the process, but you'll also have to pay any legal fees and expenses to the other party, the lender. Clearly, it can be an expensive process if a foreclosure starts against you.

As the lender, this process is to your advantage, because it means that if you're successful in the foreclosure, your legal fees and expenses are going to be included in the claim that you're able to recover. This is why I don't think it makes sense to wait very long before getting a lawyer involved in the process, if you're not getting paid as agreed.

BEING NOTIFIED OF AN ACTION

Once you are registered on title as a lender, any time a legal process starts against that property—in particular a foreclosure—you will be given proper legal notice of the foreclosure claim or lawsuit. The intent of this is to make sure all registered parties are notified of legal action that may be occurring, so that they can respond and protect their interests.

This is particularly important when you are investing in second mortgages, because you need to be aware of any problems that the first mortgage holder may have with the borrower.

As an example, let's assume that you've lent money to an investor that owns a property with a CIBC first mortgage, so you hold the second mortgage on the property behind CIBC. The borrower stops making their payments on the CIBC loan, and CIBC begins a foreclosure action against the borrower.

By law, CIBC must notify you that it is commencing foreclosure actions against the borrower, because that's going to have an impact on your interest in the property. Once you receive notice of the claim by CIBC, you'll be able to respond to the situation and step in to protect your interest.

In the case that the first mortgage is being paid but the second mortgage is not, then you won't receive a notice—but you'll know that your borrower is defaulting, because you'll be notified by your trustee. In this case, you have the right to begin a foreclosure immediately, since your mortgage is in default. The first mortgage holder will require their loan to be kept current, either by the borrower or, if they stop paying the first mortgage as well, you have the right to keep it current so that you can pursue your foreclosure or power of sale.

The Foreclosure Process

The Canadian foreclosure process itself varies from province to province, so I'll give you an overview of the general process and then outline how each province approaches it. There are really two main ways that a lender can try to recover a mortgage debt in Canada when a borrower defaults. One way this can happen is called a "**judicial sale**" and the other is called a "**power of sale.**"

A Judicial Sale

If you're lending money in British Columbia, Alberta, Manitoba, Saskatchewan or Quebec, you're going to be following the process of a judicial sale. In those provinces, the provincial court system generally forces the sale of the property, supervising the proceedings. A lender must apply to the court for the court's permission to go after the property, foreclose the borrower's rights, and sell the property to recover its debt.

A Power of Sale

The second type of process, a power of sale, essentially allows a lender to sell a property without the direct involvement of the courts. The lender has the right to sell the property based on the terms that are set out in the mortgage document that the parties sign when the mortgage is established, or according to the provincial legislation that covers power of sale. In other words, the lender has the right to sell the property from the mortgage document itself and possibly the legislation, and the process is not supervised by the court system as it is in judicial sale provinces.

Power of sale typically is used in the following provinces: Ontario, New Brunswick, Newfoundland and Prince Edward Island. Nova Scotia is unique, in that the process is similar to a judicial sale, because it does involve the court system, but the term used is "mortgage foreclosure."

The Difference Between the Two

There are three main things that distinguish between a power of sale and judicial sale.

The first difference is that a judicial sale requires the involvement of the courts, whereas a power of sale doesn't. In a judicial sale process, the court is extensively involved, and that's going to include things like ordering that the property be sold in the marketplace, overseeing the price that is set for the property sale, reviewing all offers received on the property, confirming the sales procedure and hearing any applications with respect to the foreclosure.

In a power of sale, there is virtually no court participation or involvement in the process at all. What this really means is that generally, the power of sale process is faster than the foreclosure process, so if you live in or invest in a province where the power of sale process is utilized, this may be an advantage because the process often is completed faster.

The second difference is in how the actual process is started in each case. In provinces where the power of sale process is used, the foreclosure process is started when the lender sends a notice to the borrower and the current owner of the property. In contrast, if you're looking at a judicial sale, the process formally starts when the lender files a lawsuit against the borrower (and anybody else who may be liable). As you might expect, it's generally more expensive to do a foreclosure in a judicial sale, because you have to involve lawyers throughout the process. However, keep in mind that legal fees are the responsibility of the borrower, so while you may be out of pocket during the process for legal fees, you should generally be able to recover your costs from the property when the foreclosure is complete—assuming there is sufficient equity to recover the funds.

The third difference between judicial sale and power of sale is how a deficiency judgment is achieved. A deficiency judgment basically means that if you as the lender take back and sell the property, and you can't recover all of the money that you lent the borrower, you have the added right of suing the borrower personally for the deficiency. In other words, you can try to recover your money from the borrower personally, beyond the value of the property.

In a power of sale, the lender that's seeking a deficiency judgment has to start an action against the borrower after the property's been sold, because that's when you find out whether you're going to recover the money. Even if you were successful getting a property back, if there wasn't enough equity to recover all of your funds and expenses, you're allowed to sue the owner for whatever deficiency you incurred.

In a judicial process, the deficiency judgment is part of the main action (lawsuit); there isn't a separate action to go after the deficiency. Again, each province is different. For example, in Alberta if you're lending money to someone on a primary residence, you cannot go after the borrower beyond the property. In other words, in a lot of cases you cannot sue them personally for a deficiency judgment. This is why I can't emphasize enough that you must get good legal advice and understand the process where you are!

How Long Does It Take?

To complete a foreclosure process, the judicial sale process normally takes longer because the court is involved. You're waiting for lawyers to schedule actions, do follow-up documentation, plead the case and wait for the court's decisions and orders. A typical foreclosure in a judicial sale can take anywhere from as little as three to four months, up to as much as twelve to eighteen months, depending on the complexity and the details of the case; overall, the average is in the range of about eight to ten months from start to finish.

Judicial sale foreclosure length depends on the province itself and if you're able to sell the property right away. If it's a court-ordered process and there are no buyers, then it may take longer for that property to be sold.

On the other hand, in a power of sale foreclosure, especially in Ontario (because it's known as being the most efficient jurisdiction to get a foreclosure done), it can happen in as little as forty-five days from the time the notice is first given to the borrower. Again, the timelines can vary dramatically depending on which province you're in.

In some provinces, such as Ontario, you can choose between power of sale or judicial sale foreclosure, but almost invariably, power of sale generally is preferred because it's less expensive compared to a judicial sale foreclosure, and much faster. Also, the redemption period is typically fixed and doesn't have a provision for an extension by the borrower. It follows logically that lenders are going to choose the option that's more often faster and less expensive. Additionally, in the event of a deficiency in the power of sale the lender can pursue the personal covenant for the shortfall. This means that the lender may sue the borrower personally.

As long as you've got equity and you haven't made a major mistake in your due diligence process, you should be able to rely on the process in your province, whether it's power of sale or judicial sale, to get your money back and protect your interests. If there's sufficient equity in the property, you are very well protected by the law, regardless of what type of process your specific province utilizes.

Here are some comments on the various processes across the country:

- Nova Scotia has a unique mix of the two processes.

- Alberta and Manitoba are similar in that in these provinces, the foreclosure order can only come from the court after the mortgaged property has been offered for sale—and appropriate notice must be given.

- British Columbia typically is considered the most protective province for the homeowner or the borrower. That's because the court has to approve everything about the process, including the purchase price and any terms that might be involved in a sale, and they even get to oversee the commission that's paid to a real estate agent.

- In Ontario, as I said before, the lender can choose which process to take, either judicial sale or power of sale. Of course, almost all lenders choose power of sale, because it moves a lot faster.

- New Brunswick used to have both judicial sale and power of sale. But in 1982, the province moved to power of sale, because it's allowed by legislation and tends to be a faster, easier way to get the process done.

As a case study, I want to look at one of the provinces that uses judicial sale (Alberta) and then at another that uses power of sale (Ontario).

Keep in mind that this is just an overview of the process, and it's going to be different in every province. These cases are general in nature and are used to familiarize you with the process. Therefore, it's important, even if you're in Alberta or Ontario and these cases seem to make everything clear to you, that you retain a good real estate lawyer to ensure you've got professional advice in any legal matter related to real estate.

Case in Point: The Process in Alberta

In Alberta, the process is usually started by the lender sending a demand notice to the borrower, demanding that the total amount be paid within ten to fifteen days. This letter often is triggered by a default, and is sent because the borrower has missed one or more payments. If you're holding a mortgage on a property in Alberta and you don't get paid, your first step is to send out a letter that demands the amount that wasn't paid and suggests that if the arrears are not immediately caught up by a specific date then legal proceedings are going to be taken to recover the money owing.

Typically, the big banks will send a couple of "reminder" notices to a borrower who has failed to make their payments, usually over the course of a few months. However, when you're lending money in any capacity (including mortgages), my advice to you is not to wait like the banks do. Instead, take immediate action. Send the initial letter as soon as you find out that payments are not being made as agreed, and be prepared to take action quickly.

If a demand letter is issued and no arrangements are made between the borrower and the lender, and presumably the borrower hasn't contacted the lender to try and work out a resolution, the next step in the foreclosure process is for the lender to file a statement of claim (a lawsuit) with the Court of Queen's Bench, and have that claim served on the borrower. In the statement of claim, the lender will provide an overview of what was originally agreed, what has occurred in order to give rise to the claim and what they are asking of the court. The statement of claim is written by the lender's lawyer. This isn't something that as a lender you would ever want to attempt on your own. Again, remember that your legal fees are covered by the borrower, so it's important to follow this process correctly.

In the statement of claim, the lender will ask for a number of things to be granted by the court, including

- a claim of sale of the property to the lender
- the actual foreclosure order
- an order of possession (which gives the lender legal possession of the property)
- a specific length of redemption period
- payment to the lender for all expenses and fees incurred

There also may be additional requests made of the court, depending on the circumstances.

The statement of claim is served by registered mail or in person to the borrower, who has three different options he or she may pursue.

Option 1: He or she can choose to do nothing at all (i.e., offer no response to the service and choose not to file any kind of defence).

Option 2: He or she can choose to file and serve a statement of defence, which means he or she is attempting to defend the claim and raise defences as to why they are in default. (In most cases there's not a lot of information contained in the statement of defence. Most of the information is left to be argued in the court proceedings.)

Option 3: He or she can choose to file and serve a demand of notice.

Once a borrower is served a statement of claim, he or she typically has fifteen days from the time the statement of claim was received in order to file a statement of defence or a statement of notice.

Assuming the borrower does file and doesn't ignore the statement of claim (i.e., option 2 or 3), the next step is for the lender to apply to the court for what's called an *"order nisi."* This is simply a legal term meaning "order of sale." Effectively this is a judgment from the court that the land be offered for sale if the amount owing is not paid within the period allowed for redemption. An *order nisi* is essentially the court agreeing that it is going to allow a foreclosure to proceed.

After granting the *order nisi*, the judge or the court sets the redemption period. The borrower has the right to redeem the mortgage during that time. If the borrower pays off the arrears owing under the debt of the mortgage within the redemption period, the foreclosure process is stopped and the borrower keeps both the title of the property and possession.

In many cases, the borrower spends the redemption period seeking some kind of refinancing if it's available or trying to sell the property—since they still own the property and can do whatever they want with it. If the property can be sold in time to pay off the loan, that will stop the foreclosure and terminate the need for legal action.

The redemption period is usually anywhere from six months to one year from the date the *order nisi* is granted. The length of the redemption period is going to depend on the court, which has the right to either decrease or extend that period of redemption based on the circumstances. A key element that affects the redemption period provided is the equity in the property. If you have a property and you can prove that you have a great deal of equity in it, a judge probably is going to give you more time, whereas if you've lent money on a property that now is under water and you can prove that there's no equity in the property, you can request a redemption period as short as one day.

After the redemption period expires, if the mortgage still hasn't been redeemed, the court can offer the land for sale however it wants, at any price the court considers reasonable. Typically, the price is going to be driven by the information that's brought to the court by the borrower and the lender, each party arguing for their own benefit. Obviously, the borrower is going to argue that there's a lot more value and equity in the property, whereas the lender, hoping to sell it quickly, is going to argue that there's no equity (which would mean a shorter redemption period).

The court then decides how the land will be sold. Usually the sale must be advertised or a tender must be given to the public, and there are rules about how the advertising has to be executed, such as the length of time the ad must run, what publications it can be placed within, and what language must appear in the ad. The ads are placed to notify the public that there's a judicial sale happening, and bids are invited on the property. There are some situations where advertising isn't required, but again, these are specific to the circumstances.

Another common way to sell a property in Alberta is for the court to grant the listing to a real estate agent, if the court believes that involving a real estate agent will help get the property sold faster and for a higher price.

If the public tender process is acceptable, and someone steps up and is willing to pay what the court believes the property is worth, the lender can apply for an order confirming the sale and transferring title within twenty-five days after the date that the tenders close.

The court can reject applications if tenders are a lot lower than the appraised value. The important point here is that the court is going to try and protect the homeowner's or landowner's interest and make sure that a lot of equity isn't taken away. If the court believes it's not getting offers that reflect the fair value of the property, it can order that the land be re-advertised or that it be sold by some other means. If a real estate agent was involved and didn't manage to bring solid offers, the court can appoint another real estate agent.

It's possible in some cases for the actual lender to bid on the land and have that purchase approved by the court, and that's usually done when the lender wants to avoid obtaining the final order for foreclosure. Most lenders do not want to own the property on which they provide mortgages, because they're in the lending business—not the real estate business.

The final result of a successful foreclosure or the sale, which is really the goal for the lender, is that the title and the possession of the land are granted to the new purchaser. The money received for the purchase goes to the court, and then is sent to the lenders that have claim against the land and the property. The funds will be distributed based on the order of priority that lenders may have, based on loss. What that really means is if there are multiple mortgages on the property, whoever holds the mortgage in the first position is going to be paid first. Any money left over will go to the second mortgage holder until that mortgage is satisfied (or until all the funds are distributed). If there are sufficient funds to satisfy the second mortgage holder, any additional funds go to the third mortgage, if there is one, and so on. And finally, if there is any money remaining once all the lenders are paid, it goes to the borrower, who was foreclosed out of property ownership.

Again, I want to caution you that this is a very general view of the foreclosure process in Alberta, and there are a number of variables that can affect the process and timelines.

I believe the judicial sale generally favours the homeowner or the landowner when you're being foreclosed on, because the court's role is to try to ensure that the property owner is not unduly disadvantaged by the process. It wants to make sure that the borrower gets every opportunity to keep the equity they have in the property, and avoid having the property sold at a firesale price.

Normally, in Alberta, the order for foreclosure also satisfies the debt according to the foreclosing lender. So if a lender obtains an order for foreclosure on a piece of land that it has a mortgage on, the debt is generally extinguished, and the lender is not going to be able to pursue the borrower for amounts still owing if that land doesn't fully satisfy the debt. In this way, Alberta is different than many of the other provinces.

Case in Point: The Process in Ontario

I'd like to review how the power of sale process works using Ontario as an example. As I mentioned previously, the power of sale process is generally quicker than a judicial sale. This is because the proceedings are set out in the actual mortgage documents. Because these proceedings are enforceable in the case of a default, there's no need to go to the courts to have any of the orders granted or decisions made.

> The power of sale was initially developed in Ontario, and it was set up by lenders who wanted a faster way to repossess property and recover debt. They started including the power of sale provisions in mortgages to enable them to go after the property and dispose of it without having to resort to the courts. Over time, this has become the standard, and now the power of sale is part of the *Ontario Mortgages Act*.

There are two types of powers of sale mentioned in the *Ontario Mortgages Act*: contractual and statutory. A contractual power of sale is simply when the mortgage has power of sale provisions in it, so it speaks directly to the power of sale. This makes it evident what the agreed-upon process will be, and therefore can be enacted immediately by the lender in a case of default.

If the mortgage documents don't include information or direction about the power of sale provision, then a lender would enact a statutory power of sale. A statutory power of sale is generally a rare situation, since most mortgages do contain the provisions of the power of sale. Whether the provisions are outlined or not, a lender still can exercise power of sale as long as the borrower has defaulted for more than three months—and again, this is specific to Ontario.

Both types of power of sale in Ontario are started by a notice being given to the borrower fifteen days after default. The notice has to be given to everyone who has an interest in the property, similar to a judicial sale. They're all considered to have an interest in the property, and therefore they have to be notified that they have the opportunity to protect that interest. The notice, called a "notice of sale," is attached to the *Ontario Mortgages Act*. The notice advises that a lender is intending to exercise its power of sale, and includes the details of the mortgage that was entered into, such as the date the mortgage was made, the parties involved, how much is owing, and a warning that the lender is going to repossess and sell the property if the amounts aren't paid by a certain date.

If the power of sale is a contractual one, i.e., the provisions are specified in the mortgage documents, then the borrower will be given thirty-five days to pay. This may vary if something different is outlined in the mortgage agreement. If the power of sale is statutory, i.e., it doesn't state in the mortgage that it's a power of sale, the borrower is going to be given ten extra days for a total of forty-five days. The lender can't take action until this redemption period plays itself out, but similar to the judicial sale, the borrower has the right during that period to redeem the mortgage.

Once the redemption period expires and the borrower fails to pay or cure the default, the lender can legally sell the property. In most provinces, the power of sale allows the lender to sell the property by auction, by private sale or by public tender and quite often the property is listed with a real estate agent and placed on the market. The goal is to liquidate the property, sell it and recover their funds. This process is not managed by the courts, such as it would be in a judicial sale jurisdiction.

When the property is sold, if there's any surplus (i.e., if there are funds left over after the debt and penalties are satisfied), the lender must provide an account to the borrower and to the other parties registered on title, including any other registered lien holders or junior mortgage holders. The *Ontario Mortgage Act* requires that the proceeds go first to the cost of conducting the sale, then to the interest and the cost owing on the mortgage, then to the principal owing on the mortgage itself, and then to any payments due to the encumbrances on the property. At the end of the list are the tenants' security deposits, if there are tenants.

I want to emphasize that I'm providing you general overviews of the processes, and this isn't intended to be a thorough explanation of the foreclosure process. I highly encourage you to seek out a real estate lawyer that's familiar with the foreclosure process in your province, because there are always twists and turns that a good lawyer is going to be able to help you with. Regardless of where you live or invest, there are distinctions and unique circumstances that require the advice of an experienced lawyer to ensure you are making the right decisions and taking the right actions. Remember, if you ever need to act on a default, you are not going to be doing the foreclosure process yourself; you will always be relying on a professional. And, usually, the fees and costs associated with the legal action ultimately will be paid by the borrower. As long as you properly set up your deal from the beginning and do your due diligence, the likelihood of facing a foreclosure on a loan you've provided is low—the foreclosure process really should be just a minor inconvenience and not a major setback.

RRSPS AND FORECLOSURE

Up until now, everything that I've described related to foreclosure has had nothing specific to do with RRSP mortgages; in other words, this is how virtually all foreclosures and powers of sale occur. For RRSP mortgages, it's really not that different. The only difference when your RRSP is involved is that it isn't *you* who is legally enacting the foreclosure. It's actually your RRSP account that is doing the foreclosure, and you're only acting on behalf of your account to do the work.

Remember that a registered account is considered a separate legal entity from you personally. The law sees you and your registered account as two separate entities. Therefore, if you have a mortgage that requires legal action and it's inside your registered account, it's the registered account itself that will be listed as the plaintiff in the action.

This means that when you hire a lawyer to start the legal process, you're doing it as an agent of your registered account. Eventually when the foreclosure is successful, your RRSP account will pay the legal fees. Or, alternatively, if you do not have the funds inside your registered account to pay the legal fees, you would be able to personally "loan" the money to your registered account for the legal costs. When the foreclosure was completed and the property was sold, you would recover the legal fees from the proceeds of the sale.

If you're successful in the foreclosure and you get the property back, remember it's your RRSP that's foreclosing on the property—not you personally. So if your RRSP forecloses and you're successful, the property goes back into your RRSP—you don't get it personally. An interesting component of the *Income Tax Act* is that your RRSP is not allowed to own real estate, with one general exception: your RRSP account temporarily can own real estate, if it's taken back as the result of a foreclosure. In that case, your RRSP is allowed to own that piece of real estate, but it's only allowed to own it until a year after the foreclosure.

Depending on the circumstances, foreclosure might turn out to be an advantage to you. If this were to happen, and you took back a property into your RRSP, you have one year to sell it. It's possible that between the time you take the property back and when you sell it within the year, it increases in value and results in an increase in your overall investment return. Remember that all of the proceeds from your investment, which would include the sale of the property in this case, would flow back into your RRSP as a return and not a contribution. It's possible that you could generate a profit or a positive return in your RRSP through the foreclosure and it would be tax deferred.

That's not to say I would encourage you to lend money on properties that are going to default so that you can take properties back into your RRSP; rather this simply reinforces my point that as long as you correctly set yourself up to begin with, investment in mortgages with registered accounts is a very powerful strategy to employ.

If You Hold a Second Mortgage

If you've lent your registered funds on a first mortgage, then the process is relatively easy to understand. You would enact the foreclosure on the property, get the property back and sell the property to recover your money. However, RRSP mortgages commonly are used to find second mortgages, which means there is a first mortgage in front of the second mortgage. It's important to know what your rights are as a mortgage holder when you are not in first mortgage position.

At this point, it's worth recalling the discussion about how mortgages work and the subject of "seniority" (which refers to which loan or mortgage on a property is more "senior" than the others that exist). Let me provide you another example to further illustrate this important concept, as this affects the rights you have as a mortgage holder.

Let's say that we've got a house that's worth $200,000. The owner has a mortgage from the bank for $150,000, and that mortgage is registered in first position. Based on these numbers, there is $50,000 of equity in the property, because that's what would be left over if they sold the property and paid off the existing first mortgage.

Assume that this is a real estate investor, and he or she wants to access some of that $50,000 equity, but doesn't want to sell the property. You've got some money in your RRSP and you're looking to lend out on mortgages, and you connect with this investor. You're willing to lend them another $30,000 as a second mortgage. This would mean that the total debt on the property is $180,000 because they've got the first mortgage of $150,000, and you're going to lend another $30,000, which is a total of $180,000 in debt. Since the property is worth $200,000, it has $20,000 equity in it, and that means that the loan-to-value ratio is 90% ($180,000 of debt divided by the $200,000 value). In other words, 90% of the property value is financed, leaving 10% equity.

Because your loan was registered after they already had a first mortgage in place, by definition that means that your mortgage is in second position. This means that we would refer to your loan as "junior" to the bank's mortgage, and the bank's mortgage would be considered "senior" to your mortgage, because it was registered earlier than yours.

Now let's go into the future. Everything's fine for a year, but over that year, the housing prices start to decline, and the property you've lent on goes from $200,000 in value to only $175,000 a year later.

Let's also assume that we just found out that your borrower has decided that they're not going to make any further mortgage payments, so they've stopped paying both on the first mortgage with the bank, as well as on your second mortgage. If you're the mortgage lender in second position, how does this affect you?

In the foreclosure process, the senior mortgage (which was the one that was registered earliest) takes precedence over any other mortgages that might have been registered later. In our example, the borrower stopped making payments to both the bank and to you, so who has the right to foreclose and go after the property? You're obviously going to be aware that the borrower is not paying you. In addition, because you are registered on title, you're considered to have an interest in the property so you're going to get notice that the first mortgage is not being paid either.

Because the bank mortgage is senior to your loan, the risk to you is that if the bank starts the foreclosure process and is successful, all of the registrations that occurred after their mortgage would be wiped off. And, since your loan is junior to the bank's, that means your loan would be extinguished and you'd have no further claim on that property, which means you would lose your money. Let me repeat that. If a first mortgage holder is successful in a foreclosure, any other registrations below it get wiped away.

> If you hold a second mortgage and the first mortgage on that property is successful in a foreclosure, you lose all of your money—but only if you don't take appropriate action. Provided you respond to the foreclosure, you can protect your investment.

This usually makes people say something like "Doesn't that mean that second mortgages are really high risk? If a first mortgage goes into fore-closure, then I lose all my money!"

Well, that's not how it typically works. Remember that you're con-sidered to have an interest in the property because you have a registered mortgage on the title. This also means that if the first mortgage were to go into default and the senior lender starts a foreclosure, you have the right to make up those payments to the bank and stop the foreclosure, so that you can start your own foreclosure. In other words, you can step in and make the first mortgage current, and immediately start your own foreclosure. This is true whether the borrower is making payments on your loan or not.

The good news is that if you make the payments to the first mortgage to keep it current, you will be able to claim back any of the payments you made to the bank as part of your foreclosure. While it's going to cost you money out of pocket (or from your registered account) during the fore-closure, as long as there is sufficient equity in the property, you would get all of your costs back, including whatever amounts you had to pay to the bank to satisfy their payment demands.

In this case, if you're successful in your foreclosure, you would end up with the property and the existing first mortgage, because it would survive the foreclosure, as it was a senior mortgage to your mortgage. However, you should still be in a position where you could sell the property and pay off the existing first mortgage and recoup all of your investment and expenses (including interest).

What makes a mortgage risky has less to do with whether it's a first or a second or a third mortgage, but really more to do with how much equity exists in the property. You could hold a first mortgage that is 90% loan-to-value, and that first mortgage would be more risky to hold than a second mortgage on a property with a total loan-to-value of 70%. Again, it's really driven from the amount of equity in the property, so as I keep emphasizing, the risk comes from the equity in the property or the lack thereof, and the key thing here is whether or not you're going to be able to get the property sold and recover your money if the borrower defaults.

Let's go back to our example. The property was worth $200,000 and you brought the debt up to $180,000. Now a year later, the property has declined and is worth only $175,000. What this really means is that even if you could sell the property for the full value of $175,000, you're going to take a loss of at least $5,000 because it's going to take $180,000 to pay off all of the debt, so every dollar that you don't collect back is another dollar that you're going to lose. It's worse than that, though, because in foreclosure there's going to be accrued interest and legal costs to pay. Therefore, even if you sold the property for $175,000 you would still end up losing whatever money you spent on legal fees and other expenses.

Another thing to keep in mind is that when you take back a property in a foreclosure, it usually doesn't come back to you in perfect condition. Some borrowers have been known to purposely damage the value of a property because they know they'll be losing it in a foreclosure anyway. They're upset about the bank and feeling cheated and they want to exact some revenge, and the easiest way to do that is to take it out on the property. This has happened a lot in the U.S., whereby people buy houses at a foreclosure auction, they take the house over, and they find out that the previous occupants poured cement down all of the sinks so they've got to dig up all of the pipes to repair them. The best way to avoid ever having to deal with problems like this is to do your due diligence, select your investments carefully, and make sure you keep the loan-to-value at a reasonable level.

Another way you can mitigate your risk is by investing in a solid, stable real estate market. As long as the values stay the same or go up, it's unlikely that your underlying value is going to erode. In a stable real estate market, especially investing registered funds, you shouldn't be lending more than 80% to 85% of the value of the property. You need to leave that margin of safety in case the market adjusts down a bit. In a market that's unstable or perhaps declining slightly, you want to give yourself a lot more room to move. If you lend a mortgage at 85% or 90% loan-to-value, and the property value drops by 10%, that means there's at most 5% equity left in the property. When you factor legal fees and other costs into the equation, you won't get all of your money out of that investment.

There are many solid borrowers out there looking to borrow money, so don't take a risky deal that is highly leveraged, or one with a borrower you're not fully confident about.

THE TOP SEVEN TIPS TO PROTECT YOURSELF

With all of this information, how do you as a mortgage investor protect yourself? Here's my list of the top seven things you need to do as a mortgage investor.

1. **You have to understand the process that applies in the province where you're investing.** The first thing you need to find out about is the legal process followed where you are. Make sure you understand how that process works. Source a solid real estate lawyer that's going to be on your side and is going to act for you in your transactions. The lawyer is an important part of your due diligence process, because he or she will be creating all of the documents that you require in order to both satisfy the trustee and protect yourself.

2. **Know the market value of the property that you're lending on, and know the market in which the property is.** Be sure to do an analysis on the market, and understand what kind of real estate market you're investing in. Are you in a stable real estate market? Are the indicators going in a positive direction? For example, is employment up? Are people moving to the area? Are population growths increasing? Once you have a handle on the market, look at the property itself. Get an appraisal of the property and consider going to the property so you can see it for yourself (or arrange to have someone you trust make a visit). Make sure that you do your due diligence on the property and you understand what the value is. Also make sure that you verify the title, the zoning, and the other items I outlined in chapter 8 on due diligence. Some of the due diligence is typically done by your lawyer. For example, your lawyer would pull title as part of their role, and ensure it is free of problems—and in most cases you're going to get title insurance. I definitely would recommend that, on all mortgages that you lend upon, you insist that the borrower pay for a title insurance policy. That protects you as the lender in case an unforeseen problem arises with the title.

3. **Determine what your criteria are going to be in your lending business and stick to those criteria**. What are you looking to get out of your investing and what is your risk tolerance going to be? For example, are you mostly focused on lots of security and safety? If that's the case, you might want to look more at first mortgages because they are generally lower risk and more stable (because they're usually a lower loan-to-value). As a trade-off, you're going to get lower interest rates. If you're looking to create a higher interest return, typically that's going to mean secondary financing. Again, depending on the property, the loan and other important details, it's possible that the secondary mortgage business might be considered slightly more risky simply because the loan-to-value generally is going to be higher than with a first mortgage. Decide what kinds of properties you're going to lend on, and what your specific criteria will be in terms of interest rate targets and loan-to-value ratios. By being clear on your criteria, you'll be able to quickly identify opportunities that appeal to you and disqualify deals that don't.

4. **Ensure that the mortgage is drafted by an experienced real estate lawyer and contains the clauses that you need to protect yourself**. Experienced lawyers know what to look for and usually can give you really good ideas on how best to protect yourself. Mortgages are very standard documents, and someone who is experienced in real estate law should be able to provide the necessary guidance and expertise you need. Note that not all real estate lawyers are familiar with arranging arm's length mortgages using registered accounts, so early on you should ensure they understand the process that you'll need them to undertake.

5. **Know who you're lending money to and make sure that you manage the risk of them allowing or causing the property value to decline**. I think it's important to get a basic understanding of who it is that you're lending money to, as I talked about in the due diligence section of this book. One of the risks that you're going to face is lending money to somebody you don't know and them doing something that creates an issue for you, such as turning the house into a grow-op. Spending time understanding to whom you're lending money can save you a lot of time in the long run.

6. **Keep the length of the mortgage to a maximum of two or three years**. For most private lending—especially with RRSPs—the length

of the mortgage is usually a maximum of two or three years, and it is not uncommon to see a one-year term. From a risk management perspective, this makes a lot of sense because the longer the term of a mortgage you grant, the higher the possibility that the market shifts negatively during that time. If you're only lending money for a one- or two-year term at a time, it's unlikely you'll see a sudden drop in real estate prices within that period; however, a lot can happen in five years, or even three years, so keeping the term of your mortgage in the range of two to three years is advisable.

7. **If a problem develops, act immediately**. Do not wait and hope that the borrower is going to make good on the debt. I cannot emphasize this enough. The worst thing you can do is not take action immediately. You need to jump up and down like your hair is on fire if the borrower is a day or two late with the mortgage payment, because you want that person to know that there's going to be an immediate and significant response to missed payments. If you are lax about responding to late payments, you'll have chronic late payers on your hands. Because of this, you absolutely have to take action immediately, and one of the things I suggest you do is frame the situation with the borrower. When you're first setting up the mortgage, one of the things you should do is explain to the borrower that if there's ever a problem, you absolutely must start the process immediately. That's your policy. Period. Even though you believe the borrower will make good on the missed payment, you'll have to start the process. If the borrower ever does become late on payments, simply say, "Look, I'm sorry, but I've got to start the process. I know that you're going to make good on this, but I don't have any choice. I have to start the process because it's company policy." You want to make sure that you start the clock ticking as fast as you possibly can, because time will work against you the longer that you wait. This is where so many investors allow a small problem to grow into a big one—they start thinking with their heart rather than their head. Remember, this is *your* money at risk. If you don't take good care of it, neither will anyone else! You need to communicate to the borrower that you're going to take swift action if things go sideways, and follow through on that promise if he or she is ever late with the payment.

• • •

Every type of investment carries with it some kind of risk, so it's important that you understand how to recognize, mitigate and reduce risk as much as you can.

What I like about mortgage investing is that the research and risk management process isn't overly complicated, yet you're still able to achieve attractive returns, compared to many other armchair-style investments.

If you follow the advice I've laid out for you in this book, I am confident that you'll find the same level of success that I and so many of my investors, associates, family and friends have enjoyed for many years.

Conclusions

The main reason I decided to write this book was that I was tired of watching so many of my family members, friends and associates make poor financial decisions—not because they didn't wish to make wise choices, but because they didn't have an understanding of how to properly make them.

I believe our education system fails miserably at equipping kids today with the financial skills they need to be successful in their financial lives. My hope is that this book helps you understand the system, and how you really can create a prosperous future for yourself and your family, simply by doing some simple things consistently.

The primary strategy that I laid out in this book—arm's length mortgages—continue to be one of the greatest investment strategies that you can consider, whether you're using registered funds or just cash. The unique combination of simplicity, risk mitigation and attractive returns is not offered by any other investment strategy I know.

In closing, I wanted to share with you a couple of the many success stories I've received from people who are using my strategy to build their wealth safely and predictably. This is a father and son who are involved in real estate investing, and I thought this really demonstrated the power of this strategy.

My first experience with RRSPs was in early 2002 when I purchased my first mutual funds. One year later, they had decreased in value by a total of 20%. By the end of year three they were back up to their initial purchase price. What a rollercoaster. Three full years of lost opportunity and zero gains. Not a great start. If I still owned these mutual funds today—seven years later—they'd be worth over 30% less than what I had originally purchased them for in 2002.

My trusted financial advisor's advice at the time was to convert them into back-end loaded funds so I could earn an extra 0.25% per year. "Don't worry about the 4% penalty if you sell, you're in this for the long term, right?" He neglected to mention that this would increase his commissions, and my risk. Thankfully I read an article in June 2006 that changed my RRSPs future, titled "Are Your RRSPs Earning You 13%–18% Consistently?" This article quoted Greg Habstritt, and compared investing in risky mutual funds to investing in second mortgages secured by real estate. Against the advice of my financial advisor (mutual fund salesman), I paid the 4% penalty for selling my recently loaded funds and transferred all of my RRSPs to a registered self-directed trust account. My friendly advisor was no longer friendly.

My first experience in mortgage lending was on a second mortgage on a Calgary property with a total LTV (loan-to-value) of 75%. I received an instant 6% discount (lender's fee) and an annual interest rate of 13.5%—a total first-year ROI (return on investment) of 19.5%. I still hold this mortgage today for a consistent 13.5% NET annual ROI.

I did not keep this knowledge to myself. In fact I've since helped many others secure their retirement by letting them know this valuable RRSP secret. I convinced my parents to sell all of their mutual funds alongside me in 2006 and today they're enjoying 15%–18% returns secured by real estate while mutual funds continue to drop in value. Their portfolio is up over 40% today from when they sold—I shudder to think that they would have lost at least 30%–40% of their RRSPs' value in today's market had I not learned and shared with them the secrets of RRSP investing.

—Daniel Borkowski
Calgary, Alberta

You'll note that Daniel mentions getting his parents involved in arm's length mortgage investing—and here's what Daniel's dad had to say about it.

I still remember our first meeting in 1999 at the family kitchen table. The friendly mutual fund agent asked me if I would be opposed to earning a 10% annual return towards my retirement goal. It probably would be greater than 10%, but his company likes to underpromise and overdeliver.

Nineteen ninety-nine earned 11.8%. Dang, he did not lie. Two thousand was 4.8%. Y2K, dot-com, I guess. Two thousand and one was −0.71%. No one could have foreseen 9/11. It'll rebound the next year. Two thousand and two was −12.7%. Ouch!

The market is correcting more slowly than Barry predicted, but next year look out! And if he wasn't bang on. Two thousand and three was 13.4%. We're coming back. Two thousand and four was 9.2%. See Barry, I told you—10% was about average.

The math did not seem quite right to me. The friendly mutual fund agent did not want to show me what I actually averaged over the last six years, but with prodding he eventually produced the spreadsheet. It was only a 4.3% average, not 10%. I quickly calculated that I would need to start averaging 20% returns for several years to get back on the plan he had suggested to begin with. All the while this was happening, he was earning 2.7% on his fees whether I gained or lost money.

I then learned about RRSP mortgage investing from Greg Habstritt. I called my friendly mutual fund agent, who said it was illegal. I was intrigued so I called CRA and the trustees for more information. They told me that it was perfectly legal and within the CRA guidelines.

When I presented my friendly mutual fund agent with this information he stated that it may not be exactly illegal but terribly risky, and that if I was interested in real estate investing then he has some great commercial real estate funds that have been performing fantastically the past several years. When I asked why he had not suggested this previously, he said he thought I was happy so he had never mentioned it. Happy?

I said goodbye and withdrew my funds. It was then I was further surprised to find out that there would be penalties since he had placed me in back-end loaded funds so I would be earning a greater rate of return.

For the past few years I have made short-term (six-month to one-year) second mortgage RRSP loans with those funds. They have earned from 12% to 14% annual interest rates, plus an upfront discount or fee for agreeing to the loan of approximately $5,000 for every $100,000 borrowed. Therefore, my net returns have been about 15%–18% and all were made 85% or lower LTVs, administered by the trustee. And I'm also placed on title, so I now have security if things don't go as planned.

Is this risky, as the friendly mutual fund agent stated? Investing can never be without risk, but I would rather invest my money on a real estate asset that I am registered on title for than a paper mutual fund certificate. The past year has especially proven this assertion to be true. I hate to think what those funds would be worth today.

I am well on the road to a healthy retirement fund and all thanks to an article by Greg Habstritt that I was fortunate to have forwarded to me.

—Barry Borkowski
Calgary, Alberta

This is real life, my friend, and your financial future is truly in your hands. As I like to say often, no one will take better care of your money than you will.

Reading this book has been a powerful first step in your path towards financial freedom, and creating the prosperity and wealth that you want and deserve.

I hope you've enjoyed what I've shared with you, and I welcome your comments and stories. Please be sure to visit my website at www. rrspSecret.com. Not only will you be able to download a wealth of resources as a reward for reading this book, but you'll also be able to share your stories and connect with other investors who are successfully using this strategy for their benefit.

Thank you for your trust in me. I truly hope that this book is one of the small steps along your path to financial success.

Keep investing in yourself, because you're worth it!

To your success,
Greg Habstritt

Common Questions and Answers

I thought it would be helpful for you to see some of the questions I get from people who are interested in implementing the arm's length mortgage strategy, along with my responses. Many of these questions were received from clients of mine, and in many of the responses you'll find echoes of information from previous sections of the book that you can refer back to if desired.

If you have a question that is not posed below, log on to my website, www.rrspSecret.com, and submit your question. There you'll find more Q&As, as well as the most updated information available on the various trustees/administrators and any changes or updates regarding the legislation and rules affecting this investment strategy.

GENERAL QUESTIONS

Q: I have RRSP money tied up through several plans in accounts with different institutions. Do I have to sell those assets? And is there a charge to switch my RRSPs over to one of the trustees that will allow arm's length mortgages?

A: The simple answers here are yes and yes. You have to be in a cash position to lend on a mortgage, so you may have to sell assets that are in an existing RRSP account in order to move that cash over to your self-directed account and do these kinds of investments. And if you sell the assets, you'll be selling them at whatever the market value is, so obviously if you take a loss on those assets then you'll crystallize that loss.

Keep in mind I'm not advising you to sell those assets! I'm simply saying that if you want to invest that capital in mortgages, you first would need to liquidate the assets you're invested in. Refer to page 102 where I discuss this in detail.

You're not going to pay taxes, though. If you'll have a gain—in other words you're going to sell the assets for a profit—remember that it's still inside the RRSP and therefore tax is deferred. If you sell at a loss, the disadvantage is that you can't use that loss against other investment losses outside the registered account.

You will also pay a fee to move your assets from one firm to another. Most brokerages and trustees charge an account transfer fee or an account closing fee. In the grand scheme of things, though, if you're transferring $30,000 or $70,000 out of an account, then a $100 to $150 cost is not significant when you consider that you're moving your assets from a low-return account to one that can grant you double-digit returns. This is why it's important to do a cost-benefit analysis for your specific situation, as I talk about in the book starting on page 103.

Q: Would consolidating all of the RRSP funds prior to a purchase or a deal make the process easier, or does it matter?

A: Let's say you've got someone who has RRSP accounts at three different trustees—$10,000 at one, $10,000 at another and $5,000 at a third. Does it make sense to consolidate them and move them into a self-directed account to do arm's length mortgages?

The truth is it really doesn't matter too much. At some point there's not a lot of logic in holding a whole bunch of RRSP accounts all over the place because you're incurring fees at all of the different institutions where you hold those accounts. I would think that it makes more sense to have maybe one or two accounts as opposed to several accounts. Again, refer to "The Question of Liquidating" on page 102 for more thoughts on this.

From the perspective of funding a mortgage, you'll need all of those assets consolidated into one account in order to do a mortgage for the total amount.

Q: My husband turns sixty this year and I'm turning fifty-six. Should I still be investing in RRSPs?

A: This question is best answered by your financial planner. If you don't have one, think about seeking out a fee-based planner who can offer advice without trying to earn a commission. Remember that my goal here isn't to provide you any kind of financial advice or planning. My purpose here is to show you this little-known investment strategy. It's your job to make sure you've got the right information and to plan in order to properly execute it.

Q: Can I take funds out of my RRSP and directly use them as a down payment on an investment without paying tax on them?

A: Generally speaking, the answer is no, you cannot take funds out of your RRSP and use them as a down payment on real estate. There is only one exception to this, and that's if you are buying your first home and it's going to be your principal residence. This would fall under the RRSP Home Buyers' Plan, which is a special program created by the CRA to assist first-time homebuyers. The maximum you can withdraw is $25,000, and it must be repaid over time (within a maximum of fifteen years). If you're married and your spouse also qualifies for the program, you each can take out up to $25,000 (for a total of $50,000) to buy a house together. Note that there are a series of restrictions and guidelines that you have to follow, and there are penalties if you don't execute this plan correctly. If you go to my website at www.rrspSecret.com, you'll find additional information about the Home Buyers' Plan, including a link to an information document that details this strategy.

Q: I've heard another expert refer to RRSPs as a "ticking time bomb" and "something that should only be used until you reach the age of forty, by which time all of your money should be out." Would you agree, disagree or at least elaborate?

A: RRSPs and registered accounts provide different benefits to different types of investors at different points in their lives. I don't agree with a blanket comment that RRSPs are evil and that you should get out of them by the time you're forty, and that they're a ticking time bomb. But if this statement is based on the *stock market* being a ticking time bomb, and your RRSP is filled with bad stocks, then perhaps this statement makes sense. RRSPs invested in stocks or mutual funds that you don't understand certainly can be a ticking time bomb, since there's really no way of knowing what direction the market or those investments will go in the future. This is why the arm's length mortgage strategy makes a lot of sense—because it's secure and your returns are predictable regardless of what happens in the stock market.

DEAL STRUCTURING QUESTIONS

Q: Is it legal and is there a way to structure an arm's length mortgage in a first position? Or can they only be used for second mortgages?

A: The answer is absolutely yes! In fact, there is no problem using RRSPs or a registered account to set up a first mortgage, a second mortgage or a third mortgage. The only catch is that getting a decent first mortgage on a property is usually going to require a fair amount of capital for someone to have in their RRSP. That's why it's most common for owners to get a first mortgage with a chartered bank or traditional lender, and top up that financing with a second mortgage.

For example, if you're buying a property worth $200,000 and you want to use someone's RRSP funds for the first mortgage, that person would need $160,000 in his or her account for you to obtain a traditional 80% mortgage. In addition, since the interest rates on private mortgages tend to be higher than what you can arrange from a bank or traditional lender, it's likely your borrowing costs will be higher.

In some cases, getting a private first mortgage may be your only option; for example, the banks don't like to lend against raw land, so getting a private mortgage to buy a piece of land might be your only option as the borrower.

The bottom line is that you can use RRSP arm's length mortgages for first, second and third mortgages (up to the maximum loan-to-value allowed by each trustee).

Q: Are RRSP mortgages subject to the same rules as bank mortgages? Do you have to have 5% down or can you bank finance 75% and get an RRSP loan for 25%?

A: First of all, anyone other than the chartered banks who lends money is not required to utilize mortgage insurance. The chartered banks require you to get high-ratio mortgage insurance anytime they lend over 80% (which is the conventional loan-to-value, by the way). However, a private investor could, if he wanted to, lend up to 100% of the value of a property without any mortgage insurance, although in my opinion that wouldn't be a smart thing to do. This would place your capital in serious risk, and as a result this is something you should avoid when dealing with RRSP or registered account funds.

In response to the second question, you can arrange for a second mortgage, but in most cases I would not recommend loaning up to the full value of the property. Again, this puts you in a serious position of risk. In fact, most trustees will not allow you to exceed a 90% loan-to-value ratio in terms of what is lent against a property. As I detailed earlier in the book, you also need to ensure that your first lender is aware you are planning to use a second mortgage to fund the purchase. Refer to chapter 6 for more details on this situation.

Q: What's the best way to put your own RRSP money back in your own pocket to acquire additional rental property? Will the following work? You find a swap partner in a similar position as yourself where you have RRSP funds and they have RRSP funds. You put an RRSP second mortgage on their property, and they put an RRSP mortgage on one of your properties, which has the effect of the money ending up back in your pocket.

A: This is an example of all of the creative ideas that I see out in the market and people ask me about all the time. The simple answer to this is that the *Income Tax Act* doesn't like creativity very much. On the surface, what you've described sounds like it would be a great idea, right? Let's say we both have $40,000 in our RRSPs and we don't know who to lend it to, and let's assume that we both have investment properties that have at least enough equity to support a $40,000 second mortgage.

One approach could be that I put $40,000 against your property so you get the $40,000 out. Then you give me $40,000 from your RRSP and I get the $40,000 out. We both end up with $40,000 in our pockets and now we're paying each other's RRSPs back.

On the surface that sounds pretty clever, but the CRA is going to look at the transaction and say that the only reason you lent money to me is because I lent you money back. In other words, your loan was not truly arm's length, so because we colluded together the transaction is ineligible. The CRA will force you to declare the $40,000 that you used in your RRSP, because it will take the position that you essentially removed and "deregistered" the funds since you used the funds in a non-eligible transaction—and you'll have to pay interest, penalties, and fines on it. Therefore, you need to be careful lending back and forth with another investor like this.

Q: Do you recommend doing a non-arm's length mortgage on your own property?

A: For a number of reasons, I usually don't recommend that people do this. First of all, you have to arrange mortgage insurance on the entire balance of the loan regardless of what the loan-to-value represents. Let's say you've got $100,000 in your RRSP and you want to lend your money against your primary residence or a property you own. Technically your RRSP can lend the money against your property, but in doing that, you're going to have to pay high-ratio mortgage insurance in order to insure the loan for your RRSP so that your RRSP doesn't incur the loss. There are extra costs in doing this, including a bunch of set-up fees and management fees and everything else in order to hold a non-arm's length mortgage.

Second—and here's the bigger problem—you've got your RRSP where you're trying to earn lots of interest to maximize your return, and you've got your house that you're putting the mortgage on and because it's your primary residence you can't deduct the interest on it. So here's the question. Are you better off charging a high interest rate so you're making lots of money in your RRSP, or are you better off charging a low interest rate because that's the money coming out of your pocket because you can't write it off?

I think you're better off focusing your RRSP on high return investments—in other words, on arm's length mortgages where you can generate 12%, 13%, 14%, and keep your own personal mortgage separate. There's going to be one out of a thousand examples where holding your own mortgage in your RRSP might make sense, but in most cases it won't, so I wouldn't recommend it. If you're really considering it, I'd strongly recommend getting some advice from a good financial planner who can help you calculate the pros and cons of such a strategy.

Q: If we have a loan at 12% on $100,000 and the interest payment goes into our account monthly, from what I understand you don't get any interest while the money is sitting in the account. Therefore, would it be better to hold the mortgage and get the interest yearly?

A: The challenge to lending money out of your RRSP is if you're getting monthly payments back into your RRSP, what are you going to do with that money that comes in each month? The problem is it's usually not significant enough to really do anything with it, so you've got to wait for the payments to accumulate to the point where they're significant enough to lend them out again. For example, if you're lending out $100,000 at 12%, it's going to take you a year to accumulate back $12,000. Maybe after two years you've got $24,000, and then you might consider lending that out on another mortgage. This is why the deferred interest strategy can make a lot of sense, because it allows you to increase your potential returns without having a lot of interest money sitting in your account, accumulating without generating any return. (See "Using the Deferred Interest Strategy" on page 113 in chapter 7 for more details.)

Q: Can a person be on title if he or she is using RRSP funds to invest?

A: No, because if you are on title that means that you have an interest in the property, which means by definition this is not an arm's length mortgage. For the mortgage to qualify as arm's length, you are not allowed to have an interest in the property. (For more about the definition of arm's length, see page 74.)

Q: If I use my RRSP to buy real estate for rental purposes, and the property appreciates by $100,000, when I cash in my RRSP (assuming I have to sell the property before I cash in my RRSP), will I be taxed on 100% of the income?

A: Houston, we have a problem. One of the assumptions being made in your question is that the RRSP could hold the real estate to begin with, which it is not allowed to do. You *cannot* use your RRSP to go and buy real estate. If you're interested in having your RRSP invested in a real estate-related vehicle, you can use it to invest in arm's length mortgages, real estate investment trusts, or mortgage investment corporations.

Assuming you follow my advice in this book and invest in an arm's length mortgage, your RRSP would not own the property—it only holds a mortgage on it—and if the property goes up in value, you as the mortgage holder do not benefit from that increase. It's no different than if you own a house you live in, with a mortgage from one of the big banks. If your house goes up in value over time, the bank doesn't benefit from the gains; only you do, since you're the beneficial owner.

Q: Is it possible to combine RRSP investment funds from multiple people to make one mortgage investment?

A: Absolutely. I've done that several times where I'm looking for an RRSP loan of a certain amount (say $150,000) and I know one investor who has $60,000 and another who has $90,000. One mortgage gets registered on property and it's a shared mortgage. Anybody that's involved in that mortgage has equal rights should there be a default down the road. So basically it's registered as one mortgage but it's made up of two underlying mortgages.

In fact, another thing to know is this: let's say you want to lend money on an RRSP and you've got $60,000 in your RRSP account but the person is looking to borrow $100,000. Well, if you had the $40,000 in non-registered money, in other words cash just sitting somewhere, you could lend the $60,000 in your RRSP and add the $40,000 cash and provide a $100,000 mortgage to the person. Again, this is absolutely legal and it's done quite often. For an example of this, refer to page 119 for more information.

Q: If you can't qualify for a mortgage but you want to attract money or a qualifying partner, can that person use his or her RRSP money and qualify for the loan, or would that person be required to qualify and use non-RRSP money?

A: No, that person can't use his or her RRSP funds and qualify for the property because that would mean that he or she has an interest in the property. For a lender to approve them for a mortgage, the lender will require them to be on title as an owner of the property—so that violates the arm's length rule. In a circumstance where you can't qualify for a loan, there are a couple of approaches you could take. One is to get an investor to qualify for the loan, go on title, and become a joint venture partner, and then use another investor's RRSP to get some of the cash to close and simply pay them a fixed interest rate. That's really the only way to do it, because the same person cannot both qualify and use his or her RRSP funds.

Q: As a borrower, can I register the RRSP monies I receive against two or more different properties? I'm sure the answer is yes because I only have limited equity in both, but do I only have to pay for one set of fees to the trustee?

A: Let's say you find someone who has enough capital to lend money on more than one property you have. If that lender lends you against two properties what that means is there will be two mortgages created. You're going to pay two sets of fees to the trustee because two appraisals have to be done, two mortgages have to be arranged and two sets of legal fees have to be paid. So, even though the money is coming from the same lender, if you have two or three properties that you're borrowing against, it's going to be essentially the same cost regardless of the number of lenders involved.

Q: I'm a new real estate investor and I've purchased three properties. At this point, none of my properties can carry a 12% interest on a RRSP loan from a cash flow perspective. I'm wondering if this strategy is better used in a few years when my properties are flowing cash better?

A: First of all, recognize that in today's lending environment it's not uncommon for a bank to be willing to lend you only 60% or 65% against an investment property. So for you, even as a new investor, if you're only getting a 60% or 65% loan-to-value mortgage on a property, that leaves you with a huge amount of cash that you're going to have to come up with. That's where a second mortgage can come in handy. You may only leverage the property 75% or 80%, but still you're going to get some of that cash.

Now, I understand the problem here is as you put more leverage on the property you're going to push the property into negative cash flow, and there are two ways that you can deal with that. The first is using the deferred interest payment structure (see chapter 7). Essentially you structure the loan so that in the first couple of years the interest rate that you pay is much lower—maybe it's 4% or 5%. At the end when the loan is due, you catch up the rest of the interest and you pay a bonus, which still ends up giving the lender the equivalent of 12% or 13% on their money. You pay less at the beginning and more at the end, once you've generated better cash flow.

Another thing that you can do is called an "interest reserve." Let's say that you need to borrow $30,000 in order to do renovations on a property or to close on a property. What you could do (assuming that the LTV didn't get too high) is borrow $35,000, but use only $30,000 for the renovations and put the remaining $5,000 in a bank account. That acts as a reserve to make the payments on your RRSP loan. In other words, you borrow a little more than you need for the property and you set that money aside and use it as a reserve account so that you do not have to look to the property to pay the interest on the loan. This isn't going to work in all circumstances, as it will really depend on the property that you're buying and what your plan is for it. At some point, you're going to have to come up with the $35,000 that you borrowed so you need to make sure the financial projections for the property support doing this, but if it works it's another way to get around the idea of it immediately affecting your cash flow when you first get the loan.

I'll also make a side comment here—I congratulate you on your efforts to ensure your financing doesn't push your property into negative cash flow. A lot of investors end up with major cash-sucking investment properties because they leverage them up as high as possible, which means the payments on the debt are much higher than the rent the property generates. A good rule is to never invest in properties that are negative cash flow; this means you have to work harder to find the ones that are positive cash flow. But I assure you, you'll be glad in the long run that you didn't burden yourself with a bunch of negative cash flow properties that you have to support every month!

Q: I have an investor who has some LIRA funds that I'll be putting to use for him, but the cash flow on the property won't support a 15% per year payment. So I'd like to have the same 3% plus the balance of 12% paid out later. I spoke to one of the trustees and they tell me that the Canadian government regulates that the minimum annual payment must be comparable to current 5-year fixed-mortgage rates, which would put this around 4%. So how are you able to do 3% in your example but they won't let me? What am I missing or what terminology am I messing up when I speak to the trustee?

A: Remember that the trustees all have their own guidelines and rules, so you may find that one trustee will allow slightly different terms than another. With respect to the minimum interest rate allowed on a mortgage each year, one of the guidelines in the *Income Tax Act* is that any of the assets or investments that you hold in your RRSP must be consistent with commercially reasonable terms. What that means is that you need to find the lowest mortgage rate you can find on a mortgage that's offered out in the market today, and that's what the trustee will allow you to do, because it can be proven to be "commercial reasonable" if it's currently offered in the market. Sometimes you can get 3%, and other times that's much harder to come by. Again, the trustees set their own rules, so it will be up to you to work with the trustee. If you don't feel their guidelines reflect the current market, you can always take them information from the market to encourage them to reconsider their position.

DUE DILIGENCE QUESTIONS

Q: If the borrower pulls his own credit report online and gives you a copy, how can you be sure he has not tampered with the report and reprinted it to look official?

A: There are a couple of ways you can do this. First of all, you could look to get an account with the credit bureau so that you have the legal right to pull credit reports on your own. If you don't have a purpose for that account other than doing one or two checks on somebody who wants to borrow mortgage money, it might not make sense to do that.

Another alternative would be to find someone who does have access to the credit bureau system, such as a mortgage broker, and pay that resource a small fee ($25 to $40) to access the report, assuming you've gotten permission from the person you're investigating.

There are also companies who work with real estate investors that allow you to get access to credit bureaus. Do some online research, and you'll find companies that are set up primarily for real estate landlords who want to check out the background and credit history of potential tenants.

Yet another option is to simply go online with your potential borrower and download his or her report right there so you know there's nothing funny going on.

Q: Is it better to use RRSP loans where you live to allow for easier access to the property that you're lending on, or is there some way to obtain the client's building inspection report instead of visiting the property?

A: I always recommend going and physically looking at the property so you understand what it is you're lending on. If it's not economically feasible for you to travel to a property to inspect it, find a third party that you know and trust, or someone that you can hire for a fee, to do the examination for you. For more information about doing your due diligence, refer to chapter 8.

Q: Is it risky to give all of your money to one borrower, or should you spread it out between several borrowers?

A: This is simply diversification. I would say that if you've got $100,000 of RRSP funds you're probably better off lending that against two different properties rather than lending the whole amount against one property. Note that just because you're lending a smaller amount on a property doesn't mean that the risk is any lower. For example, if I lend $100,000 on a property that with my loan is only a 60% loan-to-value, all things being equal that's going to be a much less risky investment than if I take my $100,000 and lend $50,000 against two properties that each have a loan-to-value of 80%. It's not really a matter of what the dollar amount is; what matters most is the total amount of debt on the property, compared to its true market value. As a risk-mitigation strategy, it makes sense to spread out your money against more than one property. If you do have a problem, you won't be 100% at risk on the one property.

Q: If the borrower is arranging for the purchase of a new property, can you accept the appraisal done by the bank that's providing the first mortgage?

A: I would say that's a fairly safe approach if you can get your hands on that appraisal report; however, in a lot of cases, the borrower never gets a copy of that appraisal.

If you are able to get the appraisal from the owner, one of the things I would suggest you do is to contact the appraiser and ask for an update of the existing appraisal. What this means is the appraiser will re-certify it for you. This doesn't cost the same as getting a brand-new appraisal, but it ensures that the appraisal is legitimate and that the value has not changed significantly since it was completed. The good thing about this is that if you get it updated and certified for your use, you can rely on that appraisal. If you only get a copy of the appraisal arranged by the bank, you cannot legally rely on that appraisal if something goes wrong, because the appraiser will not stand behind it for anyone other than the bank that requested it. For more information on appraisals and due diligence, see chapter 8.

Q: How can you be sure that the borrower doesn't borrow more money against the property once you've extended a loan?

A: You can't. Once you've lent the money and your mortgage is registered on that title, nothing stops the borrower from finding somebody else to lend them more money and register below you, and there's really nothing that you can do to stop that. Technically, you can place a clause in your mortgage that prohibits this and restricts the borrower from doing it, but once your loan is in place, they can still go and get more financing—and you would have to keep checking the property title to see if they've done this after the fact.

What matters is that any registration below yours (that was registered after your mortgage) is considered junior to your loan—and your mortgage will take precedence. In other words, if someone else lends them money after you do, it doesn't weaken your security or position, because their loan will not affect your ability to go after the property if your loan (or the first mortgage above you) goes into default. In fact, whoever registered the additional mortgage after you would be in third position, and would not hold very good security for their money. So the real answer is—technically yes you can restrict them, but in practice, there's not really a lot of value in doing so, because any additional financing doesn't affect your security anyway.

GENERAL ARM'S LENGTH MORTGAGE QUESTIONS

Q: My parents have more than $300,000 tied up in RRSPs that are stagnating in terms of a return. I can't do anything with this money as it is not arm's length to me, but I'm wondering what kind of finder's fee is available if I bring this money to another investor?

Good question, and I can answer it and the following question at the same time:

Q: How can I assist someone who's willing to lend money to investors with setting up an RRSP mortgage and still be compensated for my time without violating Canadian securities law?

A: You have to be careful about charging any kind of fees for essentially doing what licensed mortgage brokers do. If you think about what mortgage brokers do, they go out and try to find people who have money to invest. Sometimes it's a bank and other times it's private investors. On the other hand, they're trying to find people who need to borrow the money. Admittedly, this is a grey area. On the surface it's against the law to charge a fee for introducing somebody with money to somebody that wants to borrow that money, but again there are a lot of people that work in this world who aren't licensed and they do it by using marketing consulting contracts. I would recommend that you speak to a lawyer that's familiar with securities and real estate law.

Now to the subject of finder's fees. These fees are completely negotiable, but look at what the typical brokerage industry charges, which is typically anywhere from 1 point to 4 or 5 points, or 1% to 5% of the loan. This will depend on the type of deal you're doing, how much money is involved and whatever the broker feels is an appropriate fee to charge. The bottom line is this: get good legal advice before you start trying to introduce borrowers and lenders together, because there's a risk that you can be deemed to be acting like a mortgage agent broker, and doing so without a licence is illegal.

Q: Could you give us an example of advertising RRSP money available? Also, are there certain ways of putting the information across that will help prescreen clients and reduce being flooded by queries? Are there ways to draw out better prospects by one's wording or does the sifting process come later?

A: There is absolutely nothing wrong with putting an ad in the classifieds section in the paper (or wherever you think it's appropriate) that says something like the following:

PRIVATE INVESTOR LOOKING TO LEND FUNDS ON SECURE QUALITY REAL ESTATE. Flexible terms and rates depending on the situation. Willing to lend up to $100,000. Maximum 75% loan-to-value on current appraisal. Call John at 555-1212.

It's OK to advertise that you want to lend your own money, but you cannot advertise for somebody else's money. See chapter 8 for more details about advertising for opportunities.

Note that in the wording of my ad above, I've carefully crafted the language to pre-screen anyone who is going to be calling. I've indicated a maximum 75% LTV ratio, which tells anyone wanting to borrow 100% of the value of their property that they shouldn't call me. I've limited my lending to $100,000, so I won't get calls from people trying to borrow $250,000. By placing the major terms and conditions that I'm looking for right in the ad, it saves me a lot of time from answering the phone and talking to a lot of people that I'll never do business with, because their deal doesn't fit my criteria.

Q: Can an RRSP second mortgage be set up as part of a Joint Venture Agreement or is that a contradiction of the arm's length rule? In other words, can I promise 50% of all the profits to a Joint Venture partner if he puts his RRSP funds as second mortgages with the funds going into the RRSP taken from his 50%?

A: The simple answer is no, because you're correct in that this contradicts the arm's length rule. Using an RRSP mortgage, you cannot participate in the property value in any way; it has to be a fixed return that's specified in the mortgage. The mortgage cannot have any kind of language that says something along the lines of "the person giving the mortgage is going to receive 'X' percent of the profits on the property." That's called a "participatory mortgage" and that violates the RRSP rules. While these types of creative strategies were used in the past, the trustees have prohibited them because the CRA takes the view that if you are participating in the equity or profit of a property, then you're no longer a debt investor—you're a beneficial owner of the property.

Q: My bank has given me a home equity line of credit on my personal residence of approximately 72% loan-to-value. They say that's the maximum for houses of my type, which is acreages over a million dollars. I have no mortgage on it—the house is completely paid off. How can I secure an arm's length RRSP mortgage on my personal residence that brings the LTV up to 80% or 85% assuming that my bank allows it?

A: The answer is very simple. What you would do is go to the bank and get the 72% loan-to-value home equity line of credit. The bank would register that on your title and that essentially becomes a first mortgage. They're not going to call it a first mortgage—it's called a line of credit, but essentially it's the same thing—it's a debt that's registered against your property in first position. Let's say that to go to 85% is another $75,000. All you have to do is find an investor who has $75,000 and is willing to lend his money against your property up to 85% loan-to-value, and the second mortgage simply gets registered behind the home equity line of credit.

Q: You have said that an RRSP cannot hold real estate. If you need to foreclose, are you not temporarily taking ownership? Also, would you be able to make repairs or improvements to make the property more sellable?

A: This is a great question, by the way, because this touches on one of the unique exceptions with investing RRSPs in mortgages. Let's say in your RRSP you lend money on a property and the person stops paying you back. Your recourse is to foreclose on the property and take it back. If your RRSP owns the mortgage, when you start a foreclosure process, legally it's your RRSP that's the vehicle driving the foreclosure, and if the foreclosure proceeds successfully, it's going to take the property back into the RRSP. Your RRSP would have to sell the real estate to get your money back. The *Income Tax Act* says that you cannot own real estate in your RRSP, with one exception: your RRSP can hold property temporarily if it's acquired through a foreclosure or default. If your RRSP had to foreclose on a mortgage it holds, the RRSP would become the rightful owner of that property. Your RRSP is allowed to own that property but must dispose of it within a year of owning it.

So the ideal scenario would be that you own that property, hold it for up to a year, sell it, make a profit and put that money back into your RRSP.

Would you be able to make repairs or improvements to make the property more sellable? A tax lawyer can best answer this question, because interestingly enough, several calls to the CRA didn't get me a clear answer on this. But I do believe that there would not be an issue with you making repairs or improvements to the property because if it can't be sold in its current condition, then you would have no choice but to improve it.

This would be a very rare circumstance, but if you're interested in confirming the answer, I'd suggest you speak to a qualified and experienced tax lawyer.

For more Questions and Answers, and to post your own question for me, you can visit my website at www.rrspSecret.com.

Acknowledgments

You will never understand how hard it is to write this part of a book until you've tried to do it yourself.

To paraphrase Sir Isaac Newton, the success and growth that I've enjoyed is a direct result of standing on the shoulders of many incredible people who have taught, supported and guided me over the years.

There are literally hundreds of people that come to mind when I think to whom I owe a debt of gratitude, and I could never exhaust the list of people deserving of appreciation.

I do, however, want to specifically acknowledge those who truly have been my guiding lights, and without whom I would not be who or where I am today.

I am blessed to have the greatest parents in the world, and it all starts there. My greatest hope is to be a son that they're proud of, and to show others the humility, compassion and kindness that my mom and dad demonstrate every day. Mom, Dad, I love you both and can't express my appreciation for you always being in my corner, no matter what crazy things I did or mistakes I made.

My brother Jim has been one of the most powerful influences on me, helping me become who I am today. I picked up my entrepreneurial spirit from him, and he was always there to watch out for me and push me along when things didn't go my way. Jim, I love you and hope that you realize no matter what happens, you will always be the big brother I look up to with admiration, love and appreciation for all you've done for me.

To my beautiful wife, Raylene, who has been with me through this entire journey of learning and growth, you continue to amaze me with your spirit, your determination and your integrity. Thank you for being my biggest fan, and never letting me settle for being just average or doing "just enough," instead challenging me to be my best. I love you for helping me become a better man.

To my son, Cooper, who has redefined my purpose and shown me what love and family are about. I can only hope that one day, when you get older, you feel that I've been as good a father to you as your grandfather was to me.

And finally, to my business partner and best friend, Kourosh, who has been there through the highs and lows and continues to be my greatest advocate and mentor. Buddy, you've always been an example for me, and I'm proud to be associated with you.

And to all of those that have contributed to my growth and learning—thank you. You know who you are, and I hope that you take pride in this book getting published, because it is in part because of your love, guidance and support that it was able to happen.

Index